THE AMERICAN BAR ASSOCIATION

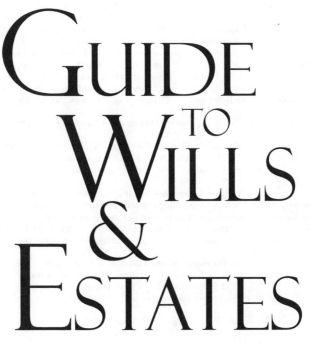

GUIDE TO WILLS & ESTATES

SECOND EDITION

Everything You Nee...

Wills, Estates, Trusts, & Taxes

RANDOM HOUSE
REFERENCE

Copyright © 2004, 2001, 1995 by the American Bar Association

All rights reserved under International and Pan-American Copyright Conventions. Published in the United States by Random House Reference, a member of The Random House Information Group, a division of Random House, Inc., New York and simultaneously in Canada by Random House of Canada Limited, Toronto. No part of this book may be reproduced in any form or by any means, electronic or mechanical, including photocopying, recording, or by any information storage and retrieval system, without the written permission of the publisher. All inquiries should be addressed to Random House Reference, 1745 Broadway, New York, NY 10019.

RANDOM HOUSE is a registered trademark of Random House, Inc.

This is a completely revised and updated edition of THE AMERICAN BAR ASSOCIATION GUIDE TO WILLS AND ESTATES, published by Times Books, a division of Random House, Inc. in 1995 and 2001.

This book is available for special discounts for bulk purchases for sales promotions or premiums. Special editions, including personalized covers, excerpts of existing books, and corporate imprints, can be created in large quantities for special needs. For more information, write to Special Markets/Premium Sales, 1745 Broadway, MD 6-2, New York, NY, 10019 or e-mail specialmarkets@randomhouse.com.

Please address inquiries about electronic licensing of reference products for use on a network, in software, or on CD-ROM to the Subsidiary Rights Department, Random House Reference, fax 212-940-7352.

Visit the Random House Reference Web site: www.randomwords.com

Printed in the United States of America.

Page design by Robert Bull.
Composition by North Market Street Graphics.

Library of Congress Cataloging-in-Publication Data
The American Bar Association guide to wills and estates: everything you need to know about wills, trusts, estates, and taxes.—Second ed.
1. Estates planning—United States—Popular works.   2. Tax planning—United States—Popular works.   3. Wills—United States—Popular works.
4. Trusts and trustees—United States—Popular works.
I. American Bar Association.
KF750.Z9 A47 2003
346.7305'2—dc21   2003008795

ISBN 0-609-80934-2

10 9 8 7 6 5 4 3 2

Second Edition

THE AMERICAN BAR ASSOCIATION

Robert A. Stein
Executive Director

Sarina A. Butler
Associate Executive Director, Communications Group

Mabel C. McKinney-Browning
Director, Division for Public Education

Charles White
Series Editor

CONTENTS

FOREWORD

Robert A. Stein
Executive Director, American Bar Association

The American Bar Association is the nation's premier source of legal information. With more than four hundred thousand members, representing every specialty and every type of legal practice, the ABA is uniquely able to deliver accurate, up-to-date, and unbiased legal information to its members, to the media, and to the general public. The ABA website—www.abanet.org—is an unrivaled database in the legal field.

An important area of the law is that governing estate planning, preparing a will or trust, and wrapping up an estate after death. Our research shows that people consult lawyers frequently for assistance in a variety of estate-planning and end-of-life matters.

This book provides you with the benefit of the ABA's network of hundreds of thousands of lawyers. *The American Bar Association Guide to Wills and Estates* was written with the aid of ABA members from all over the country. Many members of our Section of Real Property, Probate, and Trust Law—one of the largest sections in the ABA—served as reviewers of the manuscript.

The contribution of these members was especially valuable because they are experts in this area of law and have had considerable experience in dealing every day with wills, trusts, and estates. They reviewed draft chapters, providing clarifications, suggesting additional topics that would be helpful to readers, and polishing the manuscript to make it read even better.

Other ABA members reviewing the manuscript brought a rich range of experience to the project. They included professors of law and specialists in the legal problems of the elderly.

Finally, the ABA's Standing Committee on Public Education provided oversight for this project. This committee and its excellent staff contribute the perspective of experts in communicating about the law.

Thanks to all of the lawyers who worked on this book, you can be sure that the information it includes is

- useful,
- helpful,
- unbiased,
- current,
- written in a reader-friendly style that you can understand easily, and
- reflective of a national picture, since ABA members practice in all jurisdictions.

Public education and public service are two of the most important goals of the American Bar Association. This book shows how the ABA takes an active role in providing the public with information it can use.

The American Bar Association is the largest voluntary association in the world. Besides its commitment to public education, the ABA provides programs to assist lawyers and judges in their work, and initiatives to improve the legal system for the public, including promotion of fast, affordable alternatives to lawsuits, such as mediation, arbitration, conciliation, and small claims courts. Through ABA support for lawyer referral programs and pro bono services (in which lawyers donate their time), people like you have been able to find the best lawyer for their particular cases and have received quality legal help within their budgets.

Robert A. Stein is the executive director of the American Bar Association. He was formerly dean of the University of Minnesota Law School.

INTRODUCTION

Judith Billings, *Chair*
ABA Standing Committee on Public Education

According to the United Way, no more than 40 percent of adults have wills. Research by the American Association of Retired Persons (AARP) has found that only 60 percent of the population age fifty or older has a will, with only 45 percent having a durable health-care power of attorney that permits medical decisions to be made for them if they are no longer able to do so.

These figures do not seem overwhelming—yet research suggests that they represent an improvement. The percentage of Americans with wills and other estate-planning documents (including living trusts) has been going up in recent years. Even so, most of us still haven't completed this most basic of estate-planning documents.

This book is designed to help you do the planning that will very likely yield big benefits down the line: money saved, less confusion after your death, your property distributed as you want it to be, and you and your family better protected and prepared. We tell you when the services of a lawyer are particularly valuable, and how to find a lawyer that's right for the task of helping plan your estate.

One of the best aspects of this area of the law, from a consumer's perspective, is that there are so many options. For example, there are many possible answers to each of these questions:

- How can you transfer property without a will or trust?

- Should you hold property jointly with your spouse or someone else?

- **If so, how should you hold it?**
- **What's the role of insurance?**
- **Can a trust help you?**
- **How can you save on taxes?**

No matter who you are, no matter what your situation in life, you probably have these and other questions, but you may have no idea where to turn. That's where this book can help. It provides background information and suggests the pros and cons of various courses of action. It will help you decide among those options to find what's best for *your* situation, and help you craft a plan that works for *you*.

New and Improved Edition

This book is a complete revision and updating of one of the most successful books in the ABA series. We've taken into account all the latest changes in the law, and added many new chapters on estate planning for people with particular needs, such as business owners and divorced or remarried people. We've also made it easier to read, with more examples drawn from real life, shorter sentences and paragraphs, and more brief sidebars packed with interesting information.

Our principal author also wrote the first edition of *The American Bar Association Guide to Wills and Estates.* Brett Campbell is a lawyer and writer who has written on a wide range of subjects for the public, and in fact teaches journalism at the University of Oregon. His manuscript was reviewed and approved by experts on wills, trusts, and estate planning from all over the country, under the guidance of the ABA's Standing Committee on Public Education. Together, we've worked to provide you with easy-to-read information that will help you understand and use the law that affects not only your estate plan and such documents as your will or trust, but also your planning for disability, and even your planning for end-of-life health-care decisions. Our goal is to help you spot problems when they're easiest to handle—before they become major.

In this book, you'll find practical, down-to-earth information about the whole process. We take you step by step through

- figuring out how much you own and how best to leave it,
- deciding who you want to leave your property to,
- determining if you have special personal and familial circumstances that would affect your plan,
- planning for taxes,
- changing your mind if the law or your circumstances change,
- protecting yourself and your property against possible disability, and
- making life easier for those who survive you and will carry out your wishes.

We cover these topics and more in plain, direct language. You won't find legal jargon or technicalities here—just concise, straightforward discussions of your options under the law.

This guidebook can help you make decisions about writing a will, setting up a trust, using a lawyer or other professional adviser, and other matters involved in planning your estate. Remember that much of the law in this area varies according to the state in which you live, or where your property is located, so not all the information provided will necessarily apply to your state. But even in such cases, you will learn what issues to consider, what questions to ask, what pitfalls to avoid, and where to turn for information and assistance.

This book will help you save money by pointing out how the preparation you undertake—and even your willingness to do some simple administrative tasks yourself—can cut down on your lawyer's time, and thus on your legal bills. You'll also get better service by being prepared and knowledgeable, and asking the right questions. With this book's help, you should be able to ensure that you receive an estate plan tailored to fit your needs.

How to Use This Book

We've structured this book chronologically, from the first planning of your estate to the time in which your plans are put into action. It's clearly organized so that you can easily find the help you need at every stage.

Part One—First Steps gives you a pep talk about why you need to stop procrastinating and overcome your reluctance to plan *right now*. The benefits of planning your estate—in money saved and peace of mind preserved—make getting started on a plan one of the best ways to care for your loved ones and make sure that your hard-earned property will be protected and distributed as *you* want. Estate planning makes you the boss.

Part Two—Transferring Property Without a Will looks at your options for getting property to your beneficiaries directly, without a will and without probate. Life insurance is one way. Owning property jointly with right of survivorship means that the property passes automatically to the survivor as soon as one owner dies. The beneficiary designations of your IRA, pension, and 401(k) are "will substitutes," in that you designate where you want the benefit to go upon your death, and it happens independently of your will (or even if you don't have a will) and outside of the probate process. Beneficiary deeds enable you to pass tangible property in much the same way. The key point here is to be aware of all these means of transferring property and make sure they're coordinated with your master plan for distributing your property.

Part Three—Wills looks at the oldest way of passing property at death. We give you the basics of what a will is and does, suggest some of the key clauses that ought to be in *your* will, and talk about what you have to do to make sure that it is properly witnessed and effective (for example, where to leave it so that it will be found after you're gone). We also look at when you should consider changing your will—as, for example, when you've been married or divorced, had additional children or grandchildren, moved to a new state, and so on.

Part Four—Trusts and Living Trusts covers a wide range of issues arising from an alternative way of passing property and taking care of your loved ones. We begin by discussing what trusts are and how they work, then go on to the factors you need to weigh in deciding if *you* need a trust. We finish by looking at an alternative rapidly growing in popularity: the living trust. We talk about what it can do, what it can't do (beware the hype of the living-trust salespeople), and how to set one up if you decide the pros outweigh the cons.

Part Five—Putting the Tools to Work is a very practical section that will help you match your family situation—married, married with kids, kids but not married, and so forth—with some ideas about how to plan your estate. We also look at how your estate planning can (and should) dovetail with your planning for

- **the educational expenses of your children and grandchildren,**
- **retirement income for yourself and your spouse, and**
- **retirement expenses, especially for medical and long-term care.**

Part Six—Death and Taxes discusses an area of law very much in flux at the moment. The federal estate tax laws have changed and probably will change again. States may become more aggressive in imposing death taxes. We give you the basics and talk about some of the tried-and-true methods of lessening the tax burden.

Part Seven—When You Can't Make the Decision canvasses a number of issues associated with grave illness, including your right to refuse life-sustaining treatment. We tell you what you need to know about the tools—living wills, health-care advance directives, and the like—that you can use to assure that your wishes will be effective in determining your treatment, even if you can no longer speak for yourself.

Part Eight—Putting the Plan into Action After Your Death looks at how the decisions you make now affect how smoothly and successfully things go after your death. We look at the process of settling an estate (probate in most cases) and discuss some considerations to bear in mind so that you can pick the best person to be your executor or trustee. We also look at the final arrangements you can make to lessen your family's grief and spare them as many difficult decisions as possible. Once again, it's an example of how estate planning is at heart your final gift to those you love.

A resources section at the end of the book provides you with lists of websites, books, and other sources of useful information, many just the touch of a computer key away.

Finally, three appendixes wrap up the book by giving you tools to help plan your estate:

- **Appendix A is an estate-planning checklist that will help you organize your various kinds of property for planning purposes and think about where you would like it to go.**

- **Appendix B helps you understand wills by giving you typical wording for important will clauses and explaining what the purpose of each clause is.**

- **Appendix C is a health-care advance directive form that you can use to make your wishes known about organ donation and treatment you want—or do not want—if you are no longer able to speak for yourself.**

Written with You in Mind

We've made a special effort to make this book practical by using situations and problems you are likely to encounter. Each chapter is clearly laid out, with a real-life starting situation that shows the practical ramifications of its subject.

Within chapters, brief special sidebars alert you to important points. These include:

- **sidebars with this icon ▶, which generally give you practical tips that could be of benefit to you;**

- sidebars with this icon (i), which provide key additional information;

- sidebars with this icon ⚠, which generally give you a warning about a potential pitfall that you can navigate with the right information and help;

- sidebars with this icon ▤, which provide clear, plain-English definitions of legal terms. The law has its own language, and though this is a book for nonlawyers, we're occasionally forced to use some technical terms, or words to which the law assigns special meanings that may not always match our everyday usage. We'll put such terms in boldface the first time we use them, and give you a plain-language definition.

- sidebars with this icon ◖▶ indicate "Talking to a Lawyer" sections. Here, our experts respond to actual questions from people, giving legal information that may help you as you grapple with similar issues within your own family.

At the end of each chapter, in a section entitled "The World at Your Fingertips," we advise you where to go for more information if you'd like to explore a topic further—usually to free or inexpensive materials that will fill your mind without emptying your wallet. Our concluding section of each chapter—"You Must Remember This"—highlights the most important points that chapter has covered.

With this book, you'll be able to make informed decisions about a wide range of problems and opportunities. Armed with the knowledge and insights we provide, you can be confident that the decisions you make will be in your best interests.

The Honorable Judith Billings is a judge of the Utah Court of Appeals in Salt Lake City, Utah.

PART ONE

First Steps

CHAPTER 1

Why You Should Plan Your Estate

How You Can Save Money and Be Sure You've Done It Right

Things couldn't be better for Mark and Lea. They're young, doing well in their careers, and expecting a baby. The last thing they want to think about is planning their estates, right? Wrong. Estate planning can help Mark and Lea plan their financial future and save them money, now and down the line.

Estate planning. The phrase sounds so dry, distant, and foreboding. It's unfortunate so many people shy away from even the thought of it, because planning your estate is really about caring for your loved ones, seeing they are provided for, and making sure your hard-earned property is distributed according to your wishes. An **estate plan** is your blueprint for where you want your property to go after you die.

 WHAT IS AN ESTATE?

Your estate consists of all your property, including

- your home and other real estate (but how much of it is yours may depend on how title is held and who holds it),
- *tangible personal property* such as cars and furniture, and
- *intangible property* such as insurance, bank accounts, stocks and bonds, and pension and Social Security benefits.

While a will is usually the most important part of an estate plan, it's not the only part. These days, it's common for a person to have a dozen **will substitutes**—that is, various ways of distributing property regardless of whether the person has a formal will. Pensions, life insurance, gifts, joint ownership, and trusts are but a few of the ways will substitutes can transfer property at or before death quickly and inexpensively.

I'M YOUNG—WHY DO I NEED AN ESTATE PLAN?

We're all squeamish about death, but it's important to overcome our reluctance to plan for it. Millions of people of all ages and economic levels have taken steps to distribute their money and property according to a sound estate plan. The number of Americans with wills, for example, has grown by 50 percent in just fifteen years. A recent survey by the legal website Find Law determined that about half of all Americans now have wills—an all-time high. (Some studies put the number closer to 40 percent.)

Another survey, by AARP, found that 60 percent of Americans fifty and over have wills. As you would expect, the percentage is far higher among senior citizens. It is also higher among those with more education and greater assets. Click on www.research.aarp.org/econ/will.html for more on the study.

Estate planning is emphatically not just for the elderly. One glance at the news demonstrates that far too many young and middle-aged people die suddenly, often leaving behind minor children who need care and direction. Estate planning needs to be factored into your overall financial plan, along with your children's college tuition and your retirement needs. If your financial or familial circumstances change later in life, it's usually easy and inexpensive to adjust your plan.

Most people also plan for mental or physical incapacity resulting from an accident or illness. Through living wills, living trusts, durable powers of attorney, and health-care powers of attorney, you can control beforehand how you and your property are to be cared for if disaster strikes.

Estate planning also enables you to:

- **Determine what happens to your property. It enables you to coordinate gifts during your lifetime with bequests in your will or trust. You can apportion property among your family members, your friends, and charities that are important to you. If you don't have a will or trust, state law will step in and determine how to dispose of your property, in ways that you might not intend.**

- **Decide whether your business will be sold or stay in the family—and if so, who will run it.**

- **Determine who will be in charge of carrying out your wishes—your executor if you have a will, and your trustee if you have a trust. (In some jurisdictions, executors are known as "personal representatives.")**

- **Save money on probate, taxes, and other expenses of settling an estate.**

- **Be in control of your own life. A living trust or durable general power of attorney can provide a way to manage your property should you become disabled. A living will or health-care advance directive can set up a plan for your medical care, should you no longer be able to make decisions for yourself.**

- **Coordinate estate planning with other kinds of financial planning. For example, the new tax law has made significant changes in incentives to save for education (see chapter 22), making this an ideal time to look into planning for the education of children and grandchildren, as well as other financial issues.**

ⓘ TEN THINGS ESTATE PLANNING CAN DO FOR YOU

1. *Provide for your immediate family.* You can provide for your surviving spouse through life insurance, particularly if he or she doesn't work outside the home. You can pass your property on to your spouse and other members of your family, make sure you've selected a competent person to settle the estate and protect your property while the estate is being settled, and even take steps to protect your property from creditors. Without estate planning, your beneficiaries will get less, and they'll get it later.

   If you and your spouse should die before your children grow up, your will can assure your children's education and upbringing by nominating personal guardians for them. Otherwise, a court will appoint a guardian of the person and estate of your minor children without your input. The guardian of the person will decide where your children live, are educated, and worship. The court-appointed guardian of the children's estate (or property) will be required to account to the court for the administration of the child's estate, and this accounting can be costly and could prevent your children from enjoying the style of living you prefer for them. (See chapter 13.)

2. *Provide for other relatives who need help and guidance.* Do you have family members whose lives might become more difficult without you, such as an elderly parent or a disabled child, or a grandchild whose education you want to assure? You can establish a special trust fund for family members who need support that you won't be there to provide. (See chapters 9 and 10.)

3. *Get your property to beneficiaries quickly.* You want your beneficiaries to receive the property you've left them promptly. Probate may not be a problem in your jurisdiction. If it is, you can avoid or simplify probate through insurance, joint tenancy, a living trust, or other means (see chapters 3–5 and 11), or by using simplified or expedited probate. (See chapter 28.)

4. *Ease the strain on your family.* Ease the burden on your grieving survivors by planning your funeral arrangements when planning your estate (see chapter 25). You can also limit the expense of your burial or designate its place, and provide for your body to be cremated or given to medical science after you die.

5. *Minimize expenses.* Good estate planning keeps the cost of transferring property to beneficiaries as low as possible (see chapters 13–17). Choosing competent executors/trustees and giving them the necessary authority will save money, reduce the burden on your survivors, and simplify administration of your estate. It also will reduce a court's involvement and, in many states, eliminate the need to pay for a bond. (See chapters 26–27.)

6. *Reduce taxes on your estate.* Every dollar your estate has to pay in estate or inheritance taxes is a dollar that your beneficiaries won't get. A good estate plan can give the maximum allowed by law to your beneficiaries and the minimum to the government. (See chapters 20–22.)

7. *Make your retirement years easier.* Even though estate planning primarily benefits those you love and care about, you can also coordinate your estate plan with retirement, health-care, and other benefits to help you achieve the most comfortable final years while still providing for your loved ones. (See chapters 18–19.)

8. *Plan for incapacity.* **Health-care advance directives, living wills, and durable health-care powers of attorney** enable you to decide in advance about life support and pick someone to make decisions for you about medical treatment (see chapters 23–24). Some states permit you to designate a personal guardian. Disability insurance can protect you and your family should you become disabled and unable to work.

9. *Help a favorite cause.* Your estate plan can help you support religious, educational, and other charitable causes, either during your lifetime or upon your death, and at the same time take advantage of tax laws designed to encourage private philanthropy. (See chapter 22.)

10. *Make sure your business goes on smoothly.* If you have a business, you can provide for an orderly succession and continuation of its affairs by spelling out what will happen to your interest in the business. (See chapter 17.)

TALKING TO A LAWYER

Q. I'm thirty, have a pretty good job, and have a boyfriend I live with but no kids. Do I need to worry about estate planning?

A. Although you do not have any children to worry about, there are good reasons why you should consider writing a will. If you should die suddenly and not have a will, the law in most states would require that all property in your name be given to your parents. Your boyfriend, and any of your sisters or brothers, would be left out in the cold. By preparing a will, you can ensure that your property passes as you want it to.

—Answer by Harold Pskowski,
BNA Tax Management, Washington, D.C.

Q. Is there a minimum estate you have to have before making a will makes sense? In other words, if you're leaving a small amount, is it ever better just not to worry about a will?

A. Whether you need a will depends on your family circumstances. If you have a spouse and no children, the intestacy laws may work reasonably well for you. Most states have a mechanism for distributing a small estate without going through probate. However, without a will

WHAT HAPPENS IF I DIE WITHOUT A WILL?

If you die **intestate** (without a will), your property still must be distributed. By not leaving a valid will or trust, or transferring your property in some other way, such as through insurance, pension benefits, or joint ownership, you've in effect left it to state law to write your will for you. This doesn't mean that your money will go to the state. That happens only in very rare cases where the deceased leaves no surviving relatives, even very remote ones.

you lose the opportunity to name a guardian for your children, appoint the person to manage your estate, or provide for a gift to someone other than the next-of-kin specified in the intestacy laws of your state. Even if you are married, with no children, and want everything to go to your spouse, not having a will prevents you from planning how to dispose of your property should both of you die at the same time.

—Answer by Susan N. Gary, Professor of Law, University of Oregon School of Law, Eugene, Oregon

Q. *Have people showed more interest in estate planning following the 2001 terrorist attacks? Are they concerned about different issues now?*

A. The events of September 11, 2001, which cut short so many lives, convinced many people that they need to prepare a will to provide for their property and loved ones. Interest in estate planning is especially strong among those who have young children. The fact that the terrorist attacks left behind so many orphans has resulted in a new emphasis on using estate planning to ensure the financial and emotional well-being of the children of the person who is planning his or her estate.

—Answer by Harold Pskowski, BNA Tax Management, Washington, D.C.

But it does mean that the state will make certain assumptions about where you'd like your money to go—assumptions with which you might not agree. In some states, intestate descent laws take into account blood and marriage by giving a share of your estate to your children, or if there are no children, to your parents, rather than giving it all to the surviving spouse. In other states, a surviving spouse inherits the entire intestate estate and the children (or parents) are entitled to nothing. In addition, the intestacy rules in most states provide no distributive shares of your estate for family members who are not related to you by blood, marriage, or adoption. Stepchildren and unmarried domestic partners are typically excluded.

If you do not agree with the disposition imposed by the intestate laws of the state in which you reside, you need to have a will to specify who will benefit from your estate. Estate planning makes you the boss.

SAVING MONEY

A good estate plan can save your heirs plenty of money.

Probate costs

Probate is the court-supervised legal procedure that (1) determines the validity of your will, (2) gathers and distributes your assets, and (3) provides a process for paying creditors and putting a time limit on claims against your estate. Probate has been greatly improved in recent years, and may well be quick and inexpensive in your jurisdiction. If probate is a problem for you, good estate planning can minimize expense and delay by passing assets through means other than a will. (See chapters 3–5 for details.)

Executor fees

By having a will and planning well, you can minimize the executor's fees. If you name a relative who's a beneficiary under the will as executor (most likely your spouse), he or she will probably waive the fee. On the other hand, if you die without a will, the probate court will appoint a personal representative (usually an heir) to see the estate through probate, and the cost will be deducted from your estate. Similarly, if you pick a third party, such as a lawyer, to be the executor, that person is entitled to a "reasonable fee" for seeing an uncontested will through probate. While the amount varies, the fee is usually tied to what trust companies would get for performing similar duties. State law often treats this as a commission for the executor that varies with the size of the estate.

Legal fees in probate

If your estate is small and uncomplicated and your will is well drafted, your spouse or other executor may be able to reduce the costs of administration. For example, some states have "small estate" probate procedures that reduce the time and cost of probate for modest-sized estates. If things get more complex—for example, someone challenges the will, your will is out-of-date because you have a new spouse or child, the will is improperly prepared or executed, and so on—the cost of legal services becomes greater. You should count on paying whatever the going hourly rate is for a lawyer in your area. The more complex the probate process, the more hours the lawyer will have to put in—and the more it will cost your survivors.

THE WORLD AT YOUR FINGERTIPS

For further information about estate planning, the following resources are particularly helpful.

- The American Bar Association's Section of Real Property, Probate, and Trust Law has very good information for the public on its website (www.abanet.org/rppt/public/home.html).

- Nolo Press has an excellent website for the public. Check out wills and estate planning in their law center and in their online legal encyclopedia (http://www.nolopress.com/).

- FindLaw is another excellent site for the public, with plenty of information on wills and estates (consumer.pub.findlaw.com/wills/).

- Internet Law Library: Trusts and Estates contains a long list of links to estate-planning articles (www.priweb.com/internetlawlib/112.htm).

- "Crash Course in Wills and Trusts" is an introduction to the subject on a website maintained by a private law firm (www.mtpalermo.com).

- The National Association of Financial and Estate Planning
  has good information, especially for those with large estates
  (www.nafep.com/).

YOU MUST REMEMBER THIS

- Estate planning is not just for the elderly—it's a wise
  precaution at any stage of life.
- It puts you in control by letting you determine exactly how
  you want your property distributed.
- It can save you money in taxes and fees.
- It can provide a way for you to plan for any possible
  incapacity, letting you determine how you will be cared for
  when you're too ill to make decisions for yourself.

CHAPTER 2

Getting Started

Don't Procrastinate

Okay, okay, maybe estate planning is a good idea, but your financial records are shoved in boxes under your desk, you don't know a lawyer who does this kind of work, and it all seems like way too much trouble. How hard is it to plan your estate? Will you ever be able to put your feet under your desk?

Estate planning doesn't have to be a huge hassle. You don't have to be an expert on tax laws or the intricacies of wills. You have to think about what *you* want to do with your assets, and you have to gather some information—but the more you gather, the less work your lawyer may have to do, and the greater your savings.

TAKING INVENTORY

Start by writing down your basic goals—provide for your spouse and children, benefit certain charitable causes, and so on. Then it's time to get specific. Make up a checklist of assets and debts—what you own, what is owed to you, and what you owe. Don't forget to check into how assets (such as your house) are owned. If you have powers over trusts or other accounts being held for your benefit, include them, too.

One of the hardest tasks for an executor is figuring out just what money the deceased had coming in, and what bills and other payments need to be made. Think about your personal finances for a moment. If someone else suddenly had to step in and take over, would they know about (or be able to figure out) those royalties you have coming in from sales on a book you wrote three years ago? Or the payments you promised your friend Mac (orally, not in writing) for that boat of his?

Now is the time to put yourself in an outsider's shoes and write down all such expenses and income that might not otherwise be apparent to an executor. In doing so, you'll probably put your life in better order. It's another example of how estate planning is more than planning for your death. It can make your life a lot simpler, too.

"The Information You Need," a box in this chapter, lists important estate-planning data that you'll need to consider. You also may want to complete the more extensive "Estate-Planning Checklist" at the end of this book. It is detailed enough to be useful if you have a large, diversified estate, and is equally helpful if yours is a smaller, simpler estate. It also will enable you to do much of the preliminary work needed to prepare a solid estate plan. Plan on filling it out.

A FAMILY MEETING

Of course, a couple should communicate with each other so they agree on what goes to the surviving spouse and what goes to the children.

Because estate planning affects several generations, it may be a good idea, especially for families with grown children, to make your estate plan a family affair. Some families set aside a day and gather all family members who are involved in the plan. The parents can explain how this plan can have a major influence on all their lives, and why they're distributing gifts and trusts the way they are. They can also find out whether the children want to continue the family business, and ask if any property has sentimental value for them.

If you have such a meeting, encourage your family to voice their concerns and feelings about all this—remember, many people don't like to talk about death—and answer questions they may have. They may even raise issues that will lead you to call your lawyer or change your estate plan. It is easier to work through any potential conflicts while everyone is still alive than to let surprises revealed after death lead to a will contest.

▶ **MAKE SURE EVERYONE'S
ON BOARD**

Don't forget to tell the people you've selected as executors or guardians of the children, to make sure they agree to serve.

WHO CAN HELP

If your estate is relatively small and your objectives are not complicated, you might plan your estate mostly on your own, with the help of this book and other resource materials, using professional help largely for tasks like writing a will or trust. Planning for larger estates can involve the counsel of your lawyer, insurance adviser, accountant, and banker, as well as your family and friends.

WHAT WILL IT COST?

The cost of having an estate plan drawn up professionally depends on the size and complexity of your estate, the going rates for lawyers in your area, your lawyer's experience, and so on. For a basic will, some lawyers charge a flat fee that covers the costs of consulting with you, drawing up and executing the will, and any required filing fees. Most people need more than just a will, so many lawyers offer a package of estate-planning documents, including a basic will, a living will, and a durable health-care power of attorney.

More extensive estates, particularly those nearing $1 million, generally require professional help in minimizing taxes. More complex estates may involve one or more trusts, in addition to a will. With extensive estates, the lawyer often charges by the hour for the amount of work put into the estate plan.

Ask about fees at your first consultation and inquire about how much your total estate plan might cost. Make sure you have a clear understanding of the attorney's fee, preferably in writing. Some jurisdictions (e.g., the District of Columbia) now require that attorneys provide a written fee agreement to all new clients.

If you use a lawyer who charges by the hour, the more work you do in putting your wishes and the details of your estate in writing, the less work your lawyer has to do, and the lower the final costs will be.

CHOOSING A LAWYER

How do you find a lawyer to help you plan your estate and write any necessary documents? You can ask friends who have hired lawyers to draw up their wills. Or you can use any of the Internet resources listed in "The World at Your Fingertips" at the end of this chapter or elsewhere in this chapter, including lawyer referral programs and national and state groups that certify lawyers as specialists in estate planning. Lawyers will often offer a first consultation free of charge. At this get-acquainted session, you can ask about the lawyer's experience in estate planning and get a firm idea of fees.

 JUST A CLICK AWAY

The American Bar Association website has information that may help you get a referral to an estate-planning lawyer in your community. Access www.abanet.org/legalservices/public.html. The site also has information that will help you find a lawyer online, and will give you some tips on hiring a lawyer, sources of information for the public, and information about how to resolve problems with your lawyer.

By some estimates, over 100 million Americans are eligible for the benefits of **legal service plans.** These plans enable members to get legal services either free or at reduced cost. In many programs, simple wills are either free or cost far less than the going rate. More comprehensive estate planning and preparation of other documents are available from lawyers at a reduced hourly rate. About 80 percent of legal service plans are available to members of certain organizations (like the AARP, the military, or a union), or to employees of certain companies as a result of collective bargaining agreements or adoption of a plan by the employer. Plans may also be available to credit card holders, bank customers, or through individual sales agents. Some of these plans charge no fee at all to the participant; others may require payment of a monthly fee.

Legal clinics are another low-cost alternative. They can prepare your will for modest amounts because legal assistants do much of the work under a lawyer's guidance. That work often consists of adapting standard computerized forms to fit the needs of the client. If you have a small, simple estate, the cost may be modest, and you get professional advice and reassurance that your will meets the standards for validity in your state. You may be able to find a law school clinic or other clinic by looking in the Yellow Pages.

If you want to use a private lawyer, many will give you the first consultation free of charge. Ask a lawyer to give you a price or range of prices for preparing a will or estate plan; it might be cheaper than you think. Often, lawyers have a written fee schedule for various kinds of wills. If yours doesn't, before you give the final go-ahead to draw up your will, ask the estimated cost (or at least get a range of likely costs).

You should most certainly use a lawyer if you own a business, if your estate nears or exceeds $1 million (making tax planning a factor under current federal law), or if you anticipate a challenge to the will from a disgruntled relative or other person. Under current law, the federal floor for taxability of estates goes up to $1.5 million in 2004 and $2 million in 2006, but that might change within the lifetime of this book.

FIND A SPECIALIST IN YOUR STATE

In a number of states, lawyers are certified as specialists in estate-planning matters. This typically means that these lawyers have demonstrated particular competence in this area. Specialists have been recognized by an independent professional certifying organization as having an enhanced level of skill and expertise, as well as substantial involvement in an established legal specialty. These organizations require a lawyer to demonstrate special training, experience, and knowledge to ensure that the lawyer's recognition as a certified specialist is meaningful and reliable.

An ABA website—www.abanet.org/legalservices/specialization/home.html—provides links to all states having certification programs.

WHY NOT DO IT YOURSELF?

Who needs a lawyer, anyway? For as little as $20, you can buy a "will kit" in a book or on a CD-ROM that will help you fill out the forms and create your own will and perhaps other estate documents. For a steeper price, some services will even take the information customers provide and insert it into the proper form, or even check their work.

▶ FEEL COMFORTABLE WITH YOUR LAWYER

An essential: be comfortable with the lawyer you choose! A good estate lawyer will have to ask questions about many private matters, and you need to feel free to discuss these personal considerations with him or her. If you don't feel comfortable, find another lawyer who's willing to explain the options to you and who will help you do it right.

For some people—those with very small or otherwise uncomplicated estates (no real estate, for example)—such alternatives might provide sufficient help. Make sure that a given book or kit is up-to-date and thorough, especially since probate laws vary from state to state. The kits on CD-ROMs are easier than the ones in books to fit into your estate plan—they typically take you through a will with computer prompts that enable you to alter the document to fill typical needs.

But the least-expensive services don't provide anyone with legal expertise to review your work. Do-it-yourself books and kits, some lawyers say, have caused more work for lawyers (and bills for clients) than they have eliminated. Once you begin totaling up all your assets, you may be surprised to find that your estate is larger than you thought, meaning a simple will isn't enough.

What's more, most do-it-yourself alternatives can't tell you what strategies you might be able to take advantage of to save money or make sure your wishes are realized. Estate planning for most people should consist of more than just a will: IRAs, insurance, living trusts, and other elements can be a money-saving part of the mix. The precise mix that's best for you is as unique as your circumstances.

And because they cannot give legal advice, many alternative estate providers often fail to inform you when there might be a better (and cheaper) way to accomplish your goals. For example, a recent *New York Times* story recounted a reporter's experience with one such service. He wanted to leave his father part of his estate, but require the father to bequeath anything left over when he died to the reporter's children. The service "would not—could not—tell me that such a proviso is not binding (something I have since confirmed with a lawyer, who pointed out other ways to accomplish my goal)," he wrote. "I might have died in the naïve belief that my children were protected."

Law firms have other advantages—witnesses available (wills must be signed in front of witnesses to be effective), codes of conduct that protect clients' confidentiality, and, most of all, lawyers who know the various alternatives the law affords.

ⓘ WHAT AM I WORTH?

In 1995, the Federal Reserve estimated that 3 million American families had a net worth of at least $1 million. That number surely grew in the unprecedented economic boom of the 1990s. Despite the recession that followed, it is expected to more than double in the next few years.

Many people are surprised to learn what they're worth when they add it all up. To find out what you're worth, add up the current worth of all your assets, including

- liquid assets, such as certificates of deposit, money market funds, and bank accounts;
- fixed assets, including bonds;
- stocks and mutual funds;
- retirement plans, such as 401(k) plans, profit-sharing plans, and so on;
- personal assets, including your home, cars, and other property;
- insurance on your life; and
- the value of your business, rental property, or other real estate.

The next step is to subtract your mortgage and other debt. If the resulting figure approaches $1 million, then some serious estate planning is in order. Federal death taxes begin on estates totaling $1 million (scheduled to rise to $1.5 million in 2004), and these taxes can be steep, as much as 50 percent. Fortunately, your lawyer can tell you how bypass trusts, generation-skipping trusts, lifetime gifts, and other techniques can significantly lessen the tax load.

Although many people will be able to use a standard form, many more have unique situations and can benefit from the custom-made advice tailored to their specific situation by a lawyer who's obligated to represent their best interest. And since lawyers generally charge less for less complicated estates, you may be able to gain the benefits and flexibility of real legal advice at little more than the cost of a computerized will kit.

▶ THE INFORMATION YOU NEED

In planning your estate, it's helpful to have as much of the following information on hand as possible.

- The names, addresses, and birth dates of your spouse, children, and other relatives whom you might want to include in your will. List any disabilities or other special needs they may have.

- The names, addresses, and phone numbers of possible guardians (if you have young children) and executors or trustees.

- The amount and sources of your income, including interest, dividends, and other household income, such as your spouse's salary or income your children bring home, if they live with you.

- The amounts and sources of all your debts, including mortgages, installment loans, leases, and business debts.

- The amounts, sources, and beneficiaries of any retirement benefits, including IRAs, pensions, Keogh accounts, government benefits, and profit-sharing plans.

- The amounts, sources, and account numbers of other financial assets, including bank accounts, annuities, outstanding loans, and the like, and names of any joint owners or pay-on-death designees.

- A list of life insurance policies, including the account balances, issuer, owner, beneficiaries, and any amounts borrowed against the policies.

- A list (with approximate values) of valuable property you own, including real estate, jewelry, furniture, jointly-owned property (name the co-owner), collections, heirlooms, and other assets. This list could be cross-referenced with the names of the people to whom you might want to leave each item.

- The names, trustees, and assets of any trusts held for your benefit.

- Any documents that might affect your estate plan, including prenuptial agreements, marriage certificates, divorce decrees, recent tax returns, existing wills and trusts, property deeds, and so on.

TALKING TO A LAWYER

Q. *What advice do you have for clients who are just beginning the estate-planning process? What are the most important things they can do to make the process go smoothly?*

A. The most important thing is for the clients to give some serious thought to how they would like their families provided for, and their property divided, after their deaths. They also need to give some thought to who would implement these decisions for them; that is, who will be the personal representative of the estate, the guardian of their children, and the trustee of any trusts. Where minor children are involved, I often find that the question of who is to be the guardian is the most difficult one. The two spouses may disagree on this, so I usually suggest that they discuss it between themselves before they meet with me. Then, if they are still undecided, I can give them some guidelines for making a decision that they are both happy with.

The other important factor is to have an accurate listing of assets and liabilities. Unless the attorney is made aware of the nature of the client's property, it is impossible to plan for its transmission.

—Answer by Harold Pskowski,
BNA Tax Management, Washington, D.C.

Knowing that your will and estate plan will pass legal muster will help you sleep better at night—and that peace of mind is worth a few dollars more.

HOW THE PROCESS WORKS

Even if you've done a lot of thinking about your estate plan on your own, don't just expect to pile some papers on your lawyer's desk and have a will or trust magically appear in a few weeks.

Q. At best, 50 percent of Americans have wills or trusts. Why do so many people have trouble taking this step? What's the best way for people to overcome their reluctance?

A. I have found that often the reluctance to write a will is a result of fearing to face one's own mortality. I have seen seriously-ill individuals, people who are just days from death, still insist that they will get better and, therefore, do not need a will. It is very difficult to overcome such an elemental fear, and it is usually a family member or another loved one, not the attorney, who is successful in persuading such a person to prepare a will. Reading a book like this can be a helpful part of the process, since greater knowledge of wills and the probate process can help some people overcome their fears.

—Answer by Harold Pskowski,
BNA Tax Management, Washington, D.C.

Preparing these documents is seldom as simple as filling in blanks on a form. Most people will meet with their lawyer at least twice in the process, with more complicated estates requiring more consultations.

At the first meeting, you would probably discuss your financial situation and estate-planning goals. Be prepared to tell your lawyer about some rather intimate details of your life: how much money you have, how many more children you plan to have, which relatives you want to get more or less of your assets, and so on.

Your lawyer will review any documents you've brought in and ask questions that will help you think through various issues and possibilities. Then he or she will probably outline some of the options the law provides for accomplishing your goals. Though certain methods may be recommended over others, depending on your circumstances, it will still be up to you to make your own choices from among those options.

Then, based on the choices you have made, your lawyer will draft a will or trust. At a second meeting, he or she will review that document with you. If it meets with your approval, it can be signed then and there.

For more complicated estates, you may have some long phone conversations with your lawyer, and perhaps have to review several drafts of various estate-planning documents, before everything is settled.

You should review your estate plan periodically, so you'll want to stay in touch with your lawyer. Don't think of estate planning as a onetime retail transaction, but as an occasional process that works best when you have a continuing relationship with your professional advisers.

A SPECIAL NOTE FOR SPOUSES

You can't plan your estate if you don't know the facts about all the family assets. Yet, even in this era, lawyers say they still find that many clients who come to them for estate-planning advice don't have basic information about their spouse's income. All too often, the client doesn't know how much the spouse earns, what benefits he or she is entitled to, or where the money is invested. Whatever the reason for this situation, you need to know this information when planning your estate. It's especially important to find out how property you and your spouse own is titled, including insurance and other beneficiary designations.

Many people might be afraid to cause a rift in the marriage by asking a spouse about financial affairs—especially if that spouse is the primary breadwinner in the family. The need to share information and plan ahead can be raised indirectly—through another family member, an attorney, or another trusted professional—but full knowledge of the family's assets should be part of any sound estate plan.

THE WORLD AT YOUR FINGERTIPS

The following websites are among the tools that can help you find an estate-planning lawyer.

> *American Academy of Estate Planning Attorneys*
> www.aaepa.com/

> *American College of Trust and Estate Counsel*
> www.actec.org

> *The National Academy of Elder Law Attorneys*
> www.naela.org

> *National Association of Financial and Estate Planning*
> www.nafep.com/

To begin your search for a legal service plan that you might join, check the website of the not-for-profit American Prepaid Legal Services Institute (www.aplsi.org). However, not all plans are listed there, and you have to link to the plan to find out if you can join.

YOU MUST REMEMBER THIS

- Good estate planning requires good record keeping. It helps to have the essential information in one place, so that your lawyer and your family can find it if you die unexpectedly.

- Estate planning isn't a solo act—it's a group project, involving your family, your lawyer, and others whom you trust and who can help you.

PART TWO

Transferring Property Without a Will

You Have Many Ways of Getting Money

to People Without Fuss or Delay

CHAPTER 3

Lots of Little "Wills"

Your Guide to Will Substitutes

Darren and Samantha are newlyweds, each of whom has grown children from a previous marriage. They decide to buy a house together and take title to the house in joint tenancy with right of survivorship, making them co-owners.

After unpacking the last boxes, the happy couple decides to complete the remaking of their lives and rewrite their wills. Both of them want their assets to go to their own children from their first marriages. So each writes a basic will that leaves everything to his or her own children. Samantha's daughter, Tabitha, who is living in a tiny apartment with her husband and kids, will get Darren and Samantha's house when Samantha dies; Darren's children, who have nice homes already, will get the rest of the couple's assets. A few years later, Samantha dies, content because she believes she has provided for her daughter and her family.

This story does not have a happy ending, but it might have had she read this chapter.

Samantha will never know that her estate plan failed to accomplish the one thing she wanted most: giving her house to her daughter. She didn't realize that the joint tenancy she and Darren created meant that ownership of the entire house passed to Darren at the moment of her death, regardless of what her will said. She never knew that Darren was later beset by several costly illnesses and had to sell the house. His children—not hers—received what was left when Darren died two years later.

A **prenuptial agreement** (a signed contract between Darren and Samantha) would have prevented this, as would holding the house in another form of tenancy. (See chapters 14 and 15 for more on prenuptial agreements.)

A WILL ISN'T ENOUGH

Unfortunately, this situation is familiar to many estate lawyers. Too many people don't understand that there's more to estate planning than writing a will.

A will is usually the most important document in planning your estate, but it doesn't cover everything. In the **community property** states (see "Community Property: Half and Half" later in this chapter), your will can only control half of most marital assets. Other benefits not controlled by a will (or a trust being used as a will substitute) include IRAs, insurance policies, income-saving plans, retirement plans, and joint tenancy (some jurisdictions also have a special form of joint tenancy for married couples called tenancy by the entirety).

A good estate plan must coordinate these benefits with your will. Using them well can give your beneficiaries money much more efficiently than a will can. Use them badly, like Samantha, and you can negate your estate plan and frustrate your wishes.

ⓘ PROPERTY THAT DOES NOT PASS VIA A WILL

- Property held in joint tenancy (see chapter 5)
- Life insurance payable to a named beneficiary
- Property held in a trust
- Retirement plans payable to named beneficiaries, including IRAs, Keogh accounts, and pensions
- Bank accounts payable to named beneficiaries upon the death of the depositor
- Transfer-on-death stock accounts payable to a named beneficiary
- Some community property
- Income-saving plans

This chapter looks briefly at a number of the many ways you can transfer property. Two of the most common means, life insurance and joint tenancy, are examined in chapters 4 and 5.

RETIREMENT BENEFITS AND ANNUITIES: BEYOND THE GOLD WATCH

Most of us are entitled to **retirement benefits** from an employer. Typically, a retirement plan will pay benefits to beneficiaries if you die before reaching retirement age. After retirement, you can usually pick an option that will continue payments to a beneficiary after your death.

In most cases, the law requires that some portion of these retirement benefits be paid to your spouse. This right may be waived only with your spouse's properly witnessed, signed consent. Why would your spouse waive the right? There are several possible reasons. These accounts are subject to the payment of the income tax that has been deferred during their existence. Sometimes a spouse rejects benefits because of tax consequences or because there is enough income from other sources and the money might be better used by another beneficiary. Check your plan to see what is required for this waiver.

Payment options are treated differently for tax purposes. Ask your tax adviser how they'll affect your estate and tax planning. (See chapter 18.)

(i) IRAs PASS MONEY QUICKLY

IRAs (individual retirement accounts) provide a ready source of cash when one spouse dies. If your spouse is named as the beneficiary, the proceeds will immediately become your spouse's property when you die. Like retirement benefits (and unlike assets inherited via a will), they will pass without having to go through probate.

LIFE ESTATES: TEMPORARY OWNERSHIP

You can, of course, give property to beneficiaries before you die, subject to gift taxes. Often it makes sense to get an appreciated asset (such as a house that's increased in value over the years) out of your estate to save on taxes. (See chapter 22.)

Life estates are different from gifts. Many older people choose to assign the family home to the children who have expressed an interest in living there after the parents have died. The parents retain a life estate interest in the house, meaning that the parents have the right to live there until they die. The property remains in their estate for transfer tax purposes but not for probate purposes.

You can also choose to leave your children a life estate in family property that you want maintained down through the generations, like a home. The children can live in the house or rent it out during their lifetimes, but must maintain it in good condition for the ultimate beneficiaries, usually the grandchildren.

If this sounds like an option appropriate for your family, talk to your lawyer about such an assignment. Remember, though, that by conveying property through a life estate you give up control of your property; also, life estates are subject to complex legal rules and often cause more complications than they're worth. There are better planning options than life estates.

BENEFICIARY DEEDS

When you designate a beneficiary of an insurance policy or similar device, you are in effect "willing" your property to that person or institution after your death. Many jurisdictions now permit property that has a registered title (cars, trailers, airplanes, boats, etc.) to be left to beneficiaries as individuals, joint tenants, and tenants in common, and even to the descendants of deceased beneficiaries. So the beneficiary designation becomes something of a will unto itself.

In the states that have authorized them, **beneficiary deeds** have to be recorded at the appropriate office before the death of the person authorizing them (the **grantor**). In many states, this is the state department of revenue. Beneficiary deeds are not effective until the grantor's death, or the surviving grantor's in cases where there are more than one. They may be revoked at any time.

Thus a beneficiary deed has all of the advantages of a joint tenancy, and few, if any, of the disadvantages, which explains why they are becoming more and more popular as partial will substitutes. For example, a beneficiary deed naming as beneficiary the niece who has been taking care of you will ensure that she gets the property on your death but won't transfer any ownership rights while you are alive. Your lawyer can explain the ins and outs of your state's law relating to beneficiary deeds.

(In many jurisdictions, items that require a registered title can also be conveyed to someone else when you die via a **transfer-on-death** designation that accompanies the title.)

PAY-ON-DEATH DESIGNATIONS

Pay-on-death (**POD**) and **transfer-on-death** (**TOD**) designations can also apply to annuities, brokerage accounts, bank accounts, and corporate stock, depending on the state, and in fact are often used on those types of financial assets. In the case of corporate stock, it is generally used on closely held, rather than publicly traded, stock. A POD or TOD designation works in much the same way as a beneficiary deed. It, too, can be changed by the owner at any time.

The chief advantage of these designations is that they avoid probate. The disadvantage is that transmission of the TOD or POD property will not be controlled by the terms of the owner's will, which may have been his or her intent.

COMMUNITY PROPERTY: HALF AND HALF

The laws of eight states—Arizona, California, Idaho, Louisiana, Nevada, New Mexico, Texas, and Washington—and Puerto Rico provide that most property acquired during the marriage by either spouse is held equally by husband and wife as community property. (Alaska and Wisconsin have some community property elements in their law but are not true community property states. In Alaska, for example, community property is elective, and most spouses probably are not subject to the community property provisions.)

When one spouse dies, his or her half of the community property passes either by will or intestacy. The other half of the community property belongs to the surviving spouse. If you lived in one of the community property states while married, some of your property may be community property, even if you don't live there now. The major exception to marital community property is property acquired by inheritance or gift.

Unlike joint tenancy, community property isn't automatically transferred to the surviving spouse. When your spouse dies, you own only your share of the community property, and if your spouse wants you to have his share, he must give it to you in a will. Often the deceased spouse's share must be probated, but it depends on what state you live in. California, for example, no longer requires probate for property passing directly from one spouse to the other.

This arrangement can affect your estate planning in many ways. What if your spouse assumes his or her life insurance will give you enough money and leaves everything to your grown children? In a community property state, that means half of the community property goes to the children. They now own half the house, half the car, half the vacation house on the lake. If there wasn't much cash in the estate or in insurance paid to them, the only way they can really benefit from the will is to sell the property so they can share the proceeds. You'll either have to move out and get another car, or they'll have to struggle along

▶ **KNOW WHAT CONSTITUTES COMMUNITY PROPERTY**

Community property laws affect how much of your family's property you can dispose of legally. When you're planning your estate, first determine what is considered community property and what is considered separate property. This is not always easy, and the rules vary from state to state. Your lawyer can help you figure out which is which, so that you know what property you can transfer through estate planning. A lawyer may also be able to help you get income tax benefits that may apply to community property if you ever lived in a community property state.

until you die. Married people in community property states should think long and hard before leaving property to anyone other than their spouse.

INTER VIVOS GIFTS: GIVING IT AWAY BEFORE YOU DIE

Are gifts made while you're alive a good idea? Maybe, especially if you have a large estate: They can help you avoid high death taxes. Or, in some states, they might help you to make a small estate smaller and thus to avoid full-fledged probate. Another advantage of giving property away before you die is that you get to see the recipient enjoy your generosity.

You have to watch out for a few things, however. Of course, you want to be sure that gifts are only made from excess assets—don't impoverish yourself. In addition, inter vivos gifts beyond a certain size are subject to gift taxes. Current law permits you to give up to $11,000 per person per year ($22,000 if a couple makes the gift) before the tax kicks in. You can make gifts to any number of people, and they don't have to be related to you. You can also make gifts to trusts and to charities.

▤ INTER VIVOS GIFTS

Gifts made while you're alive are known as **inter vivos** gifts. Gifts made to trusts are a common means of making such transfers, but you can also make outright gifts of cash or other property.

You also have to watch out when giving a gift that has a low cost basis. The recipient of the gift takes your cost basis, so if you give someone stock that is worth $11,000 now but was worth only $1,000 when you bought it, the recipient will have to pay a healthy capital gains tax when the stock is sold. If you gave the recipient a cash gift of $11,000, there would be no tax owed.

You also have to make clear whether living gifts are advancements. Living gifts are **advancements** if you intended them to be subtracted from the amount you left a beneficiary in a will or trust. For example, suppose you write a will that leaves your son $25,000. Knowing that you have a terminal illness, you give him $10,000 to help him through a rough time. Then, a month after that, you die. If your will stated that any gifts, like the $10,000, were advancements, the probate court would subtract the $10,000 from the $25,000. If you do intend that the gift be an advancement and you put that in writing, the court will reduce the amount your son will receive even if you did not leave a will, through your state's intestate succession laws.

THE WORLD AT YOUR FINGERTIPS

- For information about pension rights and options, the administrator of your pension is a good place to start; check with your employer. For more general information about pensions, access the website of the Pension Rights Center, which has many excellent links (www.pensionrights.org/).

- For more on IRAs, check the AARP website (www.aarp.org/confacts/grandparents/ira.html). The AARP also has general information on wills (www.aarp.org/legalsolutions/faqs/wills.html).

- For beneficiary designations in general, personal finance sites often have good information. Try the Forbes website (www.forbes.com/estate_planning/), the American Express website (especially for retirement planning—www.americanexpress.com/homepage/mt_personal.shtml), and the Merrill Lynch website (www.askmerrill.ml.com/research_sub/1,2272,8,00.html?n=10&pageNum=1).

YOU MUST REMEMBER THIS

- The main thing is to be aware of the kinds of property that a will or trust doesn't cover. The various other ways of conveying property give you options that you can use in your estate planning if they're right for you.

- You should also keep records of property not conveyed by a will or trust and your other assets in a single place. To avoid confusion, mention their existence in your will or trust. This makes estate planning easier for you and locating your assets easier for your family after you die.

CHAPTER 4

Life Insurance

An Old Standby Has Lots of Uses

Brian and Paula are brand-new parents—of twins, no less! They know they need life insurance more than ever, but have plenty of questions. This chapter will provide some general guidelines.

Life insurance is often a good estate-planning tool, because you pay relatively little up front and your beneficiaries get much more when you die. When you name beneficiaries other than your estate, the money passes to them directly, without probate. If most of your money is tied up in nonliquid assets like your company or real estate, life insurance gets cash into your beneficiaries' hands without their having to resort to a fire sale of other assets. Though procedures vary by company, usually the beneficiaries receive their insurance proceeds promptly. Generally, the beneficiary informs the company in writing of the death, sends a copy of the death certificate, and receives a check, often within a few weeks.

☰ TERM INSURANCE AN OPTION

Term insurance provides protection not for your entire life, but only for a specified term of years; it's cheap when you're young, but gets more expensive as you grow older. It can be a good idea, especially if you're relatively young or are starting a business venture; banks sometimes insist that an entrepreneur's life be covered by such a policy as a condition of advancing capital.

However, be warned that life insurance isn't always the estate-planning panacea the insurance sellers claim. You need to consider what purpose the life insurance serves before you can decide which product is appropriate, how much coverage to buy, and who should own the policy.

To decide how much to purchase, begin by estimating the long- and short-term needs of your survivors. Next, estimate what will be covered by other sources such as savings, a pension, and other benefits. You'll want to buy enough life insurance to cover the difference.

HOW LIFE INSURANCE CAN PAY ESSENTIAL EXPENSES

Here are some examples of the long- and short-term needs your family may encounter. To help minimize their worries, write up a plan with categories like these. Then, when the insurance proceeds are paid, your survivors will know exactly how to budget the money they'll be receiving from life insurance.

Costs of death

Funeral, burial, and hospital bills . . . these are the most common expenses that result from death. Life insurance proceeds reach your survivors quickly and are useful for dealing with these expenses. Your family should expect to pay $5,000 to $7,500 to cover such costs—and more if the funeral arrangements are complicated or medical costs were high and not covered by insurance.

Replacing lost income

You don't want your family to have to sell property to support themselves in the absence of your paycheck. Nor do you want your working spouse to have to take a second job. Experts say that a family needs 75 percent of its former after-tax income to maintain its standard of living after the principal wage earner dies.

If you don't want your surviving spouse to have to work while raising the children, figure out how much it will take to support the family until the children are grown or at least able to care for themselves after school.

Providing liquidity

Sometimes an estate largely consists of illiquid assets, such as a closely held family business or farm. An insurance policy can provide funds so that such assets don't have to be sold to pay debts and expenses. Or an insurance trust (see chapter 22) can buy such assets from the estate, thereby infusing the estate with enough cash to pay taxes and debts.

Grief fund

Life insurance proceeds can support your family during the period of grief after your death so they don't have to go back to work too soon. This fund could equal up to several months of their normal income.

Educational expenses

You can use life insurance proceeds (especially if paid into a trust) to set up a college fund for your children.

Mortgage-canceling life insurance

Such a plan will pay off your mortgage when you die, so your survivors don't have to sell the family house. Or you can increase your life insurance by an amount sufficient to pay off the mortgage.

Emergency fund

After figuring out the other needs, you might tack on several thousand dollars to help the family cope with unexpected emergencies.

( ) TALKING TO A LAWYER

Q. Should life insurance be part of most estate plans? If so, are there rules of thumb on how much to purchase?

A. Insurance should be part of your estate plan if you anticipate that there will be a need for cash following your death. Usually, insurance is purchased to provide for the support of family members after your death, but it may also be used to pay off debts and to cover the expenses of a business temporarily until it can be sold or refinanced.

When the support of family members is your primary goal, the rule of thumb is that you should purchase insurance that is six to seven times the annual income that your family will lose as a result of your death. This amount can be reduced if you have other investments or property that can support your family after you are gone, but it may need to be increased if your family is accustomed to a high standard of living, or if you want to ensure that your children have educational opportunities at the college and postgraduate levels.

Q. There are lots of insurance products out there. What are the criteria for choosing one type of life insurance over another?

A. There is no single best insurance product. Instead, you need to look at your needs and the amount of money that you have available. Term insurance is the cheapest form of insurance and may be appropriate for someone with limited funds and only a temporary need for insurance coverage. Permanent or "whole life" insurance, on the other hand, is considerably more expensive, but it has the advantage of a level premium payment and can be used as a tax-deferred savings plan. Make sure that you are not being sold just any product, but that you are buying insurance that is appropriate for you.

—Answers by Harold Pskowski,
BNA Tax Management, Washington, D.C.

POLICY OWNERSHIP

Who should own the life insurance policy? If it's in your name, the proceeds payable on death (not the value of the premiums paid) will be included in your estate for estate tax purposes. That might force the estate to pay taxes if it pushes the value beyond the federal tax limit. If the beneficiary is your spouse, the **marital deduction** will enable your estate to escape taxes on the value of the policy, though the proceeds may push your spouse's estate over the limit, creating tax problems down the line. If someone else owns the insurance policy (commonly, a life insurance trust, see sidebar), the proceeds aren't included in your estate, enabling you to reduce its taxable value. In most cases, the recipient won't have to pay income taxes on the proceeds.

CHOOSING BENEFICIARIES

Who should get the benefits? If you own life insurance on your own life, you can have the proceeds distributed in three ways.

1. *To beneficiaries.* The company pays the proceeds directly to one or more beneficiaries named in your policy. This is the quickest way to get the money to your survivors, and the proceeds pass free of income tax and can't usually be touched by creditors. However, the beneficiaries may be liable for estate taxes if the proceeds, when added to the other assets in the estate, total more than the federal estate tax limit.

2. *To your probate estate.* If you choose this route, the proceeds will be distributed along with your other assets according to the terms of your will. (If you die without a will, your state's intestate succession laws will determine where the proceeds go.) However, they will go through the probate process and may be subject to creditors' claims. In some instances, the proceeds might add to the cost of probate by making the estate larger. You should have proceeds made payable to your probate estate only if your estate won't otherwise have enough money to pay debts and taxes.

(i) BENEFITS IF A TRUST OWNS THE POLICY

Paying the proceeds to a **life insurance trust** has several advantages:

- In many jurisdictions, creditors can't get at them.

- Generally, an estate tax will not have to be paid on the proceeds if the policy was transferred to an irrevocable trust more than three years before your death or purchased initially by the trust. Such trusts are complex, and you should surely use a lawyer to set one up.

- If the trust is for the benefit of your minor children, you can avoid the expense and court involvement of having a guardian manage this property. By having the proceeds paid to a trust, the trustee will have control over it.

See chapter 22 for more on such trusts.

3. *To a trust.* If you make the proceeds payable to a trust—either one set up after your death through your will or a trust set up during your lifetime—they will be distributed like the other trust assets.

THE WORLD AT YOUR FINGERTIPS

- One way of finding out about life insurance options—without enduring a sales pitch—is to access the website of an insurance company, such as MetLife (www.metlife.com/). Typing "life insurance" into your favorite search engine will bring up the sites of many other companies.

- Many companies offer a life insurance benefit. If yours does, speak to your company's human resources (HR) office about coverage, beneficiaries, and other related issues.

YOU MUST REMEMBER THIS

- Life insurance can be a valuable part of an estate plan; it gets money to your survivors quickly and helps them to avoid red tape.

- The decision about who should own the policy and to whom it should be paid should be coordinated with your estate plan, preferably with the assistance of your lawyer.

CHAPTER 5

Joint Tenancy

It's Easy and Cheap—but
Watch Out for Pitfalls

Ellen and Charlie are newlyweds. They just bought their first house. At the closing, the real estate agent tells them that they should take title to the property in joint tenancy. "That's what everyone does," she says. But is that really what everyone does? And, even if it is, is it a good idea for them?

Joint tenancy is owning property with someone else. **Joint tenancy** is a legal term that means, essentially, co-owner-ship. If you and your spouse (like Darren and Samantha in chapter 3) buy a house or car in both your names, each of you is considered a joint tenant and has co-ownership. When one of you dies, the other joint tenant immediately owns it all, regardless of what either of you says in your will.

Joint tenancy (sometimes called **survivorship**) can be a useful way to transfer property at death. Family cars and brokerage accounts often pass that way.

IS JOINT TENANCY FOR YOU?

Joint tenancy has its advantages. It's inexpensive to create, for example. In some jurisdictions, if one of the tenants dies, jointly held property might defeat the claims of creditors, or at least make their lives a great deal more difficult.

Should you put property in joint tenancy as part of your estate planning? The answer will vary depending on your circumstances. The current floor for federal estate taxes ($1 million in 2003; $1.5 million in 2004–2005) is high enough that tax considerations won't play a part for most people. That eliminates one source of

📋 TENANCY BY THE ENTIRETY

Some states recognize a special kind of joint tenancy called a **tenancy by the entirety.** Such a relationship can protect a married couple's assets from the claims of at least some of the creditors of only one of the spouses (tax claims, however, may take precedence). Such a tenancy can keep either spouse from being disinherited by the other. Check with your lawyer to see whether your state permits this arrangement and whether it's a good idea for your situation.

---

problems for most of us, though it's worth remembering that creation of a joint tenancy could result in a taxable gift. However, many estate planners urge caution, even for small estates where taxes aren't an issue. The next section explains why.

THE UNLUCKY EIGHT: WHEN JOINT TENANCY IS *NOT* A GOOD IDEA

1. *When you don't want to lose control.* By giving someone co-ownership, you give them co-control. If you make your son co-owner of the house, you cannot sell or mortgage it unless he agrees. (If he later marries, his wife may also have to agree.) If you do sell it, he may be entitled to part of the proceeds. Joint ownership of stock also means you've lost control. If you put your daughter on your stock accounts as a joint tenant, she can veto transactions.

2. *When you can't be sure of your co-owner.* You and your co-owner could have a falling-out, with disastrous consequences that you could do nothing about. And, in many states, someone who jointly owns real estate can force a sale of the property without the other owner's consent, no matter how small a portion he or she owns. He or she would do so by filing a suit for

⚠ NOT A FLEXIBLE TOOL

Joint tenancies deprive you of the flexibility of a will or a trust, in which you can use gifts and asset shifts to minimize taxes, and pay out money over time to beneficiaries instead of giving it to them all at once.

partition, which asks a court to separate the respective interests in property of joint owners so each may take control of his or her share of the property. A forced sale of the property is a way for each owner to have the value of his or her share of the property.

Also, if one of the co-owners becomes legally incompetent to make decisions, part of the property may go into a **guardianship** (a legal relationship between the incompetent person and the person appointed to act for him or her)—making it cumbersome at best if the other joint tenant wants to sell a house or some stock.

Finally, if creditors come after your co-owner, they may be able to get part of the house. For example, creditors could get a lien on your co-owner's half of the house, which could prevent either of you from selling it. (Of course, they couldn't sell it, either, but they'd have a club over your co-owner's head—and yours.)

3. *When you're in a shaky marriage.* In most states, your individual property becomes marital property once it's transferred into joint names. (In some community property states, simply putting property in both spouses' names does not necessarily make it marital property.)

4. *If your intentions may change.* When you transfer property into joint tenancy, you make a gift of one-half of the property to the new joint tenant. If you later change your mind, you can't undo the gift. For example, if Carol and Mark are an unmarried couple, they may put their home into joint tenancy to show their commitment to each other. If they split up a few years later, they each own half of the house, regardless of who paid for

it. And because they weren't married, they don't have the divorce rules to help them sort out their property interests.

5. *When you're using co-ownership to substitute for a will.* When people put their property in joint names, their primary goal may be to avoid probate. (See chapter 28.) However, if they overlook any of their property and leave some items in just one person's name, probate administration might be needed anyway to distribute the property not placed in joint names.

Joint tenancy doesn't help if all the joint tenants die at once. Each needs a will, or else the rules of intestacy will apply, meaning that the assets might not go where either joint tenant would choose. Nor does it answer the question of where your property goes if the younger joint tenant dies first, so you still need a will. And if you put one child's name on an account, assuming that he'll divide the money equally among the other children, you should know that legally he can do whatever he pleases with it. On top of all this, the transfer of property setting up this type of ownership could result in adverse income tax consequences when the surviving beneficiary sells the appreciated property.

6. *When it might cause confusion after your death.* Say that your mother makes you a joint owner of her bank account, so

---

(i) JOINT BANK ACCOUNTS

Particularly in old age, people often create joint bank accounts with their spouses, one or more children, or friends. The idea is that when one of the co-owners dies, joint ownership will give the other owners instant access to the account to help pay bills. However, a joint bank account is a nonprobate contractual arrangement that is similar to joint tenancy, but has important differences under the laws of many (if not most) states. For example, in many states, the joint account may belong to the party who deposited the funds, and ownership of the account may not be transferred to the surviving party until the death of the depositor. In these states, an account is more like a pay-on-death account than a joint tenancy.

⚠️ AVOIDING PITFALLS

Many of the problems associated with joint tenancies also occur with **institutional revocable trusts** and other forms of ownership of bank, broker, and mutual fund accounts and savings bonds. If you own any of these kinds of property, be sure that you understand what happens to them when you die, and plan accordingly.

---

you can help her with her shopping and bill paying. Whom does she intend to own that account when she dies? Often, nasty lawsuits ensue between the original owner's estate and the surviving joint owner. A common question: Did the owner put the property in a joint account to make a gift to the surviving tenant, or was the joint owner really a comanager of the business or property? And if the younger co-owner should die first, that might cause some unplanned tax consequences for her estate.

7. *When it won't speed the transfer of assets.* Some states automatically freeze jointly owned accounts upon the death of one of the owners until the tax collector can examine them, so the surviving partner can't count on getting to the money immediately.

8. *When it compromises tax planning.* Careful planning to minimize the taxes on an estate can be thwarted by an inadvertently created joint tenancy that passes property outright to a beneficiary.

What's more, passing property by joint tenancy can make it impossible to take advantage of other tax-saving devices, such as trusts. A joint tenancy between husband and wife may well produce an unfavorable cost basis for the surviving spouse; that's because for federal estate tax purposes, only one-half of the property involved would be included in the estate of the first spouse to die. Thus, only one-half of the property would receive a stepped-up cost basis, giving rise to potential capital gains on behalf of the surviving spouse in the event that the property should subsequently be sold. It can also increase gift taxes.

However, there may not be any gift tax implications for joint bank accounts until the co-owner makes a withdrawal or for savings bonds or stocks held by a broker.

SOME ALTERNATIVES TO JOINT TENANCY

Most of the advantages of joint tenancy can be achieved using a simple **revocable living trust.** (See chapter 11.)

For certain kinds of property, a device called a **beneficiary deed** can accomplish many of the benefits of joint tenancy with few of the risks. (Check with your attorney to see if this alternative is available in your state and useful to you.) **Transfer-on-death** designations may have the same benefits for other types of property.

In some states, the law permits **convenience accounts** that avoid some of the problems with joint tenancy while allowing the co-owner to write checks and so on. Some banks permit a co-owner addition to be "for convenience only," meaning that the co-owner will not inherit the account.

Also, your state may allow **pay-on-death bank accounts** that will give whomever you name as beneficiary access to the account at your death. This is a form of co-ownership that becomes active only when the account holder dies. It's a good way to get money to beneficiaries at death but not before. Coupled with a **power of attorney** (an instrument in which you authorize someone to act for you), it can help you retain ownership while you're alive, while giving your beneficiary management authority. It could have estate tax consequences, though, so check with your bank, accountant, or lawyer.

Note that convenience accounts and pay-on-death accounts are quite different. The first of these permits the co-owner to write checks but does not grant ownership at death. The second is just the opposite—no rights while the co-owner is alive, but possession of the property at death. Make sure that you understand the account you set up and that it can do what you want it to.

( ) TALKING TO A LAWYER

Q. We belatedly realized that holding our house in joint tenancy wasn't a good idea. How can we get it out of joint tenancy?

A. Your attorney can easily prepare a deed in which the joint tenancy owners convey the property to themselves as tenants in common. Most states exempt this type of deed from transfer taxes, and it should not be subject to the federal gift tax. Before you do this, however, make sure that this transfer is not prohibited by the terms of your mortgage and that it will not invalidate your title insurance policy. Your attorney can advise you on this.

Q. All things considered, what's the best alternative to joint tenancy?

A. In many cases, the use of a revocable living trust will be the best alternative. If properly set up, a living trust will ensure that a trusted individual will be available to manage your property if you become disabled, without giving up any of the tax benefits associated with your sole ownership of the property. As an added benefit, any property in the trust will avoid probate.

—Answers by Harold Pskowski,
BNA Tax Management, Washington, D.C.

Finally, chapters 20–22 discuss the possible tax advantages for spouses who put property in their names separately instead of owning it jointly.

ONE MORE ALTERNATIVE: TENANCY IN COMMON

Don't confuse joint tenancies with **tenancies in common.** (It's easy to do, especially when a state law deems an asset held in joint tenancy as titled "jointly as tenants in common.") In joint tenancy, you and your spouse both own the *whole* house, which means, among other things, that you both must agree to sell it. In tenancy in common, on the other hand, you each own a *half-share* of the house, and either of you may sell your half-share without the other's consent (though not many buyers are interested in purchasing half a house). In addition, with a tenancy in common, different partners can own unequal shares of the property.

Another difference: If you own an asset in joint tenancy with anyone and you die, ownership of that asset passes to the other joint tenant automatically. With a tenancy in common, your share passes as provided in your will or trust, with possible probate and other consequences.

Tenancy in common can be less risky than joint tenancy, and it is especially useful for larger estates in which you give shares of property to the children during your lifetime. Ask your lawyer if it might be useful in your estate planning.

THE WORLD AT YOUR FINGERTIPS

- The website of NebFacts (www.ianr.unl.edu/pubs/homemgt/ nf293.htm), a service of the University of Nebraska, has fact sheets that provide information on joint tenancy and a number of other estate-planning tools. The fact sheets are available online, and hard-copy versions of the service's pamphlets are also available for sale.

- A number of state bar associations have consumer pamphlets on joint tenancy and other legal topics. Contact your state's bar association (usually located in the state capital; you may be able to find its website at www.abanet.org/barserv/ stlobar.html) to request the relevant material, or enter "joint tenancy" into your favorite search engine to bring up online versions.

- A private law firm website—www.estateplancenter.com/ joint_tenancy/jointt.html—also contains information about joint tenancy and other estate-planning issues.

YOU MUST REMEMBER THIS

- Joint tenancy can have some advantages over other ways of transferring property, but it has dangers and unintended consequences, so it's best to check with a lawyer before entering into a joint tenancy agreement.

- In general, it's best to avoid a joint tenancy when you have any doubts at all about your co-owner.

- Joint tenancy is not a substitute for a will—it's virtually impossible to get all your property into a joint tenancy, so you'll still need a will or a trust.

- If you're lucky enough to be over the tax threshold, joint tenancies can cause real problems by inadvertently transferring ownership to the wrong co-owner or making it harder to transfer property to minimize taxes.

- Joint tenancies should be coordinated with your will, your trust, and other elements of your estate plan.

PART THREE

Wills

What Should Be in Yours?

CHAPTER 6
Wills 101

The Basics

Homer is a laid-back sort of guy. His heart's in the right place, but he doesn't want to go through all those formalities. He tells his wife, Marge, that he wants to leave everything to her, and he even scrawls that message on the back of a bar napkin. Any chance that this informal "will" is going to do the trick?

A will is a revocable transfer that takes effect on death. Wills have been with us since the first days of recorded history. Archaeologists have found 4,500-year-old hieroglyphics in Egyptian tombs leaving property to others. Bible readers will recall that Jacob left Joseph a larger inheritance than his brothers received, and the trouble that bequest caused.

Whether in ancient Egypt or modern America, all wills are different. What you put in yours depends on what property you have, whom you want it to go to, the dynamics of your family, and so on. You've already taken a big step toward preparing to write your will by preparing the list of objectives and inventory of assets and debts described in chapter 2. This chapter answers some of the basic questions many people ask before they start to create a will, and sets out the basic principles the law requires of them.

THE SEVEN ESSENTIALS OF A VALID WILL

To be valid, your will doesn't have to conform to a specific formula. For example, in states that recognize handwritten wills, some wills scrawled on the back of an envelope have stood up in court. However, there are certain elements that usually must be present.

1. *Legal age.* You must be of legal age to make a will. This is eighteen in most states, but you may be younger in some places and may have to be older in others.

2. *Sound mind.* You must be of sound mind, which means that you should know you're executing a will, know the general nature and extent of your property, and know the objects of your bounty (i.e., your spouse, descendants, and other relatives who would ordinarily be expected to share in your estate). The law presumes that a will maker was of sound mind, and the standard for proving otherwise is very high—much more than mere absentmindedness or forgetfulness.

Because disgruntled relatives who want to challenge a will occasionally use this sound-mind requirement to attack the will maker's mental capacity, in special cases the execution of a will is sometimes videotaped and kept on file, so if someone raises a question after the will maker dies, the videotape can be good evidence of **testamentary capacity.** (Of course, if the will maker is in the last stages of a debilitating disease, a videotape might appear to show a lack of capacity.)

3. *Intended to transfer property.* The will must have a substantive provision that disposes of property, and it must indicate your intent to make the document your final word on what happens to your property—that is, that you really intended it to *be* a will.

4. *Written.* Although **oral wills,** if witnessed, are permitted in limited circumstances in some states (see the next section), wills must usually be written and witnessed. Nevada recently authorized electronic wills, but it is still unclear how this will work and whether other states will follow suit.

5. *Properly signed.* The will must be voluntarily signed by the will maker, unless illness, an accident, or illiteracy prevents it, in which case you can direct that your lawyer or one of the witnesses sign for you. This requirement suggests the need for a lawyer's guidance, or at least knowledge of your state's law, since an invalid signature could void a will.

6. *Properly witnessed.* In almost all states, the signing of a formal will must be witnessed by at least two adults who understand what they are witnessing and are competent to testify in

court. In most states, the witnesses have to be **disinterested** (i.e., not getting anything in your will). If they aren't, you run the risk of voiding certain provisions in the will, opening it to challenge, or invalidating the entire will.

7. *Properly executed.* Your will should contain a statement at the end attesting that it is your will, the date and place of signing, and the fact that you signed it before witnesses, who then also signed it in your presence—and watched each other signing it. Most states allow so-called **self-proving affidavits,** which eliminate the necessity of having the witnesses go to court to testify that they witnessed the signing; the affidavit is proof enough. In other states, if the witnesses are dead or unavailable, the court may have to get someone else to verify the legitimacy of their signatures.

If your will doesn't meet these conditions, it may be disallowed by a court, and your estate would then be distributed according to a previous will or under your state's intestacy laws.

SOME NONSTANDARD WILLS

Do all wills have to follow these formalities? No. Depending on the state, the law *might* recognize certain kinds of other wills. However, don't rely on the fact that one of these alternatives might be valid. You're always safest with a written will that's properly signed and witnessed.

• *Oral wills* are permissible in a few states, sometimes under very limited circumstances, such as when they are uttered in your final illness. Also, oral wills often apply only to personal property.

• *Handwritten, unwitnessed wills* are valid in about half the states and effective in the disposition of all kinds of property, including real estate and personal property. Nonetheless, they're not recommended. Since such wills rarely follow legal formalities, it's sometimes hard to prove that they are intended to be wills, or intended to be your last will. Moreover, they are vulnerable to fraud and they often don't cover all the will maker's assets.

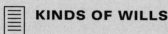

KINDS OF WILLS

Here's a brief glossary of terms used in the law for various kinds of wills.

- **Simple will.** A will that just provides for the outright distribution of assets for an uncomplicated estate.

- **Testamentary trust will.** A will that sets up one or more trusts for some of your estate assets to go to after you die.

- **Pourover will.** A will that leaves some of your assets to a trust that you had already established before your death.

- **Holographic will.** A will that is unwitnessed and in the testator's handwriting. Valid in about half the states.

- **Oral will** (also called **nuncupative will**). A will that is spoken, not written down. Few states permit these, and typically only if an oral will is made during a last illness and is for personal property of small value.

- **Joint will.** One document that covers both a husband and wife (or any two people). These are often a big mistake. See "Spouses and Joint Wills" in this chapter.

- **Living will.** A living will is not really a will at all, since it has force while you are still alive and doesn't dispose of property, but it often is executed at the same time you make your will. It tells doctors and hospitals whether you want to be kept alive on life support in the event you are terminally ill or, as a result of accident or illness, cannot be restored to consciousness. (See chapter 24.)

- *Soldiers' and seamen's wills* are permitted by about half the states. They allow people actually serving in the armed forces to dispose of their wages and personal property orally or in an informal written document. Often, they're only valid during wartime, when the will maker is in a hostile zone, and they usually cease to be valid after a certain time that varies by state.

- *Statutory wills* are another alternative available in a few states. A statutory will is a form that has been created by a state statute.

Since the statutory will includes all the formalities, all you have to do is get a copy at a stationery store, fill it out, and have it witnessed, and you have a valid will. Unfortunately, these wills are very limited. They usually assume you want to leave everything to your spouse and children and provide for few other gifts. And you must follow the form—they can't legally be changed.

THE LIMITS OF THE LAW

Before you actually sit down with your lawyer and begin allocating which property goes to which person in your will, you need to consider some of the limits the law places on your ability to transfer your property as you please. In general, you can pick whom you want your property to go to and leave it in whatever proportions you want.

There are exceptions, however. For example, in some states a surviving husband or wife may be entitled to a **statutory share** of the estate regardless of the will. This is a percentage of the estate's value as set by state law. (You or your spouse can voluntarily give up this legal protection in a prenuptial agreement.)

In some states, surviving spouses are entitled by law to the family home as a **homestead right.** Though you can try to give the family home to someone else in the will, your spouse has to approve. Without approval, your spouse will retain the property until he or she dies or abandons the homestead. As for other family members, only in Louisiana do your children have any right to be included in your estate. Otherwise, you can disinherit anyone; but if you're disinheriting a family member, you should do so specifically, not by omission. (See chapters 13–14 for details.)

Some states limit how much you can leave to a charity if you have a surviving spouse or children, or if you died soon after making the provision (under the assumption someone exerted undue influence on you).

Most states impose some restrictions on conditions listed in wills that are bizarre, illegal, or against the public policy of the state. For example, if you wanted to set up an institute to promote terrorism and the violent overthrow of the government, the probate court would probably throw out the bequest.

Some people try to make their influence felt beyond the grave by attaching conditions to a gift made in the will (as opposed to the purely advisory language in a letter of intent). Most lawyers advise against this; courts don't like such conditions, and you're inviting a will contest if you try to tie them to a gift. You can't require your daughter to divorce her husband to claim her inheritance from you; nor can you force that secular humanist son-in-law to go to church every Sunday. Similarly, your husband can't make your inheritance contingent on a promise you'll never remarry (though if the inheritance were in the form of payments from a trust, the trust agreement could provide that the payments would stop if you remarried).

For the most part, though, what you put in your will is your call.

⚠ SPOUSES AND JOINT WILLS

Both spouses should execute separate wills. A **joint will** generally provides that each spouse's property will go to the other one, and then spells out what will happen to the property when the second person dies. Because both parties have to agree to modify such wills, they often aren't revised as frequently as they should be, whether because of family disagreements or just a double dose of inertia. Joint wills can keep the survivor from using the property as he or she wishes, don't allow for circumstances that change after the will was made, and may be impossible to revoke. In addition, there could be adverse estate and gift tax consequences to a joint will upon the death of one spouse. (The marital deduction may not apply, and the survivor could be treated as making a taxable gift if he or she is unable to dispose of his or her estate as he or she chooses.)

WHICH LAW APPLIES?

The laws of your **domicile** (the state you have chosen to live in—often the state where your primary home is located) determine what happens to your personal property—car, stocks, cash. Distribution of your real estate is governed by the laws of the state in which the property is located.

If you do own homes or property in different states, it's a good idea to make sure that the provisions of your will comply with the laws of the appropriate state. You can't rely on a will drafted by a lawyer for your brother in Oregon if your primary home is located in Maine.

CAN'T A LIVING TRUST SUBSTITUTE FOR A WILL?

You might have noticed advertisements claiming that you don't really need a will, and that to avoid probate, you should avoid a will and instead use a living trust to transfer property between generations. A living trust *can* be a very useful part of estate planning. However, it alone can't accomplish many of the most important goals of estate planning. For example, you need a will to nominate a personal guardian for your children, even if you have a trust. And even with a living trust, you'll need a simple will to dispose of property that you didn't put into the trust. Also, you have to remember to put property into the trust—by transferring title and the like to the name of your trustee—to accomplish anything. In addition, many trusts are funded at death by property bequeathed in a **pourover will.**

Probate is also no longer the costly, time-consuming demon it used to be. So preparing at least a simple, auxiliary will is recommended for just about everyone.

Now that you know the basics of what the law requires in making a will, and you have your list of objectives and inventory of

( ) TALKING TO A LAWYER

Q. *Does a will have to be notarized? Would it help to notarize it, even if it's not required?*

A. Notarization of a will is essentially irrelevant in most jurisdictions, but self-proving affidavits typically require notarization.

—Answer by Susan N. Gary,
University of Oregon School of Law, Eugene, Oregon

assets and debts, you're ready to work with your lawyer to actually write your will.

THE WORLD AT YOUR FINGERTIPS

- Nolo Press's website (www.nolo.com) has much free information on wills and estate planning; many Nolo publications can be purchased through the site.

- The FindLaw estate-planning page has much information on wills: visit www.public.findlaw.com/estate_planning/.

YOU MUST REMEMBER THIS

- Even though you may not have a lot of assets, or you plan to use a living trust or other means of transferring your property to others after you die, you still need a will.

- Most of the time, you can leave your property to whomever you want under whatever conditions you desire. However, the law does impose some limits on this freedom. Your lawyer can fill you in on those limits before you write your will.

CHAPTER 7

What Goes in the Will

What to Put In and What to Leave Out

Peter's sister Jane was happily married to Ted for a decade when Peter decided to write his will, in which he left all his property to "my sister's husband." Maybe Peter was thinking of Jane's shaky marriage record—she'd had several previous husbands—and wanted his estate to go to whomever she was married to at the time he died. Or maybe he just assumed Jane and Ted would be together forever and neglected to write Ted's name in the will. They were fishing buddies as well as brothers-in-law, after all.

Whatever he intended, Peter certainly didn't intend for Jane to have to go to court to fight Ted over Peter's will. But that's exactly what happened, because between the time Peter wrote his will and the time he died (without updating it), Jane and Ted had divorced, and Jane quickly remarried. She assumed that Peter's estate would go to her and her new husband. But Ted thought that the will referred to the man who was her husband at the time Peter wrote the will—and that was Ted! After the fight went to court, not much was left for any of them.

One reason it's hard to spell out a formula for a will is that all of us have unique circumstances in our lives that resist easy, one-size-fits-all definitions—like Peter and Jane, for example. So as you read this chapter, remember that there's no set formula for what goes into a will. However, there are some things you might want to consider depending on your circumstances—whether you're single, divorced, part of an older couple, a younger couple, or an unmarried couple. We discuss some of these special considerations in chapters 13–17.

Below are the more common clauses in a basic will. See Appendix B for a sample basic will, with commentary on what each clause means.

FUNERAL EXPENSES
AND PAYMENT OF DEBTS

Your debts don't die with you; your estate is still liable for them, and your executor has the authority to pay them off if they are valid and binding.

If your debts exceed your assets, your state's law will prescribe the order in which the debts must be paid by category. Funeral expenses and expenses of administration usually get first priority. Family allowances, taxes, and last-illness expenses will also appear near the top of the list. If you want certain creditors to be paid off first, ask your lawyer how to ensure that this will happen in light of your state's particular law.

As for funeral directions and anatomical donations, while you can put them in your will, be aware that the will might not be found or admitted to probate until after you're buried. It's best to put these in a separate document. (See chapter 25.) Some states limit the amount that your executor can pay for your funeral expenses without a court order. If you don't want your executor asking for court permission to pay funeral expenses, you can waive that requirement in your will.

You can also forgive any debts someone owes you by saying so in your will. (A loan you've made is treated as an asset in your gross estate, and may be taxable if the estate is large enough, but the forgiving of the loan will not be taxable to the debtor.)

WHAT IF?

In writing your will, you should always play the "what if" game and try to figure out where a gift would go if something unexpected happened—then account for that possibility in your will. What if one of your beneficiaries dies before you do? In that event, the gift you made to the dead person is said to **lapse** (be canceled), and the gift goes back into your residuary estate (see

---

(i) CONSISTENT TO THE END

P. T. Barnum, always loquacious, wrote a fifty-three-page will, benefiting a whole range of favorites. "Silent Cal" Calvin Coolidge, ever succinct, spent only twenty-five words.

"Residuary Clause" in this chapter), to be distributed to whomever you made the residuary beneficiary.

Most states, however, have **antilapse** statutes, which provide that if a beneficiary related to you predeceases you, that beneficiary's descendants would receive the gift (particularly gifts of real and personal property). So if you left your stamp collection to your daughter, and she died before you did, the stamps would go to her descendants in a state with an antilapse statute. In a state without an antilapse statute, your stamps would go to whomever you had named to receive your residuary estate. If the person designated to receive your stamp collection was your best friend and not your daughter, the antilapse statute would not apply.

You don't have to leave all this to the law of your state. Regardless of your state's laws—lapse or antilapse—you can take into account the fact that a beneficiary might die before you by naming a **contingent beneficiary.** He or she would then get the gift if the primary recipient should die first.

GIFTS OF PERSONAL PROPERTY

It's important to identify carefully all recipients of your largesse, including their addresses and relationship to you. There are too many cases of people leaving property to "my cousin John," not realizing that more than one person might fit that description.

If you have several children or other relatives in the same category (cousins, siblings, etc.), and you want them to divide your estate or some portion of it equally, in many states you should specify that you are giving the gift to the surviving members of the class ("my surviving cousins"), not to them as individuals ("Mutt and Jeff"). That way, if one of them dies, the others would take the whole gift. Otherwise, in many states, the dead cousin's descendants would take his share of the gift. (This wouldn't work in the states where antilapse statutes apply to class gifts.)

But if you definitely do want a beneficiary's children to take a gift if he or she predeceases you, you would use language that indicates this, typically "to my cousins living at my time of death, A, B, and C and their issue, *per stirpes.*" This is technical territory (and even this language is ambiguous), but the main thing to remember about gifts to a class is this: If you have several beneficiaries, use language that will account for the possibility of one of the class members dying before you do.

Some attorneys advise leaving most items to one or two people, and then writing a **letter of intent** that advises those people about how you want them to spend that money or distribute those items. Some states have laws providing for these letters, but others do not. This means that *letters of intent may not be legally binding.* Use them only with people you can trust.

And in these days of changing definitions of what constitutes a family (see chapter 16, which discusses nontraditional families), it's a good idea to spell out in your will just who comprises your family for the purposes of administering your estate. Will you include stepchildren, foster children, unmarried partners of your children, members of the household who haven't been adopted, someone you want to leave out of the will, and so on? You may want to exclude some, include others.

Remember also that personal property can include intangible assets such as insurance policies (for instance, if you own a policy on your spouse's life, that policy and the cash value of the premiums paid into it can be passed on through your will), bank accounts, certain employee benefits, and stock options.

Finally, if you have several people whom you want to share in a gift, be careful to specify what percentage of ownership each will have. If you don't, the court will probably presume that you intended the multiple beneficiaries to share equally. Most lawyers counsel against shared gifts, because it means that several people have to agree on use of the property, and one co-owner may be able to force a sale. But there are some indivisible assets—a house, typically—which must be shared. If so, talk to the beneficiaries first and make sure they agree on how they'll jointly use and manage the gift. And be sure to designate alternative beneficiaries in case one of them dies before you do.

You can save on taxes by using gifts wisely. This section of your will can be used to give gifts to institutions and charities as well as to people.

TANGIBLE PERSONAL PROPERTY MEMORANDA

A **tangible personal property memorandum** (or **direction;** commonly abbreviated as **TPPM**) is a separate handwritten document that is incorporated into the will by reference. This means that the will says something like this: "This will incorporates the provisions of a separate tangible personal property memorandum . . ." Then the TPPM is regarded as part of the will. The TPPM is dated and lists items of tangible personal property (e.g., jewelry, artwork, furniture) and the people you want the property to go to.

Many states recognize the validity of such a signed instrument. Some require it to be in existence at the time the will is signed and will not give effect to changes made after the will is signed. For those states that do not give full effect to this type of document, a TPPM is similar to a **precatory gift** in your will or trust (that is, a gift that you request or wish be made, but not one that you command be made). If you don't direct that a certain asset go to a certain beneficiary, but merely express a hope, a wish, or a recommendation that the asset be given, most courts would hold that the language does not create a legal obligation that the gift be made.

If you do use a TPPM, it's important to remember to make provisions for what happens to any of the property listed if the people who are in line to receive those gifts should die before you do—and if you neglect to adjust the TPPM accordingly before your death. The reference in the will often specifies that the gifts are to go to the recipients still living.

In addition, the reference in the will often states that if no TPPM is found within sixty days of the will maker's death, that is conclusive evidence that it does not exist. This provision means that the estate can be settled in a timely manner, without waiting indefinitely for something that may never turn up.

GENERAL OR SPECIFIC? IT DEPENDS

In making gifts of specific property, you should be certain to identify the property carefully to avoid disputes about which items you meant. For example, specify "my grandmother's three-carat diamond engagement ring" or "the portrait of my grandfather." Such language is advisable when the item is valuable or a dispute about the property is expected.

Generally speaking, it is preferable to make gifts in broad categories of property. For example, a category can be used if the meaning is clear—for example, "all my jewelry." Similarly, "all my tangible personal property" has a reasonably clear legal meaning. The reason for this is that such wording covers the possibility that you will dispose of some items and acquire others between the time you write the will and the time you die. Another example of this kind of general bequest would be to leave your son not "my 1986 Yugo" but "the car I own when I die." The same applies to stocks or bank accounts; the bank may be taken over by another bank, or the stock may be sold. It's better to include a general description or leave a dollar amount or a fractional share.

And if you're trying to leave your children equal values of different kinds property that's liable to fluctuate in value (say, a stock portfolio or real estate), you might add a clause to the will that specifies that if one asset turns out to be worth more than the other, the difference will be made up between the children.

In fact, many lawyers discourage their clients from being too specific in their wills or trusts about the disposition of particular assets because of the possibility of **ademption** (a gift that can't be made because it is no longer in the estate) and other problems. It's better, they say, to give the executor the power to make binding decisions and/or to incorporate a dispute resolution mechanism in the will to help sort out any difficulties, or set up a procedure, such as the beneficiaries selecting items from the estate in turn. Your lawyer's advice will depend on the specifics of your family situation.

In any case, make sure the language you use in giving a gift is unambiguous: "I give . . ." or "I direct that . . ." and so on. Wishy-washy terms such as "It is my wish that . . ." might be taken to be merely an expression of hope, not an order. At the very least, such precatory language could invite a court challenge.

In general, it's simpler for your executor if you leave your property to people in broad but specific categories ("all my furniture") rather than passing it on it piece by piece ("my kitchen

---

⚠ CAREFUL, CAREFUL . . .

Be precise in the language of your will. One British soldier received from his wife's family an inter vivos gift (as we would term it today) that gave him an annual payment that would continue as long as she was "above ground." When she died, his lawyer successfully argued that the literal meaning should prevail over the colloquial; thus, much to his in-laws' consternation, the widower had her coffin encased in glass and kept above ground until he died, thirty years later, receiving the annuity all the while.

table") to many different people. If you want specific gifts of sentimental value to go to certain people, consider giving those items to those people before you die, so you can witness their pleasure (and, if your estate is large, lower estate taxes).

GIFTS OF REAL ESTATE

Most people prefer that their spouses receive the family home. If the home isn't held in joint tenancy (survivorship), you should have instructions about what will happen to it in your will.

It is possible to give what lawyers call a **life estate.** This gives something to a person to use for as long as he or she lives—but ensures that the item reverts to your estate or passes to someone else after the person dies. This is a way of ensuring, for example, that your husband will have the use of your house while he lives, but that it will pass to the children of your first marriage after he dies. The rules governing such transfers, or any transfers different from a **fee simple** outright transfer of ownership, are so complicated that you must use a lawyer to make such a gift properly. Lawyers will usually recommend a trust to accomplish the gift of a life estate.

If you die before you've paid off the mortgage on your house, your estate normally will have to pay it off. If you're afraid this will drain the estate too much, or if you want the recipient of the house to keep paying the mortgage, you must specify that in your will. If you haven't paid off the family house, and you're afraid your survivors can't afford to, you may be able to buy mortgage-canceling insurance to pay it off.

EXECUTORS

As noted in chapter 1, a skillfully drawn will generally saves money in the long run. By giving the **executor** (the person you choose to administer your estate after you die) authority to act efficiently, by saying that a surety bond will not be required, and by directing that the involvement of the probate court be kept to a minimum, which is now possible in many states, you can save your family money. It helps to spell out certain powers the executor (or, as he or she is called under the laws of some states, the **personal representative**) can have in dealing with your estate: to buy, lease, sell, and mortgage real estate; to borrow and lend money; and to exercise various tax options. Giving the executor this kind of flexibility can save months of delay and many dollars by allowing him or her to cope with unanticipated situations. If you run a business, be sure to give your executor specific power to continue the business or enter into new business arrangements. If you don't, the law may require that the business be liquidated or sold.

RESIDUARY CLAUSE

This is one of the most crucial parts of a will, covering all assets not specifically disposed of by other parts of the will. You will probably accumulate assets after you write your will, and if you haven't specifically given an asset to someone, it won't pass through the will—unless you have a **residuary clause** that covers everything. (If your will omits a residuary clause, the assets not left specifically to anyone would pass on through the intestate succession laws, possibly after long delays and extensive court involvement; in technical terms, your estate would be **partially intestate,** with some portions passing as you specified in your will and some according to state law.) No matter how small your residuary estate seems at the time you write your will, you should almost always leave it to the person you most care about.

The residuary clause distributes assets that you might not have anticipated owning. For example, normally anything you own in joint tenancy would pass automatically to the other tenant at your death, and so you wouldn't include it in your will. But what if the joint tenant has died before you? Your estate now probably owns the entire asset, and your residuary clause would ensure that it goes to someone you care about.

Residuary clauses should be used carefully, however. For example, wills and living trusts can create disasters when the tax clause of the document allocates taxes to the residue and there are significant preresiduary or nonprobate bequests. One lawyer recounts a story about a will that left a residence to one daughter and the residue to another daughter, with the boilerplate tax clause allocating taxes to the residue. One daughter was very disappointed to learn that she had to pay estate tax on her half sister's bequest. This would not have occurred if the will had not tried specifically to allocate the taxes, and that is one reason why some lawyers urge people to avoid using such specific language. (Without it, the taxes would probably have been divided between the sisters.)

TESTAMENTARY TRUSTS

As we'll see in chapter 9, you can set up a **testamentary trust** in your will, or have your will direct funds from your estate into a trust you had previously established (your will would then be a pourover will). You would normally do so in a separate clause in your will.

One of the great benefits of the estate system is the enormous flexibility it affords you in deciding just how to dispose of your property after you're gone. The possibilities are literally endless. But that same fluidity also makes it possible for your will to do things you never intended because of imprecise phrasing, neglecting to allow for changing circumstances or unexpected events, or lack of knowledge of the law of your jurisdiction. So be careful to tailor your will to your particular circumstances, and be sure to get the advice you need to help anticipate unforeseen occurrences.

THE WORLD AT YOUR FINGERTIPS

- The AARP site (www.aarp.org/estate_planning) has a wide range of good information about wills and estates.
- Who Gets Grandma's Yellow Pie Plate (www.yellowpieplate. umn.edu/07-lm.html) is an excellent website that will help you think about inheritance planning. The site also tells you how to buy a workbook and video on the topic.
- Many state bar associations offer information on wills and related topics. Consulting your own state's bar association has the advantage of providing you with information that is specific to your state. For example, the Tennessee Bar Association site, www.tba.org/LawBytes/T15.html, offers a wide variety of information. Access www.abanet.org/barserv/stlobar.html to find your state bar association's contact information.
- Books providing basic information on what goes in a will include *Everything Your Heirs Need to Know*, by David Magee (Dearborn Financial Publishing, 1995), and *Last Wishes: A Handbook to Guide Your Survivors*, by L. P. and M. D. Knox (Ulysses Press, 1995).

YOU MUST REMEMBER THIS

- When deciding just what goes in your will, it's important to think of the myriad possibilities that might occur in the future, and craft your language so that no ambiguities remain that might invite a court challenge. Your lawyer can help you do that.

CHAPTER 8

After the Will Is Written

*Follow These Steps to Be Sure
Your Will Does the Job*

Bob never paid much attention to legal matters. But when he was rushed to the hospital with a heart attack, he figured he'd better get his affairs in order before the heart surgery his doctor said he needed. Since Bob had a simple estate, he decided just to write a simple will himself, leaving all his money to his favorite son, Sam, who had taken care of Bob and his recently deceased wife, Ruth, for the past seven years.

On the morning of the operation, he called the family—all except his estranged son, Carl—into his hospital room and had them witness the signing of his will. He did not have the will notarized.

The operation failed, and Bob died. His will failed, too, because the will was not fully executed. So Bob was considered by the state to have died intestate, which meant the state law determined where his assets would go. And state law said both children had to inherit equally, even though Carl had bilked the family of thousands of dollars before skipping town. In the end, Carl inherited exactly as much as Sam did.

Okay, you've gone through all the steps, and you and your lawyer have put a lot of effort into crafting your will. But don't stop now. You need to follow a few simple but vital steps to make sure your will is kept safe and properly executed. You don't want to make a mistake like Bob's.

EXECUTING THE WILL

After you've drawn up your will, there remains one step: the formal legal procedure called **executing the will.** This step requires that you have witnesses to your signing of the will. In all states, the testimony of at least two witnesses is needed as proof of the will's validity. In some states, the witnesses must actually show up in court to attest to this; but in a growing number of states, a will that is formally executed with the signatures notarized (and a self-proving affidavit attached) is considered to be **self-proved** and may be used without testimony of witnesses or other proof, assuming there is no conflict about the will, such as a will contest.

Who should you pick to be your witnesses? The witnesses should have no potential conflict of interest—which means they should absolutely not be people who receive any gifts under the will, or who might benefit from your death. You needn't bring them with you to your lawyer's office; typically, some employees of your lawyer will witness the signing. The witnesses will watch you sign the will and then sign a statement attesting to this. (Your lawyer may ask you to sign every page of the will as a safeguard, but not all lawyers require this.)

WHERE TO KEEP YOUR WILL

You want your will to be found. If it's hidden, it may stay hidden.

In states where only the original of your will is valid, it's not a bad idea to make a few *unsigned* copies of your will and have them available for ready reference; but to avoid confusion, you should sign only one original. This—and only this—is your legally valid will. Keep it in a safe place, such as in a fireproof

 CHECK YOUR WILL

Be sure to carefully proofread your will. Does page 9 follow page 8? If you are leaving percentages of your estate to different people, do the percentages add up to 100?

box at home (you can buy one at an office or department store) or in your lawyer's office. Some jurisdictions will permit you to lodge the will with the probate court for a nominal fee; but in some places, that makes the will a public record. If privacy is paramount for you, you should ask your lawyer or the probate office how best to accomplish this.

You should also keep a record of other estate-planning documents with your will, such as a trust agreement, IRAs, insurance policies, income-saving plans such as 401(k) plans, government savings bonds (if payable to another person), and retirement plans.

What if you lose your will? Have your lawyer draw up a new will as soon as possible, and execute it with all the necessary formalities. If your family situation, state of residence, or income hasn't changed, your lawyer should be able to use copies of your lost will as a guide.

While many people keep their wills in their safe-deposit boxes at a bank, in some jurisdictions the law requires those boxes to be sealed immediately after death, until the estate is sorted out. Needless to say, if your will—or your cemetery deeds and burial instructions—is inside that box, sorting things out might get pretty complicated. If you do keep your will in a safe-deposit box, make sure to provide that someone else (and certainly the executor you name) can get it when you die. Tell your executor and your beneficiaries where the will is located, and make sure your executor, or someone you trust, has the authority (and a key!) to open the box after your death. Many estates have gone through long probate delays because the bank didn't have permission to let anyone open the safe-deposit box except the person who had just died. If you name a bank as executor or coexecutor, deliver the original will to the bank for safekeeping.

It's okay to store *copies* of the will in your home, clearly marked as copies and with a note indicating the location of the original. It's a good idea to use a fireproof box. You can also keep personal papers such as your birth certificate, citizenship records, and marriage certificate, along with coin collections, jewelry, heirlooms, medals, and so on, there or in your safe-deposit box. Finan-

▶ **A BREAK FOR THE FILING-CHALLENGED**

Many of us just can't keep track of things. That could be a real problem in states where only the signed original of your will can be admitted to probate. In some states, the law provides that a signed *copy* is acceptable if at least one witness signs an affidavit stating that the copy is a true copy of the original.

cial records such as securities, mortgage documents, contracts, leases, and deeds could also be kept in these boxes.

TRUSTS

What about a trust agreement? Unlike a will, a trust may have more than one original, in which case there will be language in it saying something to this effect: "This trust is executed in four counterparts, each of which has the force of an original." Your trustee, successor trustee, and lawyer should each have a copy.

Every time you amend the trust, be sure to have the amendment in a separate copy so indicated and signed by you. Unless the amendment is a **complete restatement of the trust** (i.e., a complete reworking of the trust), attach an executed copy to each signed copy of the trust, if possible.

KEEPING YOUR WILL UP TO DATE

Life does not stand still, and after you've crafted your initial estate plan, your circumstances are likely to change—you may have more children, acquire more assets, have a falling-out with friends, or contract a serious illness. Your children will grow up, or you and your spouse may split up. And the law may change, making some of your estate planning obsolete, or even counter-productive.

Most of these life changes will also occasion a change in your estate plan. Many people who had large portfolios in the boom years of the 1990s might have suffered setbacks in the subsequent recession, and they might want to reconsider how much of their diminished estate they want to leave to charity, for example, if it would mean that their families might suffer. Or if you left stocks to one child and an equivalent value of real estate to another, those values may change drastically with fluctuations in the stock and real estate markets. The law also changes—the recent changes to the estate tax law (which may themselves change depending on the nation's budget deficit or even military campaigns) should make many people think about updating their estate plans to reflect these new economic realities.

So it's a good idea to review your will and your inventory of assets and recipients at least once a year to make sure everything is accounted for. (You can pick a certain day, like your birthday or the Fourth of July or some other date, that will jog your memory so that you do this annually.) Remember that this area of the law differs, often drastically, from state to state, so it's especially important to check—or have your lawyer check—how your state's law covers each of these procedures.

You can change, add to, or even revoke your will any time before your death as long as you are physically and mentally competent to make the change. An amendment to a will is called a **codicil**. (It sounds like a cold medicine, and you might think of it as a cure for an obsolete will.) You can't simply cross out old provisions in your will and scribble in new ones if you want the changes to be effective; you have to formally execute a codicil, using the same formalities as when executing the will itself. Of course, it's vital that such codicils be dated so the court can tell whether they were made after your will was executed. The codicil should be kept with the will.

The same mental ability and freedom from undue influence is required for a codicil as for a will, so if the changes are substantial, it may be advisable to write a new will. On the other

> ## ▶ DO I NEED TO UPDATE MY ESTATE PLAN? A CHECKLIST

Ask yourself if any of these changes have occurred in your life since you executed your will or trust.

- Have you married or been divorced?
- Have your children married or been divorced?
- Do your children or any other beneficiaries need protection from creditors?
- Have relatives or other beneficiaries or the executor died, or have your relationships with them changed substantially?
- Has the mental or physical condition of any of your relatives or other beneficiaries or your executor changed substantially?
- Have you had more children or grandchildren, or have children gone to college or moved out of, or into, your home?
- Have you moved to another state?
- Have you bought, sold, or mortgaged a business or real estate?
- Have you acquired major assets (car, home, bank account)?
- Have you inherited significant property?
- Have your business or financial circumstances changed significantly (estate size, pension, salary, ownership)?
- Has your state's law (or have federal tax laws) changed in a way that might affect your tax and estate planning?
- Have you changed your ideas about what to do with any of your assets?
- Have you decided to do more (or less) charitable giving?
- Have you made gifts that should be taken into account, such as by reducing bequests that were to occur under the will?

When you do update your estate plan, you should also update your final instruction and will with the addresses and phone numbers of beneficiaries, trustees, executors and others mentioned in estate planning documents. It will make settling the estate much easier.

hand, if there is some question of the will maker's capacity, it may be better simply to execute a codicil, so that even if it is thrown out the remainder of the will remains valid. Decisions like this illustrate why it's a good idea to check with your lawyer before revising or revoking your will.

You will have less need for a codicil if you watched out for ademption in writing your will. **Ademption** is what happens if you will something (for example, your antique automobile) to someone but no longer own that item at the time of your death. In this case, the gift would fail completely; the beneficiary wouldn't be entitled to another vehicle. To reduce the need for a codicil, a good will uses language such as this: "I give my antique Rolls-Royce to my son-in-law, Joe, but if I don't own it at the time of my death, I give him a choice of any automobile I do own at the time of my death."

In the previous chapter, we discussed the use of tangible personal property memoranda (TPPMs) to increase your estate

---

TALKING TO A LAWYER

Q. Is it ever a good idea to videotape the signing of a will? Is that good evidence?

A. Videotaping the signing of a will may be helpful in providing evidence that the person signing had the required mental capacity and wasn't being unduly influenced by someone. The lawyer can ask some questions to establish that the person understands what he or she is doing. If you are considering videotaping the signing, however, you should be aware that the videotape could actually be used as evidence of the lack of mental capacity. Someone suffering from a debilitating illness could actually appear worse on camera than in person. Thus, you should make the decision to videotape with caution.

—Answer by Susan N. Gary,
University of Oregon School of Law, Eugene, Oregon

plan's flexibility without having to revise your will too often. To revise a TPPM, you write "revoked" across each page of the old one, sign each page, and include the date of revocation. Attach the new TPPM and make sure it's kept where it will be found after your death. If you have incorporated the TPPM in your will by reference, some states require you to amend the will to incorporate the amended document.

REVOKING A WILL

Sometimes when you undergo a major life change, such as divorce, remarriage, winning the lottery, having more children, or getting the last child out of the house, it's a better idea to rewrite your will from scratch rather than making a lot of small changes through codicils. The best way to do this is by executing a new will that states that it revokes the old one. There are two schools of thought about what to do about the old will. Some lawyers recommend that you destroy it, if possible in front of your lawyers and the witnesses of your new will. Others do not recommend destroying prior wills: A prior will is often very useful in avoiding arguments that there was undue influence exerted on you when the new will was written. If there are a number of prior wills that have similar provisions, they are very good evidence to support the new will's legitimacy.

When you write a new will, be sure to include the date that it was signed and executed, and put in a sentence that states that the new will revokes all previous wills. Otherwise, the court is likely to rule that the new one only revokes the old where the two conflict—which could cause problems.

If you fail to change or rewrite your will to account for changes in your life, the courts will give as much effect to your old will as possible. Some changes may be accommodated by the law, regardless of what your will says. For example, if you have a new child and don't explicitly say that you don't want him or her to inherit anything, then the law may give that child a share of your estate. Likewise, your spouse is entitled to a certain per-

(i) TARNISHED LEGACIES

While the rich or infamous often use their bequests to craft a posthumous public image that's nobler than their real lives (robber-baron-turned-philanthropist J. P. Morgan is a good example), sometimes it works the other way. Columnist H. L. Mencken, that great and irascible curmudgeon, left his papers (thirty thousand documents) to the New York Public Library and his diary to a library in his beloved Baltimore, both with the provision that they not be made public until years after his death. Of course, when his private writings appeared a few years ago, they revealed a troubling streak of anti-Semitism that tarnished the great writer's reputation.

President Franklin Roosevelt's infidelity was revealed to the public by a bequest to "my friend, Marguerite A. LeHand," of reasonable expenses (as determined by the trustees) for her health care. Cruelly, the money was to be paid out of Eleanor's trust account.

Lon Chaney's will revealed the existence of a heretofore unknown first wife who was actually the mother of his son—though the actor had concealed that fact for decades. The first wife was finally found, working in a field, and her situation wasn't much eased by the $1 Chaney left her, presumably to disinherit her.

centage of your estate (which varies by state), no matter what you say in your will.

In some cases, though, assets that aren't accounted for go into what's called the **residuary estate.** (See chapter 7 for more.) The residuary estate is covered by a paragraph in most wills that says that you leave all assets not specifically disposed of elsewhere to your spouse, or St. Jude's hospital, or some other person or institution. It's more likely, though, that you want that hot new roadster you bought last year to go to your twenty-five-year-old son rather than to your seventy-year-old widow, and that's why it's best to modify your will periodically to account for assets acquired since you drafted your last will.

THE WORLD AT YOUR FINGERTIPS

- You can store your will in an international registry. Click on www.willsindex.com/ for details.

- You may be able to store your will at your probate court. Check with the court in your community. Your probate court might also be online. Enter "probate court" and your community's name in your favorite search engine. The National College of Probate Judges (http://www.ncpj.org/) may be able to help.

YOU MUST REMEMBER THIS

- All the work you put into drafting your will is useless if it can't be found or accessed by your executor, or if the law's required formalities weren't followed in executing it.

- You should review your will periodically to account for changes in your income, assets, family relationships, tax laws, and the like.

- You can make small changes to your will through a codicil; for major changes, you should revoke your will and write a new one.

PART FOUR

Trusts and Living Trusts

They Can Do a Lot—

but They're Not for Everyone

CHAPTER 9

How Trusts Work

A Quick Look at
a Misunderstood Tool

We hear all the time about trust funds—or at least we do if we follow the lives of the rich and famous. Are they only for the wealthy?

Not necessarily. Like a will, a trust is a very useful instrument in the estate-planning arsenal. Estates can be as diverse as people, and the flexibility of a trust makes it useful for many different needs.

Should you have a trust? It depends on the size of your estate and the purpose of the trust. For example, if you mainly want a living trust to protect assets from taxes and probate, but your estate is under the current federal tax floor and probate is not a problem in your state (or your estate can qualify for quick and inexpensive probate in your state), some lawyers would tell you that it isn't worth the cost and administrative hassle, which can make trusts impractical for most young people unless they're relatively wealthy.

On the other hand, a trust may be a very desirable solution to many problems. A funded living trust may eliminate the need to appoint a guardian for your estate should you become disabled (although a durable general power of attorney may also avoid a guardianship proceeding). A trust for the benefit of others, such as minor children and grandchildren or disabled relatives, provides a mechanism for managing property without court supervision. A trust can also provide beneficiaries with protection from creditors.

This chapter discusses the general principles behind trusts and their common uses. It should help you determine if one is suitable for you.

WHAT IS A TRUST?

A **trust** is a legal relationship in which one person or qualified trust company (**trustee**) holds property for the benefit of him- or herself or another (**beneficiary**). The property can be any kind of real or personal property—money, real estate, stocks, bonds, collections, business interests, personal possessions, and automobiles.

A trust generally involves at least three people: the **grantor** (the person who creates the trust, also known as the **settlor** or **donor**), the **trustee** (who holds and manages the property for the benefit of the grantor and others), and one or more beneficiaries (who are entitled to the benefits).

Think of a trust as an agreement between the grantor and the trustee. The grantor makes certain property available to the trustee, for certain purposes. The trustee (who often receives a fee) agrees to manage the property in the way the grantor wants.

Putting property in trust transfers it from your personal ownership to the trustee who holds the property for you. The trustee has **legal title** to the trust property. For most purposes, the law looks at these assets as if the trustee now owned them. For example, many (but not all) trusts have separate taxpayer identification numbers.

But trustees are not the full owners of the property. Trustees have a legal duty to use the property as provided in the trust agreement and permitted by law. The beneficiaries retain what is known as **equitable title** or **beneficial title,** the right to benefit from the property as specified in the trust.

The donor may retain control of the property. If you set up a revocable living trust with yourself as trustee, you retain the rights of ownership you'd have if the assets were still in your name. You can buy anything and add it to the trust, sell anything out of the trust, and give trust property to whomever you wish.

If the terms of your will establish a trust to take effect at your death—a **testamentary trust**—you retain the title to the

TRUSTS COME IN MANY FLAVORS

In a living trust, the grantor may be the trustee *and* the beneficiary, or you, as grantor, can name someone else as trustee and establish many beneficiaries. In trusts set up in your will, the trustee is often one or more persons or, for larger estates in which investment expertise is required, a corporate trust company or a bank.

property during your lifetime, and on your death it passes to the trustee to be distributed to your beneficiaries as you designate.

We speak of putting assets "in" a trust, but they don't actually change location. Think of a trust instead as an imaginary container. It's not a geographical place that protects your car, but a form of ownership that holds it for your benefit. On your car title, the owner blank would simply read "Richard Smith, trustee of the Richard Smith trust." It's common to put bank and brokerage accounts, as well as homes and other real estate, into a trust.

After your trust comes into being, your assets will probably still be in the same place they were before you set it up—the car in the garage, the money in the bank, the land where it always was—but it will have a different owner: not simply you, but you (or someone else) as the trustee of your trust.

This may sound abstract, but as this and the next chapter show, the benefits are concrete.

There is no such thing as a "standard" trust, just as there's no standard will. You can include any provision you want as long as it doesn't conflict with state law. The provisions of a written trust instrument govern how the trustee holds and manages the property. That varies greatly, depending on why the trust was set up in the first place.

Trusts can be revocable (that is, you can legally change the terms and end the trust) or irrevocable. A **revocable trust** (see chapters 11–12) gives the donor great flexibility but no tax

KINDS OF TRUSTS

- **Revocable trusts** are simply trusts that can be changed, or even terminated, at any time by the donor. (Though most living trusts are revocable, a living trust and a revocable trust are not synonymous.)

- **Irrevocable trusts** cannot be changed or terminated before the time specified in the trust, but savings in taxes may offset the loss of flexibility.

Specific trusts include:

- **Charitable trusts** are created to support charitable purposes. Often these trusts will make annual gifts to worthy causes of your choosing, simultaneously helping good causes and reducing the taxes on your estate.

- **Discretionary trusts** permit the trustee to distribute income and principal among various beneficiaries or to control the disbursements to a single beneficiary, as he or she sees fit.

- **Dynasty trusts** (also sometimes called **wealth trusts**) can last for a number of generations, and sometimes can last forever. They can help people with great fortunes control the distribution of their wealth over a very long period of time.

- **Generation-skipping trusts** are tax-saving trusts that benefit several generations of your descendants.

advantages. If the trust is revocable and you are the trustee, you will have to report the income from the trust on your personal income tax return, instead of on a separate income tax statement for the trust. The theory is that by retaining the right to terminate the trust, you have kept enough control of the property in it to treat it for tax purposes as if you owned it in your name.

Irrevocable trusts are the other side of the coin—they have far less flexibility but possible tax benefits. The trustee must file a separate tax return.

- **Insurance trusts** are tax-saving trusts in which trust assets are used to buy a life insurance policy whose proceeds benefit the settlor's beneficiaries. (See chapter 22.)

- **Living trusts** (see chapter 11) enable you to put your assets in a trust while you are still alive. You can wear all the hats—donor, trustee, and beneficiary—or have someone else be trustee and have other beneficiaries.

- **Special needs trusts** are established for people with disabilities who want to keep their government benefits.

- **Spendthrift trusts** can be set up for people whom the grantor believes wouldn't be able to manage their own affairs—like an extravagant relative, or someone who's mentally incompetent. They may also be useful for beneficiaries who need protection from creditors.

- **Split-interest trusts** make it possible for either a charity or an individual to have an interest in the trusts for a period of time, after which the other gets the unexpended funds.

- **Support trusts** direct the trustee to spend only as much income and principal as may be needed for the education and support of the beneficiaries.

- **Testamentary trusts** are set up in wills.

- **Totten trusts** are bank accounts that pass to a beneficiary immediately upon your death.

For either type of trust, if the amount you give to fund the trust exceeds the federal unified credit, you could incur a gift tax liability. Similarly, there may be generation-skipping tax consequences in funding a generation-skipping trust. This is technical territory, where a lawyer's help is definitely recommended.

Trusts can be very simple, intended for limited purposes, or they can be quite complex, spanning two or more generations, providing tax benefits and protection from creditors of the beneficiary, and displacing a will as the primary estate-planning vehicle.

▶ ## FINE, FEATHERED, OR FURRY FRIENDS

Every pet owner knows that pets are part of the family—at least in the hearts of the owners. In eighteen states, you can provide for your companion animals directly in your will, and this trend is growing. However, in all states, you can use trusts for this purpose. In some states, you can make your pets the direct beneficiaries of a trust. In others, you can designate a friend or associate as the beneficiary and make a gift of money and the pets to that person, with instructions to expend the funds on the animals' care.

SETTING UP A TRUST

If you establish a trust in your will, its provisions are contained in that document. If you create a trust during your lifetime, its provisions are contained in the **trust agreement** or **trust declaration.** The provisions of that trust document (not your will or state law) will determine what happens to the property in the trust upon your death.

Funding the trust

This is the most important part of setting up a trust. The main reason most trusts fail is inadequate funding. A testamentary trust is funded after your death, with assets that you've specified in your will and through beneficiary designations of your life insurance, IRA, and so on. Such trusts generally receive most of the estate assets, such as the proceeds from the sale of a house.

Or you could set up an "unfunded" **standby trust.** This is a trust that could be called "minimally" funded to avoid confusion. It may have a nominal sum of money in it—$100 or so—to get it started while you're alive (and thus make it a living trust), but it only receives substantial assets when you die. Your pourover will would direct that many or all of your assets be transferred from your estate to the trust at your death. Making life insurance payable to the trust, as well as designating the trust as the beneficiary of IRAs, profit-sharing plans, and so on, will pass these assets directly to the trust outside of probate. However, other assets not already owned by the trust when you die will have to go through probate. This is why many lawyers shy away from unfunded trusts, unless probate avoidance isn't the primary goal. (See chapter 28.)

If your estate—with life insurance benefits included—will add up to more than $1 million ($1.5 million in 2004 and 2005), you can save taxes by removing the life insurance proceeds from your estate and establishing an irrevocable life insurance trust that owns the policy; all **incidents of ownership** in the policy belong to the trust, such as making decisions about the policy, including choice of beneficiary. When you die, the proceeds are

▶ ## WORKING WITH A LAWYER

When you approach a lawyer to help you set up a trust, make sure he or she is willing to work with you to tailor the trust to *your* particular needs; otherwise the primary benefit of trusts—their flexibility—is wasted. This is another reason to avoid those prefabricated, all-purpose trusts you see in self-help books and hear about at seminars.

A good lawyer will provide you with a financial analysis to show how much you might save over time by structuring your trust in certain ways. You, in return, can help by providing comprehensive lists of your assets, as determined by the form in Appendix A.

Make sure you choose a lawyer who's familiar with estate planning, trusts, and, if your trust is used for saving taxes, tax law. IRS regulations governing trusts change often, and the agency has always given trusts special scrutiny.

paid into the trust, escaping estate taxation and creditors insofar as the insurance policy is concerned. The drafting and administration of such trusts is quite complex—you will surely need a lawyer's help to do these jobs properly.

Trusts and taxes

Chapters 20–22 discuss death and taxes, and trusts are a major part of that discussion. However, there are a few basic principles worth mentioning here. While gifts under the federal tax-exempt amount (in a trust or in a will) escape federal *estate* taxation, the recipients of the trust income will still have to pay *income* tax when they receive income from the trust, just as the beneficiaries of a will would have to pay income tax on any income they might receive. They would not have to pay tax on the principal in the trust when they collected it (unless their state has an inheritance tax).

The trustee pays, out of the principal, the taxes on income from the trust that's reinvested or put back into the principal. Similarly, capital gains from the sale of stock, real estate, and the like may generate tax liabilities; the gains are generally added to the principal unless you specify otherwise.

The choice of trustee can affect the tax the trust owes. If the beneficiary is made the only trustee, some of the tax advantages of the trust can be lost. Similarly, the more powers the grantor retains, the more likely the assets in the trust will be taxable to the grantor, either during the grantor's life as income tax or after death as estate tax. Consult your attorney or a tax adviser before setting up any trust for tax purposes.

TERMINATING A TRUST

Charitable trusts can last indefinitely. Since trusts of this sort are established to accomplish a substantial benefit to the public, it is entirely appropriate that Rhodes scholarships, Pulitzer and

Nobel Prizes, and thousands of other awards and grants be funded by trusts that are expected to endure.

The old rule was that private trusts—those trusts set up to benefit private beneficiaries—could not last forever. The **rule against perpetuities,** which is embodied in state law and which varies from state to state, was designed to limit the time a trust may be operative. Usually the rule specified that a trust can last no longer than the life of a person alive at the time the trust is created, plus twenty-one years. (That person, who is called the **measuring life,** does not have to be a beneficiary.) So if you made your infant granddaughter the measuring life and set up a trust to benefit her and any children she may eventually have, and she has a long life, your trust may extend one hundred years, but not much more.

However, many states are eliminating the rule against perpetuities, which can permit longer-lasting and even perpetual trusts (called **dynasty trusts**). Check with your lawyer to see if such trusts are available in your state. You may also be able to establish a trust in another state that has no rule against perpetuities, even if yours does.

Your trust agreement should contain a clause that provides how it can be terminated. A good trust drawn up by a lawyer will certainly have such a clause.

A trust often terminates when the principal is distributed to the beneficiaries, at the time stated in the trust agreement. For example, you might provide that a trust for the benefit of your children would end when the youngest child reaches a certain age. At that time, the trustee would distribute the assets to the beneficiaries according to your instructions. The law generally allows a "windup phase" to complete the administration of trust duties (e.g., filing tax returns) after the trust has officially terminated.

You can also give your trustees the discretion to distribute the trust assets and terminate the trust when they think it's a good idea, or place some restrictions on their ability to do so. For example, you could allow the trustees to terminate the trust at

TALKING TO A LAWYER

Q. I understand that if I create a trust, I no longer own the property—the trustee does. This is profoundly unsettling to me. How can I be sure that the property won't be misappropriated?

A. The trust instrument itself, together with court decisions over the years and current laws in your state, provide rules for how the trustee must act. In legal terms, this body of law spells out the trustee's **fiduciary duties** (legal obligations to act on your behalf). To assuage your doubts, you might ask your lawyer to explain the trustee's duties and your legal rights.

—Answer by Pamela L. Rollins,
Simpson Thacher & Bartlett, New York, New York

Q. My sister and I are the beneficiaries of my grandfather's trust. I recall that it was supposed to end when the younger of us reached a certain age. What kind of an accounting will we get at that time of what's in the trust and how much will go to each of us?

their discretion, provided that your daughter has completed her education.

Your trust should have a termination provision even if it is an irrevocable trust. Irrevocability means that you, the donor, can't change your mind about how you want the trust to terminate. It doesn't mean that you can't set up termination procedures in the first place.

If you have an irrevocable trust and don't have a termination provision, the trust can usually terminate only if all beneficiaries consent and no material purpose of the trust is defeated. However, an irrevocable trust can also be terminated if there was fraud, duress, undue influence, or other problems when the trust was set up; if the trustee and the beneficiary become the

A. What happens at the end of your grandfather's trust will depend upon the provisions that he put into it. Most states would require that the trustee provide you and your sister with an accounting of the trust property and investments when the trust terminates, but trust grantors sometimes add a provision to the trust waiving this requirement. If that is the case, the trustee will have no obligation to provide an accounting. If you suspect that the trustee has mishandled the trust funds, your only recourse would be to retain a lawyer who would try to convince the local probate court that an accounting is needed.

The best approach would be for you and your sister to send a written request to the trustee several months before the trust is scheduled to terminate. In the letter, you can ask for an accounting of the trustee's activities over the life of the trust, as well as a description of the trust provisions governing the final distributions. A cooperative trustee should be willing to provide you with this information; if the trustee does not, you may wish to consult your attorney.

—Answer by Harold Pskowski,
BNA Tax Management, Washington, D.C.

same person (and there are no other beneficiaries); if the operation of the trust becomes impracticable or illegal; or if the period of time specified in state law expires. We're obviously into technical territory here, so the basic rule is this: Don't set up an irrevocable trust unless you're prepared to live—and die—by its terms.

THE WORLD AT YOUR FINGERTIPS

- There are many books about trusts, including *The Complete Book of Trusts,* by Martin M. Shenkman (John Wiley & Sons, 1997).

- Trusts are governed by state law, so it's a good idea to check out the law of your state. Bar associations often have state-specific information for the public, as do state university extension services. An example from Ohio is www.oardc.ohio-state.edu (search on "estate planning" for information on trusts and many other estate-planning topics).

YOU MUST REMEMBER THIS

- Trusts come in many different forms: some help with reducing estate taxes; others fund the education of children and grandchildren or help provide for people with disabilities or those who might have trouble managing their own affairs; still others fund charities.

- Trusts can also provide protection from your beneficiaries' creditors.

- If a trust is right for you, be sure it's funded properly and complies with all legal requirements in your state.

CHAPTER 10

Do You Need a Trust?

As Usual in the Law, It Depends

Nick loved his son, Claude, but he didn't trust Claude's wife, Livia. He was afraid she'd spend the money he gave Claude on astrologers and shoes, and maybe take the money and run after Nick died. But Nick didn't want to deprive Claude of the money he needed to run his business after Nick was gone.

So Nick's lawyer devised a plan: Nick left the money in trust for Claude instead of making a direct gift to him, and directed that Claude get only the income, so neither he nor his wife could squander the principal. In the state where Claude and Nick lived, Livia couldn't get at the assets if they divorced. Moreover, Nick was able to specify how much, if any, of the trust income or principal to leave Livia, or give Claude the choice. If she didn't turn out to be a good and faithful companion, Claude could leave the whole thing to whomever he desired.

Trusts can be useful, as they were to Nick, but they're not for everyone. If you fall into one of the following categories, you should talk to your lawyer about whether setting up a trust is a good idea for you.

PARENTS WITH YOUNG CHILDREN

If you have young children, want to assure a good education for them, and will have enough assets to do so after death (including life insurance proceeds), you should consider including trust provisions in your will or creating a living trust for their benefit. The trustee manages the property in the trust for the benefit of your children during their lifetimes or until they reach the ages that you designate. Any remaining property in the trust then may be divided among the children.

This type of arrangement has an obvious advantage over an inflexible division of property among children of different ages without regard to their respective ages or needs. Trusts are more flexible than outright gifts made to minors in your will (which require a guardian), or a gift made under the Uniform Transfer to Minors Act, which requires appointment of a custodian and, depending on state law, often transfers property to the child at age eighteen or twenty-one.

There are several issues to consider when setting up a trust for the benefit of your children.

One trust or many?

Most people will set up one trust that all the children can draw on until they've completed their educations (or reached an age by which they should have done so). Then the remaining principal is divided among them equally. This permits the trustee greater flexibility to distribute ("sprinkle") the money unequally according to need; for example, one child may choose to pursue an advanced degree at an expensive private university, while another may drop out of community college after a semester. Obviously, they will have different educational expenses.

Such an arrangement can cause friction in some families.

▶ ## THE YOUNGER THE CHILD, THE MORE FLEXIBLE THE TRUST

When very young children are involved, it's especially important to build some flexibility into a trust created for their benefit. Who knows if a two-year-old may turn out to need special counseling or education by the time he or she turns five or six?

However, your lawyer can help you craft a trust that can provide rough equality of treatment for family members whose individual circumstances differ.

There are two philosophies about what to do if there's a disparity in ages among the children. One theory is that the older children have already received the benefit of the parents' spending before they died, so the trustee should have authority to make unequal distributions in favor of the younger children to compensate. The other camp, by contrast, thinks it better to establish separate trusts, so that the older children don't have to wait until they're well into adulthood before the trust assets are distributed (which usually happens when the youngest child reaches majority age). You'll have to decide which course is best for your family's circumstances.

Generally speaking, the less money you have to distribute, the more likely you would put it all in one trust. Since there is a limited amount of money, you want to pool it to be sure that it goes for the greatest need. On the other hand, if equality is your primary consideration and there's plenty of money available to take care of each child's likely needs, then you may want to set up separate trusts for each child, to assure that each gets an equal share.

What should the assets be used for?

You can specify that the trust pay for education, health care, food, rent, and other basic support. Given life's unpredictability, however, it's often better to write a general standard (e.g., "for the support of my children") into the document and allow the trustee the discretion to decide if an expenditure is legitimate. Such a provision also gives the trustee flexibility. For example, if one of your children has an unanticipated expenditure, like a serious illness, the trustee could give that child more money that year than the other children.

Be aware, though, that in some cases a vague standard might lead to litigation, as when a beneficiary sues to receive more support.

When should the assets be distributed?

Some parents pick the age of majority (eighteen) or the age when a child will be out of college (twenty-two or so). If all the assets are in one trust that serves several children, you would usually have the assets distributed when the youngest child reaches the target age. If you have separate trusts and a pretty good idea about each child's level of maturity, you can pick the age that seems appropriate for each one to receive his or her windfall.

If you don't know when each child will be capable of handling money, you can leave the age of distribution up to the trustee (and risk friction between the trustee and the children), have the trustee distribute the assets at different times (half when the first child turns twenty-five and the rest when the youngest does so, for example), or just pick an age for each child, such as thirty.

Or you can keep the money in trust for the lifetime of the beneficiaries. This protects the assets from the claims of the beneficiaries' creditors. The trust can be flexible enough to own the children's homes, businesses, and other property to preserve assets.

▶ **IF YOU DON'T HAVE
MUCH TO PASS ALONG**

Like any trust, a children's trust costs money to set up: lawyers' fees for creating the trust, fees for preparing and filing the separate tax returns required, and so on. For families with limited assets, it might be best to give the money via a custodial account under the Uniform Gift to Minors Act or the Uniform Transfer to Minors Act. (See chapter 13.) You would lose some flexibility (in most states the child gets the assets at age eighteen), but more of the assets would be preserved to pass down to the kids.

PEOPLE WITH BENEFICIARIES
WHO NEED HELP

Trusts are especially popular among people with beneficiaries who aren't able to manage property well. This includes elderly beneficiaries with special needs or a relative who may be untrustworthy with money. For example, if you have a granddaughter who has been in a juvenile detention center, it may be a good idea to require her to obtain the money at intervals from a trustee instead of giving her a gift outright in your will. A **discretionary trust** gives the trustee leeway to give the beneficiary as much or as little as the trustee thinks appropriate.

Another type of trust has been traditionally used for improvident beneficiaries: a **spendthrift trust.** It's simply a trust in which your instructions to the trustee carefully control how much money is released from the trust and at what intervals, so you can keep an irresponsible beneficiary from the temptation of getting thousands of dollars in one stroke.

In a spendthrift trust, you can also stipulate that the trustee will pay only certain expenses for the beneficiary—those you (or the trustee) consider legitimate, such as rent and utility bills. In a spendthrift trust, the beneficiary cannot sell or borrow against his or her interest in the trust, or designate his interest in the trust to

▶ **FOR MORE THAN SPENDTHRIFTS**

Spendthrift trusts are not just for improvident beneficiaries. You could make the argument that all trusts should have such provisions, just in case a beneficiary turns out to be unreliable. In this era of asset preservation planning, provisions that prevent asset dissipation may be central to trust planning.

someone else. For example, a beneficiary might be tempted to use his interest in a trust as security for a loan or attempt to transfer the interest in exchange for some item from a seller. A properly worded spendthrift trust makes this impossible. In addition, creditors of the beneficiary can't get at the principal in a trust, but they can make a claim (if it's otherwise legal) on whatever income the beneficiary receives.

Spendthrift provisions raise a number of tricky questions and should be used cautiously. Your lawyer can tell you whether such a trust is right for your situation.

PEOPLE WHO OWN PROPERTY THAT IS HARD TO DIVIDE

Trusts help you transfer property that's not easy to divide evenly among several beneficiaries. Suppose you have a little vacation cottage on the Cape, and four children who each want to use it. You can pass it to them in a trust that

- **sets out each child's right to use the property,**
- **establishes procedures to prevent conflicts,**
- **requires that when the property is sold the trustee divide the proceeds, and**
- **sets up a procedure by which any child may buy out another's interest in the cottage.**

PEOPLE WHO WANT TO CONTROL THEIR PROPERTY

Through a trust, you can maintain more control over a gift than you can through a will. Some people use trusts to pass money to a relative when they have doubts about that person's spouse, as in the example at the beginning of this chapter.

PEOPLE CONCERNED ABOUT
ESTATE TAXES

Trusts are very useful to people with substantial assets, because they can help eliminate or reduce estate taxes. For example, by establishing a trust for their benefit, you can make tax-free gifts (up to the limit allowed by law) each year to your children or grandchildren during your lifetime, even if they're

---

( ) TALKING TO
A LAWYER

Q. *I am considering establishing a charitable trust in my name to benefit several causes that are close to my heart. Are the expenses of setting up and running a trust apt to be prohibitive? Am I better off to make a gift to an established charity and specify how I'd like the money used?*

A. The expenses of establishing and operating a charitable trust can be considerable. Unless you are interested in placing at least $100,000 in the trust, the expenses of administration will eat up most of the income, leaving little for distribution to charity.

An alternative approach is to consider a gift to a "donor-advised fund." These funds are charities that have been established by a number of well-known mutual funds and trust companies. The fund itself does not engage in charitable activities. It simply invests the funds that you have donated to it and later distributes them to your favorite charities when you request it to do so. Although the fund is not legally required to follow your directions as to which charities will receive the funds, it will almost always do so. Using a donor-advised fund gives you many of the advantages of a charitable trust, without the administrative headaches and expenses.

—Answer by Harold Pskowski,
BNA Tax Management, Washington, D.C.

---

minors. This will reduce your taxable estate and save taxes upon your death.

A properly drawn trust may also reduce estate taxes by utilizing the marital deduction or avoiding the generation-skipping tax. (See chapters 20–22.)

WHEN TRUSTS ARE BETTER THAN WILLS

A trust can do a number of things a will can't do as well.

- A trust can provide a structure under which your assets can be managed and disbursed over time for the long-term care of beneficiaries who are minor children or others not up to the responsibility of handling the estate.

- It can protect your privacy (unlike a will, a trust is confidential).

- Depending on how it is written, a trust can reduce estate taxes.

- If it is a living trust, it enables the trustee to manage property for you while you're alive, providing a way to care for you should you become disabled. A living trust also avoids probate, may lower estate administration costs, and may speed transfer of your assets to beneficiaries after your death.

- Trusts are generally more difficult to contest than wills.

- Trusts can be flexible. You can stipulate that payments fluctuate with the cost of living, authorize extra withdrawals in case of emergency, or even set a standard figure for payment each year. If the income doesn't meet that amount, the difference can be made up out of the principal.

- You can use trusts to impose discipline on the beneficiary. You could require the beneficiary to live within a set figure, getting a certain amount of income each year, regardless of inflation, need, or the stock market's effect on the principal.

- Trusts are sometimes set up to provide for the education of a divorced couple's children.
- Trusts can also be helpful if you want to make a major charitable gift but wish to retain some use of the property.

THE WORLD AT YOUR FINGERTIPS

- Whether you need a trust or not can be best answered by advisers who know your situation. Ask your lawyer if a trust is right for you.
- Websites sometimes discuss spendthrift trusts and other trust issues. See, for example, Ric Edelman's personal finance site (www.ricedelman.com/planning/estate/spendthrift.asp) and the site of the law firm Moses & Singer, LLP (www.mosessinger.com/resources/spendthrift.pdf).

YOU MUST REMEMBER THIS

- Trusts aren't for everyone, but they can make estate planning fit the needs and desires of certain people—those whose estates approach or exceed the federal tax limit, those who have family members who might not be able to manage their own affairs, and others—better than a will alone.

CHAPTER 11

Living Trusts 101

The Basics

Mary is a widow, without children or any close relatives. She is no longer able to live alone in her home or to handle her finances. In her younger days, Mary loved to hike, and wants most of her estate to support organizations that protect the environment. And she wants to leave some of her assets to her close friend, Maggie, who has been helping her as she's become more disabled.

Mary's lawyer advises her to transfer her property and other assets to a trustee, who will sell the home and invest the proceeds, along with the other assets, under a revocable (living) trust, to provide for Mary's support during her lifetime. After she dies, the living trust will direct Mary's estate to Greenpeace and the Sierra Club, and to her friend Maggie. If Mary changes her mind about who should receive her estate, she can make a simple amendment to the trust in a written letter or memo signed by her and delivered to the trustee.

A living trust—an inter vivos trust, if you want to be formal—allows you to put your assets in a trust while you're still alive. If your living trust is revocable, as almost all are, it gives you great flexibility. You or someone in whom you have confidence manages the property, usually for the benefit of you or your family. Most people name themselves as trustees, and find there is no difference between managing the trust and managing their own property—they have the right to buy, sell, or give property as before, though the property is in their name as trustee rather than simply in their own name.

Living trusts have become extremely popular in recent years. But even though they can be a useful, simple, and relatively inexpensive way to plan your estate, they do not magically solve

(i) SHOULD YOU AVOID PROBATE?

A living trust is one of the main ways to avoid probate. (Others are having property in joint tenancy with right of survivorship, transferring property through beneficiary designations in your life insurance and retirement benefits, and making gifts while you are alive.) One of the purposes of probate is to determine the disposition of the property you leave at death. Since the trustee of your living trust owns that property, there is no need for probate.

However, as more and more states have made probate quicker, easier, and less expensive—and as some states tightened their procedures for administering living trusts—living trusts have lost one of their main advantages in most jurisdictions. Now administering an estate through a living trust can in some cases take as long and cost as much as doing so under a will. But although some lawyers think living trusts have been oversold to the public, there are times when they make sense. You and your lawyer will have to weigh all the factors and decide if one is right for you.

---

all your problems. And though they're great for some people, you can't assume they're great for you.

Deciding whether a living trust is right for *you* depends on the size of your estate, what *kinds* of assets it contains, and what plans you have for yourself and your family.

HOW LIVING TRUSTS WORK

Requirements for setting up a living trust vary with each state. In general, you execute a document saying that you're creating a trust to hold property for the benefit of yourself and your family, or whomever you want it to benefit. Some trust declarations list the major assets (home, investments) that you're putting in trust;

others refer to another document (a **schedule**) in which you list the exact property that will begin the trust; or you may simply transfer the property to the trustee under the trust agreement.

In any case, you can add and subtract property whenever you want. You will have to change the ownership registration on whatever property you put into the trust—deeds, brokerage accounts, bank accounts, and so on—from your own name to the name of the trustee (e.g., John A. Smith, Trustee of The John A. Smith Trust). If you make yourself the trustee, you will have to remember to sign yourself in transactions as "John A. Smith, Trustee," instead of using only your name.

When you put property into a living trust, the trustee of the trust becomes its owner, which is why you must transfer title to the property from your own name to that of the trustee. But you retain the right to use and enjoy the property, and because you do, in the eyes of the tax authorities, the property in the trust belongs to you, the grantor, for tax purposes. If you receive income from the assets, you must still report the income from the trust directly on your income tax return. The trust itself often files a separate income tax return as well, though the IRS doesn't require one if the grantor and the trustee are the same person.

You can make anyone you want the trustee. You can also name a **successor trustee** (sometimes known as an **alternative trustee**) to take over in the event of the original trustee's death or incapacity.

 CORRECT TITLE

If you have a living trust, be sure assets are titled in the name of its trustee, not your own name. For example, if you buy a new car, be sure to take the title in the name of the trustee, not your own name. If you open a new brokerage account, do it in the trustee's name, not your own.

▶ THEY CAN LIVE A LONG TIME

Living trusts can extend long after you die. If you want the trust to bene-fit your infant grandchildren, for example, you might specify that the trustee make distributions to them or provide for their care until they are fully grown.

In a revocable living trust, you keep the right to manage your property whether you're the trustee or not, since you have a right to change the terms of the trust, the trustee, and the property in the trust at any time. When you die, your successor trustee dis-tributes the property according to the terms of the trust. Usually, your successor trustee is your surviving spouse or an adult child, but you can name a bank or a trust company if you are willing to pay their fees. (See chapter 28 for more information.)

Living trusts, like wills, give you wide flexibility in distribut-ing your property. For example, the trust agreement could say "at my death, my trustee is to give my car to my son Bill, my boat to my son Jacob," and so on. Your instructions can tell the trustee to continue managing assets for the benefit of someone else, dis-tribute them to any beneficiaries you choose, or perform some combination of these actions. If beneficiaries of your living trust die before you do, what happens to the property depends on the terms of the trust and state law. For example, the property might revert to you or go to the deceased beneficiary's estate. To avoid confusion, make sure your trust clearly states what will happen under these circumstances by naming **contingent beneficiaries** for those gifts.

Unless taxes are a worry—and they won't be in the vast major-ity of estates—you should be sure to retain the right to revoke or amend your trust whenever you wish. Have your lawyer create a revocable trust agreement, which allows you to change the terms or trustee, or just to forget the whole thing if it's too much trouble.

It can be a bother to set up and fund the living trust, but the payoff for your family comes when you die. If Ilsa wanted her property to go to her friend Rick, for example, she would put it in a trust and name him cotrustee or successor trustee. Then, when she dies, he becomes sole trustee and, acting in that capacity, transfers the trust property to the beneficiary—himself. Since the property does not have to go through probate, there's no break in continuity.

A living trust can contain other, separate trusts, which gives you a nice flexibility. For example, if you plan to leave some of your property to your minor children in trust (see chapter 12), you could specify in your trust that the children's property goes into a separate irrevocable children's trust. You can design separate trusts for several beneficiaries, all funded (usually at your death) by the assets in your living trust.

ADVANTAGES OF A LIVING TRUST

It helps in managing your affairs

A living trust provides a way to care for you and your property in case you become disabled. You'd typically set up a revocable living trust, fund it adequately, and name a reliable successor trustee (often an adult child) to manage it should you become ill. This avoids the delay and red tape of expensive, court-ordered guardianship. At the same time, the trustee can take over any duties you had in providing for other family members.

Of course, living trusts can help even if you're not disabled. For example, if you have a trustee, a living trust can manage your property. Say you rent out condos; your trustee can take over the management while you receive the income, minus the trustee's fees.

It protects your privacy

Living trusts maintain your privacy more than wills, since there's typically no public record required. However, if the trust is funded through a pourover provision in your will, the items transferred from your probate estate will appear in a public record. And in some states, if you put certain kinds of property in the trust, such as real estate, securities, or a safe-deposit box, you may have to register the trust, which creates a public record of its contents. You may be able to get around the requirement of recording the full revocable trust through use of a **nominee trust** or a **nominee partnership.** Your lawyer can fill you in on whether these are possible, but be aware that you cannot have a partnership (nominee or otherwise) if there is only one partner.

It's easy to create and change

For most simple estates, it's not that hard for a lawyer to create a living trust tailored to your estate objectives, and you don't have to go through the formalities required to execute or change wills. There are a few caveats. You do have to be competent, of course, just as you would if you were to write a will. And if real estate is involved, it may be necessary to have documents notarized so that they can be recorded. Some states require that your living trust be registered with the state, but that's a simple procedure.

However, most states require no witnesses to execute the living trust or an amendment to it. Just have your lawyer write it, and then you sign your name. (Of course, there may be times when you want witnesses to ensure that the trust will withstand a challenge to its authenticity, but the point is that you're not required to have them in most jurisdictions, so it's your call.)

It provides more options than a simple will

Living trusts give you wide flexibility in distributing your property. Your instructions can tell the trustee to continue managing assets for the benefit of someone else, distribute them to any beneficiaries you choose, or perform some combination of these actions.

Also, you can use your living trust to make gifts over a period of time. (You can't do that in a simple will.) In fact, living trusts can extend long after you die. If you want the trust to benefit your infant grandchildren, for example, you might specify that the trustee make gifts to them as needed until they are fully grown. (You can also get the benefits of a trust by creating one in your will—a testamentary trust.)

It's good for far-flung family and assets

Say you want your estate administered by someone who doesn't live in your state (usually a child who has grown up and moved away). A living trust might be better than a will because the trustee probably won't have to meet the residency requirements some state laws impose upon executors.

If you have property in another state, many lawyers recommend setting up a living trust to hold the title to that property. This helps you avoid **ancillary probate** procedures.

It avoids probate

This used to be a main reason for having a living will, but probate is now far less burdensome than it was in most states. Moreover, unless you have *all* of your property in the trust, you will still need a will, and your estate will still have to go through probate, though only for the property left out of the trust.

DISADVANTAGES OF A LIVING TRUST

Title problems

People often neglect to put all of their assets in the name of the trustee. Moreover, not all items may be easily transferred into a trust. For example, jewelry can be a problem because it typically does not have a title indicating ownership, like a car, boat, or home. Sometimes lawyers draft a **deed of gift** for the donor to get jewelry into the trust. And in Maryland and some other

SCAM ARTISTS

A number of scam artists, playing on elderly people's fear of probate and suspicion of lawyers, have taken to hawking living-trust kits door-to-door or through seminars. Some of these hucksters deliberately exaggerate the costs and difficulties of the probate process, even though probate procedures and fees in many states aren't onerous anymore. Authorities in several states have filed consumer fraud suits against these outfits for misrepresenting themselves as part of the AARP and not informing consumers that they could cancel contracts signed in the home within three days after the agreement.

Most lawyers and financial advisers say to avoid such pitches, whether they're made via unsolicited phone calls, postcards, or seminars. Such products seldom live up to their promoter's promises and often cost $2,500 or more—far above what you'd typically pay to get a good personalized trust done by a lawyer. Because living trusts should be crafted to fit your particular situation, it's next to impossible to find a prepackaged one that will suit your needs as well as one prepared by your lawyer.

states, transferring your home to a living trust will have the effect of voiding your title insurance, requiring the purchase of a supplemental policy.

It's burdensome to maintain

Trusts often spawn administrative chores that need to be attended to from time to time—and it's easy to forget to keep them up to date. For example, revocable trusts may not be automatically revoked or amended on divorce, unlike wills. If you don't amend the trust, your ex could end up being the beneficiary. It's also a good idea to amend the trust when you and your spouse have separated.

It could undermine other legal benefits

If you're in certain specialized situations, you might ask your lawyer whether a living trust is a good idea. It can, if not properly drafted (and this is a very technical area), jeopardize Medicaid qualifications. Depending on the state in which the property is located, putting your home in a revocable trust might jeopardize a homestead exemption, might require a transfer fee, or might cause your property to be reevaluated for property tax purposes.

Though a living trust you write while living in one state remains valid if you move to another, it's a good idea to check with a lawyer familiar with the statutes of your new state to see whether the trust should be revised to account for differences in the law. This is especially so if you're moving from a community property state to a common-law state or vice versa.

It provides less protection in the administration process

Because the administration of trust estates (that is, wrapping them up after death) has fewer formalities, abuses have occurred, such as not adhering to the terms of the trust, not maintaining adequate records of disbursements, and the like. In other words, what you may gain in speed and flexibility may be outweighed by what you could lose.

It provides less protection generally

If you have a will and your estate goes through probate, it is before a court, which has its advantages. A trust is not administered in court, so there is no quick way to get the case to court to settle disputes or issues of facts regarding status of beneficiaries. In other words, if a court is to determine those issues in a trust administration, a separate legal case needs to be filed—which entails a summons, related costs, and a time delay. In contentious situations, an estate administration is best.

Possible tax problems

Some states charge income taxes on trusts but not estates. Check your state law for such traps before setting up a living trust.

Cost

It can cost more to draft a living trust than a will. Though there *may* be some eventual savings in reduced or eliminated probate costs, registration fees and other incidental costs of the trust are incurred up front; the savings generally don't accrue until your death.

SHOULD YOU HAVE A LIVING TRUST?

The debate over living trusts has often focused on controlling costs and avoiding probate, but with probate reform so wide-

---

( ) TALKING TO A LAWYER

Q. *I'm one of the beneficiaries of my uncle's living trust—or at least I think I am. Is there any way (short of asking him) that I can find out what may be in store for me?*

A. Privacy is one of the key features of a living trust. In most states, your uncle would not be required to file the trust as a public document and would be under no obligation to reveal the nature of the trust. So treat your uncle well and hope for the best.

—Answer by Harold Pskowski,
BNA Tax Management, Washington, D.C.

⚠️ **WHAT A LIVING TRUST WON'T DO**

Living trusts are obviously an important estate-planning tool. In recent years, many people have come to expect them to work wonders. Here's a list of miracles they won't perform.

1. *They won't help you avoid taxes.* A revocable living trust doesn't save any income or estate taxes that couldn't also be saved by a properly prepared will. The property in the revocable living trust is still counted as part of your estate for tax purposes. Your successor trustee still has to pay income taxes on income generated by trust property. (Your executor would have to pay such taxes out of your estate if you had disposed of the property by a will instead of a trust.) And if the estate is large enough to trigger state and federal estate or inheritance taxes, your successor trustee has to file the appropriate tax returns. These and other duties can make the cost of administering some estates distributed by living trusts as high as traditional estate administration.

   You may be able to avoid or lower taxes by using one of the tax-saving trusts briefly discussed in chapters 21 and 22. *But a simple revocable living trust, by itself, will not save taxes.*

2. *They won't make a will unnecessary.* You still need a simple will to take care of assets you fail to transfer to the trust, or that you acquire shortly before your death. If you have minor children, you probably need a will to nominate a guardian for them.

3. *They won't affect other nonprobate assets.* Like a will, a living trust won't control the disposition of jointly owned property, life insurance payable to a beneficiary, or other nonprobate property.

spread, many lawyers think the emphasis on probate misses the far more significant features of living trusts.

The living trust, while offering advantages over probate, isn't guaranteed to save you money. If your records are well organized, your assets are simple (not necessarily small, just easily identified), your beneficiaries aren't contentious, your state has simple and inexpensive probate procedures for estates of your

4. *They won't protect your assets from creditors*. Creditors can attach living trust assets while you are alive, and in some—if not most—states after you die. In fact, the assets you put in a living trust don't have a probate administration, and thus lose the protection of the probate statute of limitations—in other words, your creditors have longer to get at them. And your family doesn't receive the **family allowance** granted for a probate estate, which sets aside a certain amount of money for family support that takes priority over creditors' claims. An *irrevocable* trust may help shield your assets from creditors, but this involves complicated legal provisions that require a lawyer's advice. And, of course, you lose control over the assets.

5. *They won't absolutely protect your assets from disgruntled heirs*. While it is harder to challenge a living trust than a will, a relative can still bring suit in trial court to challenge a living trust on the grounds of lack of mental capacity, undue influence, duress, or other reasons.

6. *They won't necessarily prevent delays*. In most states, a will and a living trust could take about the same time to administer (i.e., pay taxes and distribute your assets after you die). Many state laws impose a waiting period for creditors to file claims against estates of people with living trusts. The period usually isn't as long as the time required to probate a will, but it can stretch into many months. The trustee will still have to collect debts owed your estate after you die, prepare tax returns, and pay bills and distribute assets, just as an executor would. All that takes time. In addition, there may not be hardships caused by delays if you leave your property in a will. In most states, the assets of an estate are quickly available to the executor after the testator's death, so your family could probably get enough money to live on soon after you die.

size, and your probate court and lawyer are efficient, the legal costs of probate might be so low that it costs less to pass the property through a will than via a living trust.

Besides, since you should have a will even if you do use a living trust, you may be paying some court fees anyway, even though most of your property will be controlled by the living trust. And it might be possible to use other probate-avoidance techniques—joint tenancy, pay-on-death accounts, life insurance, and others mentioned in chapters 3–5—that don't entail the costs of a living trust.

You may want to determine how much probate will cost your estate and compare it to the costs, financial and otherwise, of a living trust for the same-size estate. An easy way to decide whether a living trust is right for you is to show your lawyer your list of assets (see Appendix A) and ask if, under all the circumstances, a living trust will save you money.

However, don't forget the many situations in which the benefits of a living trust outweigh any cost savings. For example, the advantage to an older or ill person is that a living trust eliminates the need for an expensive and undesirable court proceeding with a court-appointed guardian or conservator. (Another way to avoid a conservatorship is a **durable general power of attorney** authorizing someone to act for you in financial matters; you may wish to explore this alternative with your lawyer.)

Not everyone needs a living trust. When talking to a lawyer, ask what goals you can accomplish by setting one up. Then ask about the downsides mentioned here.

Eventually, you'll have to balance the advantages and disadvantages, but you can't do that until they're spelled out. Encouraging your lawyer to think clearly about your estate-planning goals—and express them clearly to you—will help you make the critical decisions that lie ahead.

THE WORLD AT YOUR FINGERTIPS

Living trust books tend to gush, but nonetheless you may find useful information in the following titles:

- *The Living Trust: The Failproof Way to Pass Along Your Estate to Your Heirs,* by Henry W. Abts (McGraw-Hill, 2002)

- *Your Living Trust and Estate Plan: How to Maximize Your Family's Assets and Protect Your Loved Ones,* by Harvey J. Platt (Allworth Press, 2002)

- *Understanding Living Trusts; How You Can Avoid Probate, Save Taxes, and Enjoy Peace of Mind,* by Vickie Schumacher and Jim Schumacher (Schumacher & Co., 1999)

YOU MUST REMEMBER THIS

- Living trusts can be a useful estate-planning tool, but check with your lawyer before believing the hype—they can't perform the miracles that many claim for them.

CHAPTER 12

Setting Up a Living Trust

Your Guide to Doing It Right

John is a doctor in his early forties. He lives with his wife, Jane, and their five children, ages 2, 5, 7, 10, and 13 (with expectation of more), in their home. He has a good income from his practice and is gradually building up an estate. However, in the event of his death or disability, John knows that he would not be able to support his family in the same lifestyle they're enjoying today. He is able to purchase a large life insurance policy on his life.

Then he takes another step. His lawyer helps him set up a revocable trust agreement with himself and Jane as trustees, and with Jane's brother and their trust company as successor trustees. The life insurance contract provides that the proceeds of the life insurance policy be payable to the trustees. Now, regardless of what happens to him, John can provide for Jane and the support and education of their children.

John's example shows how living trusts can work with other estate-planning tools such as life insurance. When you write your living trust, make sure you consider these issues.

Coordinated estate plan

It's important to make sure to coordinate the trust with the rest of your estate plan. The executor of your will still must pay income

---

(i) COST OF PREPARING A TRUST

A lawyer's fee for preparing a living trust will probably be higher than that for preparing a simple will, but in some states you may save money in the long run by avoiding probate costs.

and inheritance taxes and various probate expenses, but if too many of the estate assets are in the trust, he or she may not have enough money to do so. One way to meet this contingency is to give the trustee (and successor) power to make these payments from trust assets.

Coordinated disability plan

Most lawyers will help you plan for your possible incapacity. Sometimes they'll draft a durable power of attorney (see chapter 23) to go with the revocable trust, which will give the **attorney in fact** (the person you've selected to act for you) the power to receive assets from and transfer assets to the trust in case you become incompetent. The conditions placed on the power will vary depending on your family and financial situation. In many— perhaps most—cases, the attorney in fact will also be a cotrustee. Both are often your spouse, especially in smaller estates.

However, when different people are carrying out those functions, lawyers caution not to give the attorney in fact actual control over the trust; usually, they write that limitation into the power of attorney. The reason? It sets up a potential conflict of interest between one family member who's charged with looking out for your benefit and another, perhaps more distant relative who stands to benefit from the trust. That person would have a vested interest in keeping more of the money in the trust, even though you might need it to pay for, say, a better nursing home.

Finally, your lawyer will probably prepare and coordinate a living will or a health-care power of attorney (see chapters 23–24) with your living trust.

One trust or two?

Some lawyers say it works fine for a couple to use one living trust for all their shared property, whether in a community property state or common-law state. Most couples prefer to keep the ownership of important assets shared. That way, they don't have

≣ BY ANY OTHER NAME

In law, many words are **terms of art;** that is, they have special legal meanings. However, in talking about trusts, you find a bewildering array of names, some of which refer to the same kind of entity. In part, this is because trusts are generally governed by the diverse laws of fifty states and the federal government; in part because lawyers (and authors) often make up their own names for various clever trusts that take advantage of changes in the law. So don't worry if you go to a lawyer and you've never heard of the kind of trust he or she is talking about (or vice versa). What matters is how it works, not what it's called.

to worry about dividing part ownership of various assets. Nor, in the event of marital discord, does one spouse have to worry that the other's trust owns their house.

Such a joint marital trust will commonly provide that the property of the first spouse to die will go to the surviving spouse. Therefore, it winds up back in the living trust anyway, combined with the surviving spouse's property. (When tax considerations come into play, this might change.)

Remember that such a setup transfers the property to the other spouse with no conditions of any kind. Also remember that *in most states, divorce does not automatically invalidate a living trust.* If you want to maintain more control over your property, talk to your lawyer about alternatives to a joint trust.

Other lawyers disagree with the one-trust idea. If your lawyer doesn't carefully arrange the joint trust, the couple might be exposed to the gift tax (see chapter 20). A joint marital trust can also cause estate tax problems and is not recommended if there are assets larger than the federal exemption amount.

State laws vary in this area, so be sure to check with your lawyer before deciding whether to set up one trust or two.

Revocable or irrevocable?

As with other trusts, living trusts can be revocable (changeable) or irrevocable. Most living trusts are revocable. But some people (usually those with a lot of money) do use irrevocable living trusts to avoid taxes. You give up control over the assets in the trust, in return for escaping some estate, income, or gift taxes. Irrevocable living trusts are often used to give money to charity (**charitable remainder trusts**). Other common irrevocable trusts are **2505(c) trusts, Crummey trusts,** and **life insurance trusts.**

An irrevocable trust doesn't avoid taxes entirely; it merely sets up a separate taxable entity that might be able to pay taxes at a lower rate than if all the assets were combined in one estate. It can also offer a bit more protection from creditors.

FUNDING THE LIVING TRUST

Setting up the trust is actually the easy part. The harder part is putting something in it—what's called funding the trust. This includes not just depositing money in the trust account, but also transferring title of assets to the name of the trustee.

Living trusts can be funded now, while you're living, or after you are dead. If you want to fund it before you die (a **funded trust**), you transfer title of your assets to the trustee

---

⚠ IRREVOCABLE MEANS NO DO-OVERS!

If you make the trust irrevocable to reduce taxes and avoid creditors, prepare for a lot of paperwork. And understand that you lose the flexibility of a revocable living trust. *Be sure to consult a lawyer before setting up an irrevocable trust.*

---

and make the trustee the owner of any newly acquired assets you want to go into the trust. Any assets in the trust will avoid probate.

How do you transfer titles to the trustee? You have to reregister title documents—for example, transfer title of your bank accounts and stocks to the trustee's name, and prepare and sign a new deed to your house designating the trustee as owner. If you have any doubts about how to proceed, consult your lawyer. Make sure to keep a record of these transfers; it will make your successor trustee's job easier when you die.

What should you leave out? The special tax treatment given IRAs might encourage you to leave them in your name. The fees your state charges to transfer title of a mortgage or other property increase the cost of transfer.

Some people are just afraid to take the family house out of the husband and wife's names in joint tenancy and put it in the name of just one of the spouses as trustee. Maybe that's because they then don't own their house (the trustee of their trust does), or because the spouse who isn't a trustee doesn't trust the spouse who is the trustee to hold and manage it for the benefit of both. In such cases, a lawyer may suggest putting the living trust in both your names—for example, "the James and Ima Hogg Trust," instead of in just one name—and making both spouses cotrustees.

If the trust is in one name only, and the other spouse is not a cotrustee or a successor trustee, many lawyers recommend leaving one checking account with ample funds out of the living trust, and not having it poured over into the trust when that person dies. This is as much for psychological as financial reasons, since it reassures the spouse who is not a trustee that he or she will have access to funds upon the death of the other. The checking account should be a joint account with rights of survivorship, in the name of both spouses. That way, if one dies, the other will have the right to write checks on the account.

The important point is to be sure to go through each of your

⚠ MAKE SURE IT'S NOT AN EMPTY SHELL

If the purpose of the trust is to avoid probate, funding the trust improperly or inadequately is probably the single most common mistake people can make. If, however, the trust is being used primarily to keep the dispositive provisions private (i.e., to keep bequests out of the public record), then you can use an unfunded trust that is funded just before or after death. The reason for this is that in some jurisdictions the probate court retains jurisdiction over trusts set up in a will.

---

assets with your lawyer to determine whether it's wise to transfer that asset to the trust.

THE UNFUNDED LIVING TRUST

The other way to fund a trust when needed or after your death is the **unfunded living trust.** Many people choose to fund it through their will. To do this, you set up a revocable trust and a pourover will, which transfers the assets into the trust upon your death. You can add some assets to the trust before you die, but generally, the will would specify that all estate property would pour over into the trust, including life insurance and other death benefits.

Obviously, you can't avoid probate this way. So who would use this approach? Perhaps people who don't want to go through the hassle of funding a living trust while they're alive, but also don't want their after-death gifts to be a matter of public record. They could give their estate to a trust via their will, and specify named beneficiaries through the privacy of the trust.

The other option is to have it funded when you're facing death or disability. You give someone (often your spouse, an adult child, or a friend; see chapter 23) a durable power of attorney. Then, if you should become disabled, that person has the authority to fund the trust and transfer assets into it. The trustee can then use the assets to care for you in your final illness.

Many lawyers caution against trying to fund unfunded trusts at the last minute. Your state may not allow you to grant such powers of attorney. If you should die or become incompetent before you or your trustee can transfer your assets into an unfunded trust (a process that can take weeks), then those assets will go through probate as your will pours them over to the trust. All in all, you may be better off funding the trust when it is created.

SAVE YOUR LAWYER TIME . . . AND YOURSELF MONEY

Your involvement shouldn't stop after the trust document is executed. In a living trust, someone must take charge of funding (transferring assets into) the trust. This can involve changing car titles, executing deeds or bills of sale, reregistering stocks, and so on. Some lawyers describe the often onerous process as "going through probate before you die."

Usually, you don't want to pay a lawyer's hourly fee to undertake these sorts of routine clerical tasks. Sometimes lawyers will delegate them to their paralegals, who will charge you less, but it still costs you money.

On the other hand, lawyers complain that clients often (and understandably) neglect this tedious process after they walk out of the office with an elegantly crafted revocable living trust in hand. If you neglect it, and disaster strikes, much of the estate still has to go through probate, because you failed to complete the funding process.

What to do? If you're short on money, long on time (as many retired people are), have few assets that need retitling, or are

⚠ DON'T TRY THIS ON YOUR OWN

Who should advise you about living trusts? Your lawyer is the obvious choice. After all, trusts are complex legal documents, and a mistake could be costly if not catastrophic.

It's especially good to have a lawyer's help in figuring out which assets to put in the living trust and which to put elsewhere and leave for disposition via your will. By providing money-saving advice like this, lawyers often save you more than they charge you in legal fees.

By doing some preparation, you can minimize the time the lawyer spends on setting up the trust and thus reduce your legal costs. Just as you would when making a will, you should ask your lawyer what documents you should bring with you. After collecting all the needed records, deeds, bank statements, and the like, make a list of what you have and where you want it to go when you die.

certain you're willing to do the legwork, then do it yourself. Or you and a paralegal could split up the work, with the lawyer supervising the process by checking with you a few times after the trust is executed. Because of the vagaries of real estate law, many lawyers will want to take care of transferring real property themselves.

THE WORLD AT YOUR FINGERTIPS

Books on the mechanics of setting up a living trust include:

- *The Living Trust Workbook,* by Robert A. Esperti, David K. Cahoone, and Renno L. Peterson (Penguin, 2001)
- *Loving Trust: The Right Way to Provide for Yourself and Guarantee the Future of Your Loved Ones,* by Robert A. Esperti and Renno L. Peterson (Viking, 1994)

YOU MUST REMEMBER THIS

- A living trust can be a useful device—but it doesn't work automatically and all by itself.
- To avoid probate, a living trust must be properly funded.
- Be sure to coordinate a living trust with the rest of your estate plan.
- A living trust must be maintained after it's set up—newly acquired assets must be put into it, the beneficiary designations must be kept up-to-date, and so on.

PART FIVE

Putting the Tools to Work

Some Tips for People with Particular Needs

CHAPTER 13

Providing for the Kids

Tips for Every Age of Offspring

Charles and Emily were both hardworking, industrious people, yet devoted plenty of time to their only son, Oliver, who was a top student in his fifth-grade class. Then Charles died in an auto accident, only months after Emily had succumbed to cancer. Charles's best friend, David, badly wanted to help Oliver; David was a successful graphic designer, and he and his wife had plenty of room in their home after their only child left for college. But because his parents hadn't provided for a guardian in their will, custody of Oliver went to his closest relative, Emily's sister, Holly. Holly had always been irresponsible, and David was concerned. David could do nothing as Oliver's grades plummeted, and the once-promising student started to struggle.

Most people want their estate plan to take care of their children after they (the parents) are gone. Many different methods are available to accomplish this, but choosing the right one depends upon your particular circumstances—financial, familial, and otherwise. Here are some common strategies; your lawyer can help you decide which one—or which combination—is best for your family.

PERSONAL GUARDIANS

If you die and your spouse survives you, he or she will naturally have custody of your minor children, so you might think there'll be no need for a personal guardian for them. Even if you're divorced, it's almost impossible for the custodial parent to deny the noncustodial parent custody of their child if the custodial parent should die (there are rare exceptions, such as if the surviving parent is in jail or has been found incompetent by a court).

If you leave all your estate to your spouse, the children will presumably have no property to manage, so you might think there'll also be no need for a guardian of their property.

The difficulty with property guardians is that the law usually requires the guardian to put up a bond, file all sorts of legal papers, account for finances, and negotiate a maze of legal requirements—all of which would be at least doubled if that guardian dies or resigns and a successor guardian is appointed. For example, all but twelve states require that the property guardian post a bond, and in some of those states you can't waive the requirement in your will. There may also be restrictions on who may serve as the children's property guardian.

But what if you both should die, say, in a car accident? Your will should provide for that real—if remote—possibility by nominating one or more persons to fill the role of the guardian.

TALKING TO A LAWYER

Q. Besides naming the best possible people to serve as guardians for our kids, what else can we do to assure that they will be raised with our values in mind?

A. While nominating guardians is important, parents should also consider drafting a memorandum to their guardians that express their hopes, dreams, and aspirations for their children. Such memoranda can cover personal beliefs, spiritual beliefs, educational preferences, views about what the children should be taught about money, and other values and routines that the parents may not want to express in their plan documents. Parents should review this document, like their other plan documents, on a regular basis.

—Answer by Lena Barnett,
Attorney-at-Law, Silver Spring, Maryland

If both parents die, the law requires a minor child to have a **personal guardian** to step in and in effect become the child's parent. Who would be the guardian for your children? Many people haven't given this question enough thought. Questions to consider: Who would provide the best care for your children if you die? Is the home you choose large enough for them? Will their guardians have enough money to provide your children with the kind of education and environment you prefer? What sort of financial provisions should you make for the children?

Sometimes people delay their estate plans over the selection of the guardian. While this can be a difficult decision, it is better for the parents to select the guardian than it would be to have a judge make the selection. Parents know their children much better than any judge. A less-than-perfect decision is going to be much better than no decision.

Your will can nominate a personal guardian. The probate judge doesn't have to accept your choice—although the court will almost always go along, unless someone challenges that choice as not being in the child's best interest.

It's better to nominate an individual as personal guardian; if you name a couple and they split up, what happens to the child? Be sure to consult with the person you name to be sure he or she wants the job, and name an alternative guardian in case your first choice should have a change of heart or die before the child is grown.

PROPERTY GUARDIANS

It's one thing to find someone who'll provide the adult guidance and supervision your minor children will need after you and your spouse are gone. It can be quite a different—and difficult—task to manage the children's property. Children under eighteen can't legally own (without supervision) more than a minimal amount of property; the law requires that an adult take responsibility for managing all property above that minimal limit for the children's benefit. That person is called the **property guardian** or **property**

▶ **GO THE PERSONAL ROUTE**

Consider an alternative to a bank or other institution as property manager, particularly for a small or medium-sized estate; their fees are often too high, and they are too impersonal to provide the level of service you want and need.

manager. You should definitely name a property guardian for your children, even if you don't leave them any money in your will, in case the other parent dies, too.

Who should be the property guardian? Often, it's the same person you name to be the child's personal guardian. That obviously simplifies matters, allowing one person to control the assets used for the child's benefit and spend them for that purpose.

However, you can appoint two different people to manage the child's money and personal affairs. If the personal guardian lacks the financial expertise or inclination to manage money, it may be worthwhile to consider another relative or friend to be the property guardian. Some lawyers caution that conflicts can arise if you split authority this way. Others look at it the opposite way—that it is a good thing to separate the child's care from the care of the child's property because self-interest cannot then play a major role in the choices made by the personal guardian.

TRUSTS AS AN ALTERNATIVE

It's best to minimize the role of the property guardian by setting up a simple trust for your children in your will. The trust would probably be funded by life insurance policies on each parent's life, payable to the surviving spouse, or to the children's trust if both parents die simultaneously. It would come into being at the death of the second parent.

◯ TALKING TO A LAWYER

Q. How can we ensure that the guardians we've named for our children have the resources to raise them well?

A. If you have an estate plan that involves a living trust, the trustee will take the role of the property guardian. The trust will contain instructions for the financial well-being of the children. Just as parents can draft a memorandum to their guardians, they can also draft a memorandum to their trustee that goes beyond what has been stated in the trust.

A trust document can give the trustee authority to assist guardians of the children with the financial burdens associated with raising additional children. Such burdens may include the need to buy a bigger car or put an addition on a house.

Whether you have a will-based or trust-based plan, it is important that your documents enable your trustees/property guardians and personal guardians to act in the best interest of the children in a manner consistent with your wishes, directions, and values.

—Answer by Lena Barnett,
Attorney-at-Law, Silver Spring, Maryland

In such a **testamentary trust** (set up in your will) or other properly drafted and funded revocable trust, you transfer assets to a trustee to manage for the benefit of your children, set forth the conditions under which money would be paid to them, and give the trustee authority to spend, sell, or invest the assets for the children's benefit.

As noted in the discussion of personal guardians, you can name the trustee to be the guardian of the children as well, or you can split the job—there are arguments on both sides of the question.

Typically, the trust would provide for the children's care and education and make money available to them as they reach certain ages indicative of maturity—18, 21, 25, or 30. However, for both estate-planning reasons and as protection from creditors, some people prefer to keep the money in trust for the lifetimes of their children.

Trusts are far more flexible than guardianships. Guardianships require court approval of actions by the guardian and usually must follow strict rules for paying out funds to children. You might not agree with these rules, which could limit your ability to specify which of your children should receive which of your assets and when.

Testamentary trusts established in your will or a variety of trusts that you can establish through your living trust can provide you with a wealth of opportunities regarding the upbringing of your children. This is where the professional guidance of your attorney can really make a difference. Do you want to have a common trust until your youngest child attains a certain age or meets some other requirement? Do you want to have a separate trust for each child? There are advantages and disadvantages to both options. Once the children have reached the age of maturity, how should assets be left them? How much protection do you wish to give them? For example, are you concerned about mismanagement, divorce protection, or predator protection? How rapidly do you want to pass the responsibility of owning assets to them?

CUSTODIAN ACCOUNTS

Suppose your estate is modest and you don't think it warrants setting up a trust for your children. But you still want to convey property to them upon your death. You can set up a custodian account for them while you are still alive and bequeath funds to that account through your will. The **Uniform Gift to Minors Act (UGMA)** or the **Uniform Transfer to Minors Act (UTMA)** have been adopted by almost all the states. Most states permit you to make gifts to these accounts in your will.

The UGMA and UTMA authorize the creation of custodian accounts for minors. Thus, they're different from bank accounts

▶ **AN ESTATE TAX TIP**

If you are the custodian for your children's accounts, their accounts will be included in your estate for estate tax purposes if you die before the child reaches the age of majority. If the purpose of the gifting is to remove assets from your estate, consider other gifting alternatives, have someone else serve as custodian, or name a successor custodian.

you'd open in a child's name. But the mechanism they authorize is so simple that you can probably set up custodian accounts using just a bank or a brokerage firm. These laws allow you to open an account and deposit money or property in it while you are still alive. You can make yourself custodian of the account, and set up a successor in case you die while the child is under eighteen (or up to twenty-one or even twenty-five in some states). Use the child's Social Security number.

Both laws give the custodian broad powers, with the powers under the UTMA being somewhat wider. For example, a UGMA custodian cannot take title to real property unless the statute has been modified.

When your children are over age thirteen, the federal government taxes income in these accounts at the children's rate, which will almost certainly be lower than yours. For younger children, through the "kiddie tax," the federal government taxes income from the account at *your* tax rate.

The drawbacks? Some parents might be uncomfortable with the fact that in many states the funds become the child's property when he or she reaches age eighteen, leaving them no control over the funds after that.

Using an UGMA or UTMA account or trust will reduce the amount of supervision and paperwork required by the court, and thus lower expenses to your estate. If most of the assets you

▶ ## LEAVING GIFTS TO SOMEONE ELSE'S KIDS

In the states that allow you to leave a gift in your will to UGMA and UTMA accounts, you can use a custodian account to leave a gift to children who aren't yours—say, a favorite nephew. Or you could set up a trust for that child just as you would for your own children. Or you could leave money to the child's parents to be used for his benefit (although this wouldn't legally bind the parents to spend it on the child).

leave to the child are handled by these methods, it can reduce the probate court's involvement to almost nothing.

But even if you make gifts to your child in any of these ways, you still must name a personal guardian in your will. You must also name a property guardian to manage property the child receives after you die and property inadvertently left out of the trust or UGMA / UTMA gift. You can make the same person the personal guardian, the property guardian, the custodian, and the trustee.

There are also a number of minors' trusts that can be set up to benefit your children. See chapter 22 for a brief discussion of them.

WHEN CHANGES COME: CONTINGENCY PLANS FOR YOUR CHILDREN

Of course, you want to provide for your children, but sometimes you don't get around to changing your will when you have a new child. The law helps you out in that case. If you've made a will, and then have another child and die before you can change your will to include him or her, most states provide for a share of your property to go to this **pretermitted child.**

The share a pretermitted child is entitled to take varies from

---

ⓘ IF YOU DON'T APPOINT A GUARDIAN

If you don't appoint a guardian for your children, someone (usually a friend or relative) may ask the court to name him or her as guardian. If no one volunteers, the court can choose someone, generally the nearest adult relative.

---

state to state. The amount also may depend on whether you left him or her a gift through some means other than a will (such as a living trust), and whether you had other children who received gifts in the will.

Generally, if you had no other children, the pretermitted child would receive the same share he or she would have received had you died intestate (without a will). If you had other children, yet gave them nothing under the will (often people leave everything to the spouse), the pretermitted child would receive nothing, just like the other children.

If, however, you left property to the other children, the omitted child may be entitled to what he or she would have received had you given each child an equal share. Let's say that you had two children and provided for them in the will, and a third was born later but left out of the will. The court would give the pretermitted child one-third of the total amount of the estate you left to the other two children.

If you want to avoid this result, the best way is to keep your will up-to-date and specifically disinherit any children you don't want to provide for. Obviously, if it could be shown that you had intentionally disinherited any children yet to be born—usually by language in the will—no pretermitted child laws apply. Those laws also usually don't apply to nonprobate instruments like a living trust; thus, the unintentional disinheriting of a child born after the living trust is executed is a potential disadvantage of that instrument.

⟲ TALKING TO A LAWYER

Q. In a UGMA or a UTMA, the custodian manages the property for the benefit of the child, and state law determines at what age the custodianship has to end. What happens then? Does the beneficiary get the full amount of what's in the account? What if I think the beneficiary is too immature to use the money wisely?

A. Your child will receive the full amount in the account when he or she reaches the age specified by state law. That age is eighteen in some states, twenty-one in others. If you are concerned about what your child might do with the account, you should consult an attorney before that time arrives. You may be able to persuade your child, on termination of the UGMA or UTMA account, to place the money into a trust that will continue for the child's benefit until he or she is able to handle the funds. Another approach is the creation of a family partnership that you or your spouse can control. If the UGMA or UTMA account is placed into the partnership before it is required to be paid to your child, you would be able to continue to control the investment of the account and any distributions made to your child. Either approach would require the assistance of an attorney.

—Answer by Harold Pskowski,
BNA Tax Management, Washington, D.C.

What happens if you will some of your property to one of your children, but he or she dies before you do? Generally, a will can't make a gift to a dead person, so if a beneficiary dies before you, the gift **lapses** or fails (i.e., it goes back into your estate). However, many states have **antilapse** laws that provide that a gift to a beneficiary who dies before you passes on to that person's descendants.

There are at least a couple of ways to plan for such contingencies. One way to accommodate late arrivals or early departures is not to bequeath your assets to children by name, but as a class (for example, "I leave all my property in equal shares to

Q. What are some other ways of keeping the money in the custodial account out of the hands of kids just barely above the age of majority?

A. The beneficiary is entitled to everything in the account at the age of majority, but a parent can spend down funds for the benefit of the child using funds to cover tuition, for example. Or the parent may want to consider establishing a restricted 529 plan account by transferring the assets to the account. The funds will then be limited to educational purposes, but they will not come under the full control of the beneficiary at majority.

—Answer by Lena Barnett,
Attorney-at-Law, Silver Spring, Maryland

Q. Our two kids are not close to each other in age or emotionally. Can we specify different guardians for them?

A. Yes. One alternative that might bring them closer together is to specify that if one of them is of age when you die, that person should become the guardian of the younger sibling.

—Answer by Pamela L. Rollins,
Simpson Thacher & Bartlett, New York, New York

my children living at my death and to the then living descendants of each deceased child, the descendants of a deceased child to take their ancestor's share, *per stirpes*"). Under a clause such as this, if you have three children when you make the will, and one dies before you do, the remaining two children will inherit one-third of your estate, instead of one-half. The children of the deceased child will split the remaining third. The two living children won't get half unless the deceased child leaves no descendants.

Another way is for the person making the will to specify what he or she wants to do about afterborn and adopted children. Perhaps the will maker wants to handle such contingencies in a particular way. If so, he or she can establish the terms for what happens if one or more of the children should die before the will maker does, or die before the complete distribution of their inheritance.

DO BEQUESTS TO CHILDREN HAVE TO BE EQUAL?

If you have more than one child, keep in mind that the law does not require you to leave money or property to your children in equal shares, although this is the most common arrangement.

Rather, you can leave each child the kind and amount of assets that best suit his or her situation. The grown child who just graduated from medical school, for example, would probably need less of an inheritance from you than the learning-disabled child who just turned nineteen. The son who shares your interest in ichthyology would probably appreciate your aquarium more than your daughter, the stock car driver.

However, many estate-planning lawyers caution that even though you have the legal right to leave your children unequal shares, such an arrangement might cause hard feelings among

▶ **FAMILY DISCUSSIONS ARE ESSENTIAL**

If you do contemplate making unequal gifts to your children, make sure you discuss your plans with them first. Assure them of your love for all of them, and tell them the reasons you are thinking about unequal gifts. Their reactions will probably tell you whether your plan will fly. It's best to get their agreement before making an unequal distribution.

the kids and even invite litigation. Children understand that they have different needs, but even so they may take unequal gifts to mean that their parents prefer some over the others.

Whether you leave equal or unequal shares to your children, you do not have to establish the same terms for each share. You may want to leave assets in different ways to children that have differing life circumstances and needs.

BEQUEATHING REAL ESTATE TO CHILDREN

Besides their homes, many Americans own other real property, some of it located out-of-state. Maybe it's a vacation home, or a farm, or rental property, or even investment property. It's not always easy to know how to handle this kind of asset for estate-planning purposes.

A main issue is how the beneficiaries view the property. That vacation home may have fond associations for the now-grown-up kids, so of course you'll want to keep it in the family. One way to do this is through a trust that sets out each child's right to use the property, lays down guidelines to prevent conflicts, and sets up a procedure by which any child may buy out another's interest in the property.

But if you're not sure whether the kids have the time or interest to manage real estate, especially if it's far from home, you may want to explore other options.

A good first step is to get the property appraised to find out what it's worth, what income-producing potential it has, and so on. Then it's important to talk through the issue within the family so that all the generations are on the same page.

And, of course, you'll want to involve your lawyer, since the decisions you make—such as whether to sell some of your property now to convert it into more liquid assets or allow it to pass to the next generation and then be sold—could have significant tax consequences.

(i) DISINHERITING CHILDREN

Children may be disinherited. In case your state has standards of specificity for disinheriting children, you should be sure to name in your will the children you intend to disinherit: for example, "I intentionally make no provision for my son, Oedipus." In a few states, you must leave the disinherited children a token amount, usually a dollar, to make sure they don't get a share against your wishes. Louisiana is an exception to the general rule. It has a "forced heirship" policy that, absent certain exceptions, requires parents to leave a share of their estate to their children.

NONTRADITIONAL KIDS

What about children who don't fit the traditional categories, such as adoptees, children of a previous marriage, and so-called illegitimate children?

In most states, adopted children are treated just like natural children unless you indicate otherwise in your will. To avoid problems, specify in your will that words such as "child," "children," "sons," or "daughters" include (or exclude, as you wish) an adopted child.

If your will simply indicates that gifts will go to your children (without indicating which children), children from all your marriages will be included in that term. However, if you marry someone with children from a previous marriage and don't formally adopt these stepchildren as your own, they are not included in your bequest to your children unless you specifically say so.

If you're a male, in most states a bequest to children includes only legitimate children. But in the case of a mother, a bequest to children usually includes illegitimate children.

Note that these rules don't just apply to your own children.

If you leave bequests to your beneficiaries' children, the same rules would determine who is (and is not) included.

THE WORLD AT YOUR FINGERTIPS

- *Best Intentions: Ensuring Your Estate Plan Delivers Both Wealth and Wisdom,* by Colleen Barney and Victoria F. Collins (Dearborn Trade Publishing, 2002). The authors stress that values, ideals, and feelings should be incorporated into an estate plan intended to benefit children.

- *Beyond the Grave: The Right Way and the Wrong Way of Leaving Money to your Children (and Others),* by Gerald M. Condon and Jeffrey L. Condon (HarperBusiness, 2001). The Condons, who are father and son and both lawyers, look at traditional estate planning but also consider the psychological and emotional aspects of leaving money.

- *Silver Spoon Kids: How Successful Parents Raise Responsible Children,* by Eileen Gallo, Jon J. Gallo, and Kevin J. Gallo (McGraw Hill/Contemporary Books, 2001). Eileen Gallo is a psychotherapist, and her husband, Jon J. Gallo, is an attorney. The book is oriented more toward teaching your kids how to handle money (and their potential inheritance) while the parents are still around, rather than estate planning per se.

YOU MUST REMEMBER THIS

- Although as parents you don't like to think about what would happen to your kids if both of you were to die, you must construct your estate plan to account for that possibility.

- You can use guardianships, trusts, and other legal devices to make sure your kids are taken care of if the worst happens.

CHAPTER 14

Married . . . with or Without Children

Most of Us Want to See That Our Spouse Is Taken Care of, but How?

This chapter discusses the most common estate-planning situations: those involving a married couple. How can you use the basic tools of estate planning to fit your particular needs?

While no two marriages are alike, most married couples share some basic estate-planning needs, some of which are outlined below. What's more critical than the specifics that appear here, however, is that you discuss these matters with your partner.

Often, a couple will arrive at a lawyer's office only to discover that the partners have different fears and desires about where their money should go after they die. The husband might want some of his property to go to the couple's grown children, to help them get started in life. The wife, on the other hand, might see the limited job market for herself and want more of his money to go to support her. These are intimate matters that will have to be hammered out between you and your partner—preferably before you talk to a lawyer.

Many married couples with modest estates (and that's by far the majority of them) will execute simple wills in which each partner leaves everything to the surviving spouse. This is especially true if the couple is past the prime earning years, or if one of them has depended on the other for support and the children are grown and earning money.

However, even couples with modest estates should consider estate plans centered around living trusts. As noted earlier, the advantages of such revocable trusts include protection for your

▶ KEEP YOUR WILL AND REVOCABLE TRUST UP TO DATE

When you get married, you should be sure to rewrite your will or trust, or at least modify it. In some states a will is **revoked** (that is, canceled) by marriage, unless the will expressly declares that it was executed in contemplation of the particular marriage and that it shall not be revoked by that marriage. In all states, the law provides that your spouse can take a share of your estate, no matter what your will says (see chapter 15), though a prenuptial contract typically waives this right. You'll want to factor your marriage into your estate plan, and you may want to alter your will to account for it.

assets in the event that you are disabled, as well as probate avoidance and privacy. Such plans may utilize a joint trust for the couple, or a separate trust for each spouse.

A married couple's estate plan will usually change over time: They accumulate more assets, children are born and then leave the household, and the chances diminish that one spouse will long outlive the other. Here are some considerations for both young and middle-aged couples, assuming that one or both spouses work outside the home and that together they have a middle-class income.

YOUNGER COUPLES

Marianne and Gilligan are in their thirties. They are concerned about things like taking care of their minor children if they both die and making sure there's money set aside to pay for college and, if one of them dies, giving the other an adequate income.

Because they haven't paid off their house, they bought life insurance to cover the mortgage. For their other debts, they've arranged a debt-payment schedule and a life insurance plan so their children won't be burdened with this duty if they die soon. They haven't yet earned enough money to worry about estate tax planning.

For all these reasons, each needs a relatively simple basic will or trust that leaves everything to the surviving spouse. The principal goal is to protect the surviving partner, who may have several decades to live if the other dies unexpectedly. In addition, they make each other beneficiary of their life insurance policies and other benefit plans.

This estate plan and will or revocable trust are interim documents, which Marianne and Gilligan will update as their assets and incomes grow.

Thurston and Luvey, on the other hand, have substantial assets, including a family business. Their plan includes a funded revocable living trust that enables the trustee to administer the assets for the benefit of the surviving spouse. This type of trust will avoid probate for all the assets put in the trust. (Probate is likely to be more complicated and costly for a larger estate than a smaller one). They also have life insurance for liquid assets. Finally, each also has a will that leaves the residue of the estate to the trust; that arrangement will pick up any assets somehow left out of the trust.

Both couples have health-care powers of attorney that let each spouse make decisions for the other if either becomes incapacitated, and a living will.

Neither Marianne and Gilligan nor Thurston and Luvey use a **reciprocal power of attorney.** Young couples (whose marriages statistically are most likely to collapse) should generally not execute reciprocal powers of attorney as a way of planning for incapacity. Should a breakup turn nasty, one partner who is legally entitled to act on the other's behalf might drain the other's savings account or squander his or her assets out of spite or greed.

If you have executed such powers and your marriage is collapsing, both partners should revoke them immediately. The same goes for any jointly held rights over property, such as a joint bank account or a joint revocable trust.

Many lawyers believe that a **springing general power of attorney** is far safer. These become effective ("spring" into being)

(i) JOINT TENANCY FOR MARRIED COUPLES

If your combined estate falls under the estate tax limit, and you don't expect it to exceed that amount by the time the second spouse dies, you may think it's simpler just to leave all the property in joint tenancy. In that case, the surviving spouse receives all the assets without worrying about estate taxes, and there's no probate.

However, you still need to take into account the drawbacks of joint tenancy discussed in chapter 5. These include the fear that the surviving spouse will squander the money instead of spending it on the children, or will remarry and leave all the money to the new family. Joint tenancy makes tax planning harder (just in case taxes suddenly become a problem). If you die together, the jointly held assets would have to go through probate. Since joint tenancy doesn't let you control the distribution of your money after you die, you will have to use a trust or a will if you want the money to go to anyone but your spouse.

---

when the principal (the person creating the power) has been certified as incompetent. Since the power is not granted until it is needed, in theory it is safer than executing a general power of attorney.

However, there could be problems in creating a springing power. In marginal circumstances (for example, one in which the principal was not comatose) the doctor you ask to certify to the client's incompetence may legitimately refuse to do so. Moreover, the doctor is likely going to have to update his or her opinion constantly. And what would happen to your springing power if the principal were simply missing? Because of such difficulties, some lawyers caution against using such powers. Their reasoning is that you simply shouldn't give such authority to someone you don't trust. Your lawyer can tell you which option works best in your particular situation.

OLDER COUPLES

Archie and Edith have paid off the mortgage on their home. They've accumulated many more assets than they had when they were young, but not so many that they have to worry about taxes on their estate. With retirement near, they're concerned with assuring that the surviving spouse has enough funds for a comfortable life for his or her remaining years.

Like most older couples, they have left everything to the surviving spouse, with the expectation that the property will pass to the children or grandchildren upon his or her death.

Fred and Ethel, whose children have already established themselves well in the world, are less concerned about providing for their children and want instead to concentrate on leaving a gift (probably in trust) for their grandchildren, with the parents to administer it. Since the surviving spouse will likely not live many years beyond the first spouse, each has set up a **marital trust** effective upon his or her death. The surviving spouse would live off the income of the trust if it were sufficient, and could get to the principal if the trust is drafted with the appropriate **encroachment provisions.** At death, the remaining principal would go to the children or grandchildren. And, as shown in chapter 21, the marital trust could also save on estate taxes.

Lucy and Ricky have enough assets to worry more about tax planning. To accomplish this goal, they create separate trusts or a joint trust that would bring a **bypass** and/or a marital trust to life at the death of the first spouse to die. This arrangement will avoid probate for those assets placed in the trust and help protect assets from taxes. The surviving spouse receives the income (and might be able to receive principal) from that trust for the rest of his or her life. When the second spouse dies, the property remaining in this trust will pass on to their children or grandchildren. The successor trustee could be a child (and/or a professional trustee, if the estate is large enough) who is capable of managing the money for the grandchildren's benefit. This type of

▶ **ASSUMING THE WORST**

No one wants to consider the possibility that his children might die before he does, but your estate plan must take this tragic contingency into account. If you have grandchildren, you'll want a provision that sets up a contingent gift for any of them in case your child—your grandchildren's parent—dies before you do. That way, the gift that would have gone to that child will instead pass to his or her children when they reach age eighteen or twenty-one. Sometimes the gift will be structured so that a contingent trust comes into being when you die; that way, the gift will be held in trust for the grandchildren till they reach majority age. Or the trustee can pay it out over time, so that the grandchildren don't suddenly have thousands of dollars at their disposal when they are still relatively young.

vehicle requires the advice and active participation of a lawyer and other professional advisers.

TROUBLED MARRIAGES

In a perfect world, all marriages would be blissful—but the reality is that many aren't. The next chapter discusses estate planning for divorced or divorcing couples, but some issues are worth considering even before a marriage reaches such a state. Some spouses are shocked to learn that their partners, for whatever reason, wanted to cut them out of their wills. However, the law usually doesn't permit this. In the days when wives were totally dependent on their husbands, disinheritance could leave widows destitute. Even though the law may have originally been intended to protect widows, it applies both ways. Women can't cut their husbands out of wills, either.

If a husband or a wife dies and his or her will makes no provision for the surviving spouse, or conveys to that person less than a certain percentage of the deceased spouse's assets (the percentage varies by state), a widow(er) can **take against the will.** This means that he or she can choose to accept the amount allowed by law (usually a third or a half of the estate) instead of the amount bequeathed in the will. The surviving spouse doesn't have to take against the will. If he or she chooses not to, the property is bequeathed as stated in the will.

This **elective or forced share provision** is troubling to many people considering second marriages late in life. Many have avoided marriage out of fear that the surviving spouse of only a few years could take half their property, though they want to give it to their own children. Recent revisions to the Uniform Probate Code have adopted a sliding scale for widow(ers) who take against the will—that is, the longer the marriage, the higher the elective share. If the marriage lasted only a few years, the percentage could be quite low, minimizing one source of worry for older couples. However, as of this writing fewer than half the states have adopted even a portion of the suggested code (see sidebar).

What about people who have a living trust instead of a will? In some states, spouses aren't entitled to a forced share of living-trust assets. In those states, one spouse might be able to disinherit the other. Your lawyer can tell you about the law in your state.

(i) UP TO CODE

The Uniform Probate Code (UPC) is the work of the National Conference of Commissioners on Uniform State Laws, a group that encourages state legislatures to modify their laws to bring them into accord with the models. A minority of states have adopted all or some of the Uniform Probate Code. Check out the commission's excellent website (www.nccusl.org/) to learn more, and check with your lawyer to see if your state has adopted these revisions.

⚠️ DIFFERENT STATES, DIFFERENT FATES

There are sometimes big differences in state laws regarding marital property, so if you own property in different states, or if you've moved since you planned your estate, you should check to be sure your estate plan comports with the applicable state laws.

For example, what if you live in a separate-property state but own real estate in a community property state? Often, state laws will treat such real estate as community property for estate-planning purposes. Thus, if you live in Arkansas (a separate-property state) but own land in Texas, an Arkansas court probating your will would treat the Texas property just as Texas would—as community property. But not every state would extend the same courtesy.

Obviously, this separate-property/community property division can get pretty complicated—and it's only one example of how state laws are different. If you own property in more than one state, use a professional adviser who is conversant with the estate laws of all of them.

What if the statutory share is too little? The statutory protection for spouses is often inadequate, especially if one spouse thinks he or she deserves certain items of property, such as the family home. People getting married might benefit from executing a **contract to make a will,** which guarantees how the property will be bequeathed (see chapter 15), or a prenuptial agreement (see below). But beware of possible gift tax issues that may arise in such contracts.

PRENUPTIAL/POSTNUPTIAL AGREEMENTS

Another way to prevent a spouse from taking against the will is to execute an agreement in which the partners voluntarily give up

( ) TALKING TO A LAWYER

Q. *I understand the benefits of springing powers of attorney, but I understand, too, that there can be problems in determining when the powers should "spring." What are some solutions?*

A. We often prepare springing powers of attorney that specify that the incompetency be determined by two physicians, one of whom, if possible, should be the family's doctor.

—Answer by Edgar Farmer,
Husch & Eppenberger, St. Louis, Missouri

A. I tell my clients to use an instructions letter with the power of attorney, which I prepare. The letter says that the power of attorney is immediately effective, but the donor of the power asks that it not be used except in case of incapacity.

—Answer by Rik Huhtanen,
Attorney-at-Law, Eugene, Oregon

Q. *Is it true that the tax laws give spouses tax-saving opportunities that others don't have? What are some of the things they can do to avoid taxes?*

A. It is true that spouses have a privileged position under the tax law. Any gift that you make to your spouse, either during your life or at your death, is exempt from federal gift and estate taxes, regardless of the amount. Almost all states extend this same favorable treatment to gifts between husbands and wives. The only exception is if your spouse is not a U.S. citizen. Then the gift is taxable unless it meets special requirements to ensure that your spouse does not take the property offshore.

—Answer by Harold Pskowski,
BNA Tax Management, Washington, D.C.

the right to a statutory share of the other's estate and agree on how much—or how little—of the other's estate each will inherit. These agreements can be made before the marriage ceremony (**prenuptial**) or after it (**postnuptial**). They usually supersede statutory set-asides for spouses.

Actually, any couple in which one partner is substantially older or wealthier than the other should consider such an agreement. To assure fairness and enforceability, each partner should retain a different lawyer to represent him or her when drawing up these agreements, and each should make a full disclosure of his or her assets. In general, the courts look more critically at postnuptial agreements; prenuptial are preferable.

THE WORLD AT YOUR FINGERTIPS

- Another book in this series, *The American Bar Association Guide to Family Law* (Times Books, 1998) looks at the rights and responsibilities of marriage in greater detail.

- On the Web, both Nolo.com and FindLaw.com have good free information on a variety of family law topics.

- Typing the key words from this chapter into your favorite search engine will lead you to many sites on the Web.

YOU MUST REMEMBER THIS

- You have many options regarding how to provide for your spouse, depending on your age, the assets you have accumulated, and your particular situation.

- The law also takes into account troubled marriages, making it impossible for spouses to disinherit each other totally, unless they have executed a premarital agreement or a similar document.

CHAPTER 15

Splitting Up

Divorce and Remarriage

Chuck and Di started out as the perfect couple. Everybody around them knew that each of them brought into the marriage something the other lacked—her glamour, his powerful family connections. But after a few years and a few kids, it became clear that their marriage wasn't so perfect after all, and both began seeing other people on the side. They separated and began tentative talks about the divorce; their marriage was over in all but name. And Di was in love with someone else.

But when Di was killed in an accident along with her lover, her estate didn't go to her kids or family, or even to her sister or parents. It went to Chuck, because they had the usual arrangement in which the spouse receives everything in the dead partner's estate. And Chuck spent a good deal of that money on his mother (who had never liked Di and interfered in their marriage) and his new lover, Camie, whom Di had detested.

E ven "perfect" couples don't always make it till death does them part. It's hard to imagine in the glow of the wedding photos, the scent of the bouquets, and the showers of rice—but realistically, everyone should consider what happens if the perfect marriage doesn't last.

WHEN YOUR MARRIAGE STARTS TO HEAD SOUTH

Let's begin with a marriage that is experiencing difficulties but is not irretrievably broken. If you're in this unhappy state, you and your spouse might take some steps that could make a divorce less uncertain financially.

Execute a postnuptial agreement

Couples who didn't execute a premarital agreement might consider a postmarriage agreement that accomplishes some of the same objectives. Through such a document, you can set forth the division of property and estate in the event the marriage dissolves. Not a subject that you and your spouse will enjoy talking about, surely, but one that at least can remove the uncertainty of a divorce case—this way, you'll know going in how much each spouse will get. Courts scrutinize such agreements carefully; if each person is represented by an attorney, the agreement is more likely to be the product of negotiations between equals, and thus be enforceable in court.

Execute a contract to make a will

Such a contract prevents your spouse from changing arrangements in his or her will without your knowledge and consent. These can supersede any updated will, and can be written so that they expire if the marriage officially ends in divorce or annulment. In effect, such a contract guarantees that each person will stick to the jointly agreed-upon estate plan, instead of changing a will without the other's knowledge. The contract's obvious drawback is that it cannot be changed without the other person's permission no matter how much your circumstances change. It surrenders the flexibility that a will provides. These contracts are usually prepared in anticipation that some conflict will occur. Therefore, you surely should involve a lawyer in drawing one up. Be aware, too, that contracts to make wills can involve some serious gift tax issues. Ask your lawyer to look into what those potential problems might be for you.

WHEN YOUR MARRIAGE IS REALLY BROKEN

If you haven't taken one of the steps in the previous section, and it's clear that your marriage is heading for divorce, be sure to change your estate-planning documents. Do it now. Even before the divorce is final.

When the divorce is final, depending on the details of your state's law, divorce or annulment revokes either the entire will or those provisions that favor the former spouse. However, this doesn't necessarily apply if you're separated (officially or otherwise). A divorce can take years to become final. Changing your estate-planning documents will ensure that your current wishes will be respected if you should die before you're officially divorced.

Also remember to change the provisions that relate to your former spouse's family, especially the residuary clause. Even if state law revokes that part of your will benefiting your ex, it may do nothing about provisions benefiting your spouse's family. And what if you'd chosen your spouse's sister to be your executor?

Under recent revisions of the Uniform Probate Code, your state *may* also automatically revoke provisions of other estate documents, such as life insurance policies, in which the proceeds previously would have gone to the ex-spouse. But the odds are against this. Few states have adopted all the provisions of the UPC. It's best to change any such documents, including IRAs, living wills, and survivorships, or have your lawyer do it. If your spouse is the beneficiary on your employer's retirement plan, federal law prohibits you from removing him or her until the divorce is final. But be sure to make this change (if per-

▶ **SHARING A LIFE DOESN'T MEAN SHARING A WILL**

The high divorce rate is another good reason for both partners to have separate wills. If they have joint wills, *both* parties have to agree to modify such wills, which means that revisions can be caught up in the disagreements leading to a split-up, and your estate can become just one more battlefield in what's already a potentially nasty war.

▶ **DIVORCE AND TAXES**

The so-called **marital deduction** is one of the most important parts of estate tax planning, and when you divorce, you lose it. If your estate is worth over $1 million, you will certainly need to revise your tax planning after a divorce.

mitted by the divorce settlement) as soon as things have been finalized.

Trusts may need to be specifically amended, including replacing trustees if they were members of your ex-spouse's family.

Finally, if you're in a relationship that's breaking up and you have given each other powers of attorney, be sure to revoke those immediately. Obviously, it's hard to agree on anything at this stage, but perhaps through negotiation you and your spouse can convert any jointly held assets (bank accounts, living trusts, property, etc.) into separate holdings.

One thing to keep in mind: Patchwork families are a prime category for will contests, because children from different marriages may be more likely to disagree about the distribution of estate assets. People in this category should be especially careful that their wills, prenuptial/postnuptial agreements, or contracts to make a will are properly prepared.

REMARRIAGE

Sometimes divorces have a happy ending, and one or both spouses find happiness in a new marriage. But remarriage brings with it some estate-planning issues, especially when children are involved. If you're one member of a couple in which both spouses have children from a previous marriage, you might want to arrange things so your own money goes to your own children, and your spouse's money goes to his or her children. If those children are well-off and earning their own incomes, then you might consider leaving more to your surviving spouse, or to other family members, such as by setting up a trust for your grandchildren. Here is a brief discussion of some of the transfer techniques.

Qualified terminable interest property trusts (QTIP trusts)

Providing for children from different marriages may conflict with tax planning. The marital deduction allows spouses to leave their entire estates to each other without paying taxes. What if you and your spouse have children (especially grown children) from other marriages? You might naturally prefer that your biological children receive more of your estate than your spouse's children from a previous marriage. Your spouse might not agree with your wishes—and if you leave your entire estate to your spouse, he or she has the final decision on how to dispose of the property after you're gone.

That's why some "patchwork" families are using QTIPs. The **qualified terminable interest property trust** allows you to leave your property in trust for your spouse, but then it goes to whomever you wish after your spouse dies. You still get the marital deduction, your spouse gets to live off the income from the trust if sufficient (and, depending on how the trust is written, may be able to get at the principal as well), and your children get the property upon your spouse's death. The problem is that no one else can benefit from the assets in the trust until your spouse dies, which might not leave other family members enough money for their comfort until then. Insurance can ease the blow. If you have a large-enough estate, you can leave up to $1 million (tax-free under current law) to your children or put that amount into a credit shelter trust for their benefit on your death, and put the rest into the QTIP trust.

Mutual wills

Mutual wills provide another option in those cases in which children from different marriages (or anyone else that you want to inherit some of your property) are involved. Each spouse leaves all property to the survivor, who, after death, will leave specified property to the friends or relatives the other designates. A warning is in order here: The use of mutual wills might jeopardize the marital tax deduction and also involves issues of contract law that vary among states. Moreover, the second to die might be able to change the will after the death of the first spouse to die. (A contract to make a will, on the other hand, can't be changed.) Get professional advice before using either mutual wills or contracts to make a will.

Life estates

What if you want your surviving spouse to be able to live in the family home, but want to make sure that the house will ultimately pass to your children? In that case, a life estate is an option. A **life estate** ensures that the recipient only gets to use the property for as long as he or she lives; after the spouse's death, the property is then passed to a third party (or occasionally reverts to your estate). The property can't be sold or substantially modified by the life tenant. Your will can include a life estate provision, but check with a lawyer before trying such property conveyances; they can be quite complex. A better method is to leave it in trust for your spouse so long as he or she is able and desires to occupy it.

 THEY SOUND ALIKE, BUT . . .

Don't confuse **mutual wills** (two separate wills that refer to each other and are trying to accomplish the same purpose) with a **joint will,** which is one will that attempts, usually unsuccessfully, to cover two people.

Life insurance

Life insurance is another tool you can use to distribute assets among children from different marriages. You can set up an irrevocable trust for your children that will ultimately be funded from the proceeds of a life insurance policy. You pay the premiums, but the trust actually owns the policy. When you die, your children receive the benefits from the trust tax free, while your spouse gets the rest of your estate.

Trusts

The versatility of trusts makes them useful instruments for allocating assets among different families, because you can set up a separate trust for the children of different marriages, or even for each family member. Imagine the complexities of the Brady Bunch trooping down to their lawyer's office and trying to decide who gets what!

Spouses often want the surviving spouse to be happy, and expect that a new marriage might be in the cards. However, they are often concerned about the failure of a subsequent marriage by the surviving spouse. Through a trust, a spouse can make provisions to protect the surviving spouse and the estate from a failed subsequent marriage. This can ensure that assets will end up with the children or other chosen beneficiaries.

Prenuptial or postnuptial agreements

If you're an older person with grown children from another marriage, you should strongly consider asking your lawyer, as part of your estate plan, to prepare a prenuptial or postnuptial agreement that specifies that the separate property of each party should remain separate at death. Then your wills or will substitutes can leave your assets directly to your respective children on your deaths. They're already adults, and it's unlikely your spouse will survive you long enough to require large amounts of money from your estate to live on.

THE WORLD AT YOUR FINGERTIPS

The Internet is awash with divorce sites, and just about all book-stores include a whole section on the topic. Here are just a few resources.

- The website of *Divorce* magazine (www.divorcemagazine.com/) has many articles on the legal side of divorce.

- Another website dealing with divorce issues (www.divorceonline.com/) also contains many legal articles.

- A website sponsored by Cornell University (www.law.cornell.edu/topics/divorce.html) includes basic legal information about divorce as well as a state-by-state listing of laws.

YOU MUST REMEMBER THIS

- The bottom line is to revise your will and your trust when you feel the marriage is irretrievably broken.

- Remember, even if state law revokes provisions in favor of your spouse for you when the divorce is final, it probably doesn't help you at all in the months and years it takes to become legally divorced. Change your will or trust now.

- Many people remarry, creating patchwork families that can be ripe for conflict. A number of estate-planning devices can help you deal with potential problems.

CHAPTER 16

Beyond Ozzie and Harriet

Straight Talk and Otherwise

Al and Gertrude were very much in love. In fact, they'd spent three decades together as committed partners, sharing their home and their lives. They even raised two children. But when Gertrude died, her estate didn't pass to Al, who needed the money badly. Instead, it went to Gertrude's brother, Leo, and Al—whose full name was Alice—lost the house she and Gertrude shared.

So far, this book has dealt mostly with the "typical" estate-planning situations—those involving a married couple. But times are changing, and plenty of family arrangements don't fit into that old cookie-cutter pattern of a man, a woman, and 2.3 kids. Unfortunately, however, the law is almost always written with conventional families in mind.

Because the law often assumes that families are traditional, it has provisions such as those setting forth the spouse's elective share and the rules of intestacy. The first of these guarantees that your spouse will have the chance to claim a share of your estate, no matter what your will says. The second leaves your property to your family if you die without a will.

For other couples to do all that married couples can do in the eyes of the law, they must have a will or a trust and use contractual agreements that set out the rights and responsibilities of each partner. Read on to find out what you need to do.

UNMARRIED COUPLES

If you're part of an unmarried couple, you'll probably have many of the same estate-planning objectives as married couples. For example, each of you will probably want to provide immediate help for your partner if you die, possibly through life insurance. Depending on what assets you have, you may want a revocable trust with a pourover will, just as married couples do.

Whether you use a will or a trust, you'll have to figure out what will happen to your bank account, to your partner's bank account, to a joint bank account, and to other property should one of you die. It's especially important to make provision for property acquired while you and your partner have been living together. The real problems in cases like this are often expensive items of personal property: collectibles, art collections, furniture, and so on. If you don't include these items in your estate plan specifically, and there are relatives that the law presumes would take your estate under the laws of intestacy, a court fight could ensue, with the survivor battling the legally presumed heirs of the dead partner.

Here's a quick rundown of the most important documents that you'll need.

Wills

It's especially important for unmarried partners to have wills because state intestacy laws presume that your blood relatives will inherit your property after you die, when in fact you may want your property to go to your partner.

Trusts

Unmarried partners may decide to use revocable trusts. These trusts can protect them in the event of disability, avoid probate, and enable assets to go to chosen beneficiaries. Each partner might set up a separate living trust for his or her separate property, and the couple might set up a third one for shared property. Each individual trust can be used to make gifts for friends or relatives of each partner. The shared trust can leave property to the couple's mutual friends, as well as to the surviving partner.

You don't need a lot of money to have a living trust. They serve smaller estates just as well.

Cohabitation or domestic partnership agreements

Cohabitation agreements, which can cover a wide range of topics, are also worth considering. To deal with each partner's possible disability, for example, cohabitation agreements often contain mutual powers of attorney that enable partners to act on each other's behalf. However, as is the case whenever you assign anyone a power of attorney, you should carefully consider the consequences of giving anyone the legal power to act on your behalf.

Durable powers of attorney

A durable power of attorney (DPA), which is usually used for business transactions, enables the other person to spend your money, sign your name to binding documents, and so on. Many unmarried people might want their partners to have this kind of authority should they become disabled by age, injury, or disease, but not when they are in full possession of their faculties. If you don't want your partner to have all this power (and you may not if the relationship is tenuous), have your lawyer write the power of attorney so that it is springing; that is, so that it takes effect only when you have been certified incompetent by your physician. But make sure your state's law allows this.

And be warned that some attorneys don't like springing powers, reasoning that if you don't trust the person you appoint, you should not appoint him or her in the first place. Moreover, there are circumstances in which it might be hard to determine incompetence, or in which the incompetence is intermittent. There could even be situations in which the ill person is out of the country and hard to diagnose, or is simply missing.

One possible solution to these problems may be to appoint co-agents, on the theory that one provides a check on the other's exercise of discretion.

LIVING SINGLE

Married people aren't the only ones who need to plan their estates. If you're single and have minor children, you'll want to provide for their guardianship using one of the techniques described in chapter 13.

Whether or not you have children, you'll probably want to use a health-care power of attorney, a living will, or another device discussed in chapters 23 and 24 to plan for your possible incapacity or terminal illness. You may want to pass certain property to certain people—your antique dresser to the niece who so admires it, your Cajun accordion to a music-loving friend—which you can do with your will or a living trust.

And if you're wealthy, you'll want to use tax-avoidance techniques to give your property to relatives, friends, or charities instead of the government. In short, as you read this book—whether you're thoroughly single, utterly married, or somewhere in between—look for estate-planning techniques that seem appropriate to your circumstances.

Health-care powers of attorney

A health-care power of attorney allows your significant other to make medical decisions should you become incapacitated, but doesn't provide him or her control over your bank account and other nonmedical affairs. Or, as an alternative, you can execute a living will specifying treatments that you want or don't want, and not authorize someone to make health-care decisions for you.

Guardianships or conservatorships

A cohabitation agreement might also provide for mutual guardianships, so that if one partner becomes disabled, the other can take care of him or her. This is especially important if one partner's family doesn't accept the validity of his or her

(i) A TRUST MIGHT BE BETTER

Because of the difficulty of determining incompetence under a springing power of attorney, many lawyers prefer using a funded revocable trust as a method of planning for management of assets in the event of disability.

Of course, there may be a similar problem of determining when you (the trustee) have become incompetent and the successor or cotrustee should step in to replace you. But the **trust instrument** (document establishing the trust) may provide that you are deemed to have resigned only when there is certification of your disability, or it may authorize the cotrustee or successor trustee to act on his or her own certification.

---

lifestyle. Without an agreement, the courts can appoint a guardian should you become disabled. They will often lean to a family member over someone with no legal status.

Contract to make a will

You can change your will at any time. But each partner in a marriage is somewhat protected against sudden, capricious changes of mind by state laws that allow spouses to take against the will—that is, to receive a percentage of the deceased spouse's estate, regardless of what the will says. The law doesn't yet extend this sort of protection to unmarried partners.

Suppose you're putting your partner through medical school, and you stand to inherit a lot of her property. After making such a sacrifice, you don't want her to change her mind without your knowing it and rewrite her will, leaving her property to someone else.

To prevent this, you might, as part of your cohabitation agreement, execute a contract to make a will, which legally binds both of you to its terms. The contract can only be changed by attacking the contract in court, a much more difficult procedure than re-

(i) WHEN IT'S OVER

The law frequently revokes wills (and sometimes other documents) when a couple's marriage ends. It doesn't provide such a fail-safe mechanism for the wills of unmarried partners or their cohabitation agreements, contracts to make a will, and the like. You can write into a cohabitation agreement or a contract to make a will a provision that alters the will and other documents if the parties agree that the relationship is over. If you don't, you must remember to deal with these documents should the relationship dissolve.

In any event, you should certainly rewrite your estate plan when this happens, as you would when any other major life change occurs.

---

writing a will. Usually, these contracts contain a provision that dissolves them when the partners agree in writing that the relationship is over. These contracts might also provide that the wills of both parties be kept at the lawyer's office, and that neither can obtain access to them without the other being present. Obviously, these documents should be custom-tailored to the particular concerns and circumstances of each relationship—and they require a lawyer to do them right.

GAY COUPLES

Most of the information in the preceding section applies to gay and lesbian couples as well as to unmarried heterosexual partners. Since gay couples face legal barriers that heterosexuals don't, estate planning is even more critical for them.

When it comes to relationships, the law is basically written for people who are married. You may recall the Sharon Kowalski case, in which the courts gave custody of a nearly comatose young woman to her family, despite evidence that she would have preferred that important decisions be made by her lesbian partner. Had she been married, a court would probably have given custody to her husband.

You can't count on the law or a judge to be sympathetic to gay relationships. If you are gay and in a relationship with someone whom you want to include in your estate plan, you have to take extra steps to prevent family members (some of whom might not approve of homosexual relationships) from interfering with your wishes.

Much of what heterosexual partners take for granted—the ability to take out family life insurance policies, file joint tax returns, inherit pension benefits, or make medical decisions for each other in the event of disability—will not automatically apply to homosexual relationships. You have to take extra, affirmative steps to protect your rights and make certain you have an estate plan that meets your needs.

It's important to realize that the rules in this area are changing along with society. Vermont allows civil unions between partners of the same sex, and many communities have adopted domestic-partner registries that may be mostly symbolic, but may also carry some legal rights. Many employers, including some of America's largest companies, are permitting same-sex or other unmarried partners to qualify for health and other benefits, just as a spouse would. The dynamic and varied nature of the law and rules in this area make it even more imperative that gay and other people in relationships not recognized by the state as officially married consult a lawyer familiar with the rules of their jurisdiction to help them craft an estate plan that protects both partners.

Here is a brief look at some of the legal tools at your disposal.

Wills

It's especially important to write a will if you're involved in a same-sex relationship, because a will lets you leave your property to anyone or any organization you wish, despite the fact that the law does not recognize gay relationships. Most important, a will

lets you name an executor for your estate to supervise distribution of your assets. If, as is likely, you want your partner to
inherit a good share of your property, naming your partner or
someone sympathetic to the relationship as executor will help
ensure that your wishes are carried out.

Trusts

As noted in the prior section, each partner could execute a living
trust. This could be useful in the event of disability, is private,
and enables you to make gifts of property, like a will.

Beneficiary designations

As important as it is to write a will or set up a trust, remember
that that's not enough to ensure that all your property goes to
your partner. As discussed in chapter 3, many assets pass by
means other than a will. So if you want your partner to receive
the proceeds from a life insurance policy, an IRA, a bank
account, and so on, you need to name your partner as the beneficiary in each of those documents separately.

The advantage of using beneficiary designations and other
nonprobate arrangements (such as holding property in joint tenancy with your partner) is that the transfers take place automatically upon your death. No disgruntled relatives can hold up
your desires, as they can in a will contest.

Funeral instructions

Funeral instructions can be especially important to homosexual
couples. The law often gives the deceased person's blood relatives—not the same-sex partner—the right to determine what
will be said at the funeral. That also means they control what
will appear in a newspaper notice. Many surviving partners have
been disappointed to find that no mention has been made of the
relationship, or even the fact that the deceased was gay. To prevent this, write up a list of funeral instructions (see chapter 25)

naming your partner (if that's what you want) as the person responsible for carrying out those instructions.

You might mention the instructions in your will as well, although you should remember that sometimes a funeral is over before the will is read. Still, the mention of your wishes in a will and a signed statement of funeral instructions should go a long way toward convincing funeral directors of your partner's authority in the event of a dispute.

Powers of attorney

A durable power of attorney gives your partner, or anyone else you choose, the legal authority to handle your financial affairs, pay the bills, deposit and withdraw money from the bank, and so on if you become incompetent. A health-care durable power of attorney lets you decide who has the right to make medical decisions for you should you become incapacitated.

ESTATE PLANNING
FOR PEOPLE WITH AIDS

The devastating AIDS epidemic has raised all sorts of legal issues, including those relating to health-care maintenance. Proper estate planning gives people with AIDS (PWAs) a sense of control over their lives and deaths that can help ease the trauma of the disease.

A person with AIDS needs the following estate-planning documents:

- **A general power of attorney, which will give a trusted friend or relative the authority to make decisions should the person become incompetent or restricted to a hospital or home.**

- **A health-care power of attorney, which designates someone to make health-care decisions and tells everyone your wishes regarding medical treatment.**

- **A living will.**

▶ **FIND THE RIGHT LAWYER**

For all these arrangements between gay partners, especially cohabitation agreements, you should seek out a lawyer who's experienced in nonspousal domestic partnerships. Your local gay-rights organization may keep a listing of attorneys who specialize in such situations.

- **A will or trust that disposes of the rest of your property. This is especially important for gay men or women who want to make sure that people who are not family members are provided for.**

A will can also provide for a guardianship of any children, which can be important if a family member challenges your wishes for your children. For example, the mother of a person with AIDS might not want that person's surviving partner to bring up her grandchild. However, a guardianship that is specified in your will can't ensure that your wishes will be carried out, because it's not binding on a court. An **inter vivos guardianship** (a guardianship that is set up in your lifetime) may be better, but that means you may have to give up control of the children before your death. If you anticipate a challenge to a guardianship, it's a good idea to execute an affidavit expressing your desires and stating why other possible guardians are inappropriate. The complexity of such issues makes the help of a lawyer essential.

THE WORLD AT YOUR FINGERTIPS

- Many gay-rights groups offer publications and other information about the legal rights and needs of people who are in nontraditional relationships. A good place to start is the Lambda Legal Foundation (www.lambdalegal.org/).
- *Prenups for Lovers,* by Arlene G. Dubin (Villard Books, 2001), discusses the need for cohabitation agreements.
- Search on "cohabitation agreements" on the Internet to find many sources of information. A particularly useful site is the Equality in Marriage Institute (www.equalityinmarriage.org).

YOU MUST REMEMBER THIS

- Although society is slowly recognizing nontraditional partnerships, the law in most places is still written under the assumption that people in committed relationships will be legally married to a person of the opposite sex.
- If your partnership doesn't fit this traditional pattern, it's crucial to work with your lawyer to craft an estate plan that protects you and your partner in a way that you both prefer.

CHAPTER 17

Estate Planning
for Business Owners

The Law Gives You Lots of Options—
but You Have to Use Them Well

Hank's company was doing well, but Hank wasn't. When he went to the doctor and found out that he had only weeks to live, he didn't have time to think about what would happen to the propane business he'd built over thirty-five years. And like most entrepreneurs, he'd been too busy getting his business going and growing during that time to worry about what would happen to it after he was gone. And now with the press of medical and funeral arrangements, he'd never get the chance.

Hank's wife, Peggy, a teacher, knew nothing about the company and wasn't interested in taking it over, even if she'd been able to, while his son Bobby's interests tended more toward stand-up comedy than propane accessories. While they tried to sell the operation, the business languished. The accountant kept up with the bills, but no one was hustling new accounts. As a result, when the family finally did sell the business, it was worth hardly anything at all.

Unfortunately, approximately 70 percent of family-owned businesses fail to make a successful transition into the second generation. About 90 percent fail to be transferred successfully to a third generation of family members. These statistics reveal both the difficulty of transferring business property from one generation to the next and the lack of planning for successorship.

Small-business owners have a host of special needs. Who will take over the business after you die? Does the surviving spouse get control of the stock or do the children? Which ones run the company, and which merely share in the profits? How shall the value of the business be passed to the next generation?

The principal issues your estate plan should address are these: Do you want the business to continue after your death? If so, who will run the business after you die? Will your beneficiaries be capable of taking over the business—and will they even want to? Do you want it sold at your death? If so, what's the best way to transfer ownership to the new owners?

Before you meet with your lawyer to plan your estate (and the legal issues involved here are so touchy that a lawyer's expertise is essential), you should sit down with your beneficiaries and business partners to try to answer these and other critical questions, including how the business will be operated in the immediate aftermath of your death.

OPERATING THE BUSINESS
AFTER THE OWNER DIES

Customers, bankers, suppliers, competitors, and predators are all very interested in what will happen with the business now that the owner and president has died. What's worse, the death of the owner may bring on some serious crises. Loan documents, franchise agreements, and other legal contracts often contain termination or renegotiation clauses in the event of the death of the majority or sole business owner. Can there be any worse time for the business to renegotiate financing or defend its opportunity to continue a favorable franchise or distributorship relationship? And many relationships with key customers were dependent upon personal contact with the owner. Now that the owner is dead, all those accounts are up in the air.

If your business loses key customers or distributorships because of the uncertainty following your death, it will be difficult to sell the business for an optimal price. Some distributorship agreements require preapproved successors, in effect forcing you to plan for your succession. You should also plan ahead to make sure that customers feel comfortable dealing with

▶ ## WHAT IF YOU BECOME DISABLED?

Don't limit your estate planning to preparing for your death. Keep in mind the possibility that you might suffer significant physical or mental disability that could impair important decision making. Disability may even be worse than death, because you might not recognize the seriousness of your impairment. The law makes it extremely difficult for others to take away your freedom of choice and responsibility for making decisions. Great damage to the business can be done before you return to good health or before control is transferred through legal proceedings that result in conservatorship. Ask your attorney what steps you can take now to avoid harm to your business if you should become disabled.

at least one other person in the business—especially as you get older and the risk of your death or disability increases. When renewing contracts with franchisers and suppliers, ask for a modification of any clauses stating that the contract be terminated or renegotiated upon the death of the owner. Perhaps you could amend them to specify renegotiation three months after the death of the owner, to give your business a chance to get over the hump. There is no guarantee that franchisers and suppliers will agree to these changes, but you'll never know unless you try—and the time to try is *now.*

CONTROL

Any prospective buyer will want to see a business that's running smoothly. Make sure that the people named in your plan to succeed you are granted specific authority to make decisions concerning the business immediately after your death or disability. The issue of control should be addressed through a will, a living trust, or another appropriate legal document. Appoint one or more competent, experienced individuals or entities to make business decisions.

VALUE

If you're anticipating the sale of the business after your retirement or death, you may want to maximize business value to attract maximum interest from potential buyers. Let's say you've been operating the business to maximize compensation and minimize taxable income. That's fine, but annual earnings may suffer under such a plan. Even though the buyer may well adjust the profit potential in light of excessive compensation, you might want to bump the profits up if you anticipate selling the business.

In many cases, key managers and employees have an interest in purchasing the business. These potential buyers may ask the estate and surviving family members to finance the purchase

---

(i) BUSINESS AND PROBATE

Emily Dickinson wrote, "Because I could not stop for Death, / He kindly stopped for me." But you and your employees don't want your business to stop when you die. That's why avoiding probate might be important where a business is concerned, since even relatively short interruptions in transferring title to bank accounts and other assets through probate can be devastating to a business that must pay its bills on time. Probate laws vary greatly by state, but in some states the people who take over from you might find they have to get probate court approval for major business decisions unless you have made adequate arrangements to avoid this. In those states, you might do well to arrange for the business assets to pass outside your will, usually through a trust or a contractual agreement.

price. A sale to an employee stock ownership plan sounds fine on paper until family members realize that financial security for the surviving spouse and the children depends upon the future success of the business enterprise.

CONTINUE FAMILY OWNERSHIP OR SELL?

Your plan should provide a legacy for your children and future generations of family members after your death or disability. At the same time, it must adequately address the financial needs of a surviving spouse. It must also provide for the fair distribution of estate assets among children and other family members. Will one or more children receive ownership interests in the business to the exclusion of other children? How do you compare the value of an illiquid business interest with cash or marketable securities? Should one child receive a controlling interest in the business or, alternatively, should it be shared among several children? If one child receives the business, how will that affect that child's total share of the estate? Is that child's share of the remainder of the estate adjusted? What is the impact of these decisions on family relationships?

Only you and your family can answer these questions. As always, communication is the key—be sure you involve your family in these decisions so you know their concerns and they know your evolving thinking. If your beneficiaries (usually we're talking about a spouse and children) are interested in taking over the business and, in your judgment, possess the expertise to do so, it's relatively simple to transfer your interest directly to them. If stock is involved, you might want to leave voting stock to the children who will be involved in operating the business, and leave nonvoting stock to the others. Or you can leave the child who will be running the business enough cash (perhaps through life insurance proceeds) to enable him or her to buy out the rest of the estate, and thus avoid conflicts.

PAYING ESTATE TAXES

The owner's death may well trigger estate taxes, and these have to be factored into the family's decision to retain or sell the business. Chapters 20–22 discuss a number of ways of lessening the tax burden.

Gifts you make during your lifetime are another good way of avoiding or limiting taxes on larger estates. The law allows you to give up to $11,000 worth of assets *per recipient* to as many people as you wish each year (married donors giving a gift as a couple are allowed $22,000 per recipient per year in gift tax exclusions).

For example, Tom, a business owner, could give $22,000 a year (if his spouse participated in the gifts) to each of his three children and seven grandchildren (possibly in trust to the young grandkids). That's as much as $220,000 *a year* that could escape taxes.

ⓘ DEATH, TAXES, AND BUSINESS

The estate tax gives tax breaks to estates owning interests in small businesses. Consult a lawyer or a Certified Financial Planner, a chartered financial consultant, or other professional with experience in this difficult area of law and finance.

The key law was passed by Congress in 1997. It provided special benefits for family business owners by reducing estate taxes. A tax exclusion available to them but not available to nonfamily business owners can save thousands in estate tax liabilities. Also, in certain situations, estate tax obligations can be deferred for a period of up to fifteen years with installment payments payable at an interest rate of 2 percent. As might be expected, there are a number of complex rules and requirements that must be met in order to qualify for these special tax provisions. This should be part of your estate-planning process; but remember to get advice from a qualified attorney.

Tom could also transfer some of the value and control of the business during his lifetime (e.g., give shares of stock). It may be possible to do so at a discounted value for minority interests. If the beneficiaries were too young to handle the money wisely, Tom could give the money or stock via a trust.

IF THE BUSINESS IS SOLD

Sometimes your beneficiaries will want no part of the business after you're gone. Things get more complicated if you decide to pass management or ownership to people who are not beneficiaries of your will or trust. If so, and if your business is a partnership, you'll usually want the other partners to remain in operational control of the company. The most common device used for transferring ownership of a business on the death of a partner is the **buy-sell agreement,** in which all the remaining partners agree to purchase the interest of any partner who dies. This allows the business to continue running smoothly with the same people in charge, minus one.

Buy-sell agreements typically provide that at the owner's death, his or her interest in the business will be acquired by the remaining partners or shareholders, leaving the dead partner's relatives with the proceeds of the sale. Life insurance is usually the vehicle used to finance these arrangements, which lets the business itself avoid a drain on its cash. The partners buy life insurance on each other's lives, and the proceeds go to the surviving spouses, children, or whomever, in return for the deceased partner's share of the business.

There are two principal ways to structure such agreements. An **entity purchase** allows the business entity itself to take out a policy on the life of each owner and use the proceeds to purchase the share of a deceased owner. In a **cross-purchase,** the co-owners each take out insurance on each other and buy a share of the dead partner's interest. While an entity purchase is simpler, a cross-purchase may provide a substantial tax advantage. (If life insurance on the business owners is held by the

▶ **SPELL IT OUT**

A lengthy and more comprehensive buy-sell agreement will probably answer more questions than a relatively short and simple agreement. Don't be satisfied with a cheap Band-Aid document that leaves many questions unanswered.

business, the proceeds will increase the value of the business in the estate, possibly triggering taxes.) Ask your lawyer which kind of agreement is best for your business.

Review old buy-sell agreements and make certain that their terms and provisions continue to provide a reasonable and clear result in each circumstance. As a rule of thumb, you should review your buy-sell agreements at least every other year, or immediately if there are significant changes in the law or in the business itself.

Buy-sell agreements can be tailored to fit your needs. Consider the following issues in the context of your particular facts and circumstances and with the advice of a competent attorney.

Force-out provisions

This type of provision, unlike the others described below, operates while all the principals are still alive. It allows individuals, during the administration of the business, to buy out other owners. One helpful provision is to allow any owner to offer to buy out another owner's share. The owner making the offer has to come up with the dollar figure. The owner receiving the offer either accepts the offer or buys out the owner proposing the offer at the price proposed. This provision guarantees that a fair price is offered, provided that all parties have equal capacity to consummate a purchase.

Right-of-first-refusal provisions

A buy-sell agreement may simply provide that the company or other business owners have a right of first refusal to purchase an owner's interest in the event of death. Typical provisions include a specified price at which the business interest may be purchased and whether payment must be in cash or, alternatively, paid over a term of years at a specified rate of interest. Collateral and security provisions should be included if installment payments are allowed. The price or price formula, of course, is very important to purchasers and sellers of the business interest. In addition to death, buy-sell provisions and a right of first refusal can be granted under other circumstances such as disability,

▶ FOR THE NEXT GENERATION

Are you hoping that your family business will continue into the next generation, providing employment and prosperity for your children and grandchildren? Avoid dissension in the family with a carefully drafted buy-sell agreement.

One variation of the standard right-of-first-refusal agreement is to provide an opportunity for the ownership interest to remain in the same branch of the family before it is offered to either the company or other branches of the family. This can be extremely important when the balance of control between or among different branches of the family is an issue.

Buy-sell agreements for family-owned businesses should address lifetime gifts of stock, sales, and other transfers. Lifetime transfers to family members, as well as bequests at death, are typically permitted under the terms of the buy-sell agreement without invoking a right of first refusal that would otherwise apply. Gifts and other transfers to trusts may also be addressed in the buy-sell agreement. Nevertheless, these specific provisions must be clearly spelled out in the agreement in order to avoid later controversy.

attempted sale to another party, retirement, bankruptcy, or termination of employment.

Mandatory-purchase provisions

Mandatory-purchase provisions in a buy-sell agreement provide for certainty that the business interests will be sold by the heirs of a deceased business owner and purchased by the company or other business owners. This element of certainty is very important for all parties. As long as all of the detailed terms and provisions

---

( ) TALKING TO A LAWYER

Q. *Is it advantageous, from a tax standpoint, to make gifts during my lifetime or just through my will at death? How can I gift portions of my business?*

A. If you are interested in saving taxes, it definitely makes sense to make gifts of portions of your business now, rather than waiting until your death. First, you can make tax-free gifts of up to $11,000 per recipient each year, with this limit doubling to $22,000 if your spouse agrees to join in the gift. There is no such exemption for gifts made at death through your will. Second, by making lifetime gifts of partial interests in the business, you can reduce the value of the gift for tax purposes by claiming **minority** and **lack of marketability discounts.** Don't try to claim such discounts on your own; the services of an estate-planning attorney and a qualified appraiser will be needed to protect you from any challenge by the IRS. Making the gifts should not be difficult if the business is held as a corporation. The gift can be made by transferring shares in the corporation from your name to the names of your intended recipients.

—Answer by Harold Pskowski,
BNA Tax Management, Washington, D.C.

---

are clearly spelled out in the agreement, action is automatic. There is no room for concern, conflict, anxiety, and further negotiation at a difficult time. Again, mandatory-purchase provisions may also be provided for circumstances and events other than death—such as retirement or incapacity of the owner—as desired by the parties to the agreement.

Price and value provisions

The specified price or value contained in a buy-sell agreement may be dramatically less than the value of the business interest if the entire business were sold under favorable circumstances. Be sure you carefully consider the price and value provisions in your buy-sell agreement, and update the language from time to time to reflect changes in facts and circumstances. Does the agreement distinguish between minority ownership interests and majority ownership interests? If an appraisal is required, is the appraiser given guidelines concerning discounts for minority interest or lack of marketability? Who gets to pick the appraiser? Does the agreement provide that the company picks one appraiser and your family picks a second appraiser?

Note that family buy-sell agreements may not be binding in terms of how the IRS sets the business's value in the estate. In other words, the estate might have to pay taxes on the full value of the business, even though the estate receives much-smaller amounts per the buy-sell agreement.

Funding provisions

When you die, how will the company and remaining business owners finance the purchase of your interest in the business? Life insurance is an obvious solution. Another method is seller financing through installment payments over a number of years. Does the company (or do the other business owners) have the capacity to borrow additional funds to finance the obligatory purchase? Will your family members be protected from financial risks associ-

(i) WHAT HAPPENS TO THE BUSINESS'S DEBTS?

Most estate planning assumes that you have assets to distribute when you die. But what if you're in debt, and there's only red ink in your estate account?

First, don't fear that you family will "inherit" your debts through your will. Only if they co-signed on notes or otherwise made some contractual agreement to assume liability for debts can any of your beneficiaries be stuck with any of your debts.

If you should will someone an asset that's burdened by debt (a business, for example), the recipient may **disclaim** the gift, and therefore not receive it—or the debt attached to it.

ated with installment payments? Is their risk increased if remaining business owners dramatically increase the indebtedness of the company for expansion and acquisitions?

THE WORLD AT YOUR FINGERTIPS

- Several chapters in *The American Bar Association Legal Guide for Small Business,* a companion book in this series, include discussions of retirement and estate planning for business owners. The book also describes the various forms of ownership—sole proprietorship, partnership, corporation, limited liability company—that will affect tax liabilities and how the business is conveyed at death.

- The *Inc.* magazine website—www.inc.com/home/—includes many articles on estate planning. Just search the site using that term.

- You may wish to consult books on this topic, including Karen Ann Rolick's *Family Limited Partnership: How to Protect Your*

Family Business and Provide for Your Children (Sphinx Books, 2003), Denis Clifford and Cora Jordan's *Plan Your Estate,* 6th edition (Nolo Press, 2002), and George C. Shattuck's *Estate Planning for Small Business Owners* (Prentice-Hall, 1993).

YOU MUST REMEMBER THIS

- If you own a business, your estate plan will involve issues quite different from those covered by typical wills and other devices.

- Not only do you have to plan ahead for what will happen at your death, you've also got to make plans for the business in case your health deteriorates and you become disabled.

- Regardless of whether the business interest will be sold or continued, the estate-planning process is not for your personal benefit. It's for the benefit of family members and employees who are left behind. Good tax planning can benefit them to the tune of hundreds of thousands of dollars.

- With the help of your lawyer, you can create documents— a will, a trust, a business successorship plan—that will ease the transition for your partners and employees, provide for your family, and reduce the chances that people will fight over the assets.

CHAPTER 18

Providing Income for Your Final Years

Estate Planning and Retirement

Americans are living longer than ever, and that often means that we face unprecedented decisions about how our assets and estates should be arranged to provide us with maximum comfort and care in the often-difficult years near the end of life. Traditional estate planning focused on our family and survivors, but today's estate plans must take into account the opportunities and potential problems of extended life.

America is getting older. Because of the baby boom and other demographic changes, the number of Americans over age sixty-five will double over the next forty years. Many of them will have serious health problems, and 14 million will have Alzheimer's disease. By 2050, the elderly will number 67 million, 22 percent of the population.

These changes have spawned a whole new legal specialty called "elder law." This book isn't the place to discuss the whole panoply of elder law issues—another book in this series, *The American Bar Association Legal Guide for Older Americans,* covers that subject in detail—but estate planning makes up a significant component of legal concerns for those of retirement age, and we briefly discuss some important considerations here.

In today's complex environment, decisions you make while writing your will or trust can affect your pension or retirement plan, your insurance purchases, and even where you choose to live in retirement. Most lawyers recommend that you try to coordinate retirement planning, planning for educational expenses of children and grandchildren, and estate planning.

⚠ PLAN NOW

Older Americans have mostly small estates, often poorly organized. Too many widowed spouses are left impoverished, often by poor estate planning. Clearly, many older Americans need to combine estate planning with retirement planning, money management, and other devices that will help them maximize what they have.

RETIREMENT PLANS

The changes to the federal tax laws make this a good time to look into the attractive possibilities for financing your own retirement. The annual limits for contributions to both traditional and Roth IRAs have gone from $2,000 to $3,000 ($3,500 if you're over fifty).

Moreover, there is now greater portability to move your retirement money among a variety of plans. This is a boon to employees who have worked for a variety of employers and have different kinds of plans. Now they can roll them over more easily to one employer's plan or an IRA.

For self-employed workers and others using such retirement vehicles as SEP IRAs and SIMPLE IRAs, restrictions have been lessened and the plans generally permit you to save more and have greater flexibility to roll the accounts over.

Another recent phenomenon has been the rise in reliance upon 401(k) plans from private employers. These plans offer you more control and flexibility than traditional defined-benefit pensions. While it's not possible to protect your retirement plans entirely from economic downturns, having a wide variety of retirement vehicles—IRAs, 401(k)s, and traditional pensions— might lessen risk by increasing the diversity of your holdings.

What does all this mean for your estate plan? These retirement accounts will have their own beneficiary designations that will determine how quickly they must be paid out after your death, as well as the tax consequences. You need to take these factors into account when crafting your plan with your lawyer.

BEYOND IRAS: RETIREMENT PLANNING FOR BUSINESS OWNERS

Business owners have additional ways to save money for retirement. Effective in 2002, the law governing **tax-qualified retirement plans** allows an employer to contribute 25 percent of the first $200,000 of each employee's salary up to $40,000. As a business owner, you wear two hats. As the employer, you receive a current tax deduction for all contributions to the plan. As an employee, you are not currently taxed on the contribution when it is made on your behalf, but only when you actually receive the money—upon your retirement, death, disability, or termination. Generally, when you receive the proceeds at the later date you have less income, and therefore you pay a lesser tax rate on these distributions. Moreover, you can continue to defer this tax until age seventy and a half by not taking distributions. Even if you're the sole employee, or if you have self-employed income from moonlighting while you have a job, or if your business is unincorporated, you can set up a **Keogh plan.**

These plans require the services of a lawyer to set up. And they have distinct advantages.

• A retirement plan could give you a competitive advantage over other businesses to attract and keep qualified employees.

• The funds contributed to the plan by you as the business owner are held in a separate trust account. These assets may not be touched by the business, and they are exempt from creditors of both your business and your employees. The funds in this tax-sheltered trust are to be invested by you as a trustee of the retirement plan.

• All of the income generated by investment of these funds is also tax deferred. The trust will not pay any tax when the income is earned, and the tax will be deferred until the investment income is actually distributed to you.

Such retirement plans can be expensive to administer, and you will be required to file a complicated annual form with the Internal Revenue Service and notify the Department of Labor. However, the expenses of administration and filing annual reports will be paid from the plan assets and not out of your business.

There are several types of plans available that do not require approval. These include **volume submitter plans, prototype plans,** and **SIMPLE** plans. Check with your lawyer to see if any of these would work for you.

CONTROLLING YOUR EXPENSES IN RETIREMENT

Up to this point, this chapter has focused on increasing your income in retirement. Obviously, reducing your expenses is the other part of the equation. Planning *now* can help you put a lid on costs. We focus here on housing expenses, since they are likely to be your largest single outlay. And, if you own your own home, certain programs can give you income while you continue to live there.

RETIREMENT HOUSING AND ESTATE PLANNING

Whether you decide to stay in your own home or move to a shared-housing facility, the decision will affect your estate planning. Here are some of the options available, and their possible effect on your estate plan.

Congregate housing

More and more older Americans are living in various forms of group housing, including so-called retirement villages and others that offer semi-independent living options, including some or all of the following: housecleaning, meals, recreational facilities, nursing care, social programs, and so on. These communities may include hospice-care facilities for people with terminal illnesses. Residents of such congregate-housing facilities typically sign a binding lifetime contract to pay a lump sum for admission and a monthly fee for operating expenses, and possibly fees for other services. Some require residents to sign over their Medicare benefits. In return, the residents receive a license to occupy a unit and get the services and health care they require while they live there, but they do not acquire an ownership interest in the property; when a resident dies, another one takes over his or her apartment.

How does the advent of such living arrangements affect estate planning? Some of these facilities require residents to disclose all their assets and set rates based on the ability to pay. This requires residents to consider whether and to what extent to distribute assets before death in order to make sure that more of their assets reach their families rather than the living facility. Some middle-income people now put a sizable portion of their estates into entry fees for retirement communities. This means that choosing to live in one of these facilities may make less of your accumulated wealth available to your heirs, since you'll be committed to spending it on significant retirement living expenses.

All of which means that it's a good idea to have your estate-planning attorney review any such agreement before signing it, and adjust your estate plan accordingly. Your lawyer can also help you be sure of the terms of the complex agreement, including such issues as

- whether the fees can be increased or services can be changed;

- the right to eviction or transfer of the right to live there;

- right of appeal of decisions;

- responsibility for injury; and

- what happens if your health conditions change, or if you move out or die prematurely.

Supportive housing

These forms of congregate housing vary from single-family homes that offer board and care to large institutional complexes, but all provide some combination of housing and supportive services, such as help with the activities of daily living (eating, dressing, transferring from one position to another [e.g., sitting to standing], using a toilet, and bathing), help with the instrumental activities of daily living (preparing meals, taking medications, walking outside, using the telephone, managing money, shopping, and housekeeping), or protective oversight (monitoring, memory assistance, or other supervision, particularly for someone with cognitive impairment).

There are many types of supportive housing, of which three are the most common.

• **Board and care homes** (also called residential-care facilities, domiciliary-care facilities, homes for the aged, and community-based residential facilities) which are group residences that provide room, board, twenty-four-hour protective oversight, and some assistance.

• **Assisted-living facilities,** which offer the same services but also provide more social and recreational opportunities, a more individualized approach to care, and more emphasis on encouraging independence, autonomy, privacy, and the right to make choices in a homelike setting.

• **Continuing-care retirement communities (CCRCs),** which offer a broader (and more expensive) level of care. The living options in such communities range from independent-living apartments to assisted living (either in an apartment or in an assisted-living wing or unit) to skilled nursing-home care.

STAYING IN YOUR OWN HOME

If you don't want or need to move into shared housing, your own home can provide you with retirement income. Several options are available.

RETIREMENT HOUSING BY ANY OTHER NAME . . .

Housing programs for older persons have many names. But for the consumer, the questions are the same. What will your living conditions be, how much will it cost, what will you get for your money, will the program meet your health and safety needs, who will be making the decisions, and how much independence will you have?

Reverse mortgages

A **reverse mortgage** lets you borrow against the equity in your home, without having to repay the loan right away. You can get the money in a lump sum, in monthly cash payments for life, or by drawing on a line of credit—or you can choose a combination of these options. These loans can be costly, but the relative costs lessen over time, and you will never owe more than the value of your home. When you sell your home or move, or at the end of the term, you must repay the money you have borrowed plus the accrued interest and fees. The house can be sold to repay the loan, or the funds collected some other way. The lender is not permitted to collect more than the appraised value of the house at the time the loan is repaid, even if the loan exceeds that amount.

Income from a reverse mortgage will not affect your eligibility for Social Security, Medicare or other retirement benefits, or pensions that are not based on need. But unless you plan carefully, reverse-mortgage payments may affect your eligibility for supplemental security income (SSI), Medicaid, food stamps, and some state benefit programs.

Reverse mortgages will affect your estate plan. They allow you to spend your home equity while you are alive. You may end up using all of your equity, and not have any left to pass down to your heirs. Some plans allow you to set aside some of the equity so that it is not used. Reverse mortgages may have an effect on estate taxes, so you should consult your lawyer and tax adviser. So far, the IRS has not taxed reverse-mortgage payments, on the grounds that the money is a loan.

Reverse mortgages are very complex and involve difficult financial, legal, and personal decisions. Talk to a lawyer who is familiar with the issues, and discuss your aims and concerns with your family.

Sale-leasebacks

In a sale-leaseback, you sell your home but retain the right to live there while paying rent. The buyer usually makes a substantial down payment to you. You act as a lender by giving the buyer a mortgage. You get the buyer's mortgage payments; the buyer gets your rent payments. You remain in the home, and you can use the down payment and the mortgage payments as income. The buyer can deduct the mortgage interest payment from his or her income and will also benefit if the value of the property increases. Sale-leasebacks used to be good investments, especially within families for adult children, but today there are fewer tax advantages, so finding an investor may be difficult.

Life estates

In a life estate, or **sale of a remainder interest** plan, you sell your home but retain the right to live there during your lifetime. The buyer pays you a lump sum, or monthly payments, or both. You are usually responsible for taxes and repairs while you live in the house. At your death, full ownership passes automatically to the buyer. This arrangement is used most commonly within families, as part of an estate plan. As with a sale-leaseback, it might be difficult to find an outside investor.

Regular home equity loans

A home equity loan is very different from a reverse mortgage and can be risky for an older person on a fixed income. As with a reverse mortgage, you borrow against the equity you have built up in your home. But in a home equity loan, you must make regular monthly payments, or you may lose your home. Home equity loans do have tax advantages: You can borrow up to $100,000 on the equity in your first and second homes, use the money for any purpose, and deduct the interest you pay on the loan. You can deduct the interest on a home equity loan that exceeds $100,000 if you use the money for home improvements.

THE WORLD AT YOUR FINGERTIPS

You can get more information on some or all of the topics in this chapter from the following sources.

Retirement plans

- IRS Publication 560, "Retirement Plans for Small Businesses," is a good guide to the tax implications of various plans.

- The Employee Benefits Security Administration Home Page (www.dol.gov/ebsa) provides a good starting point as you research your options.

- The American Savings Education Council Home Page (www.asec.org) is useful in helping you figure out how much to save to get to that retirement nest egg you want.

- The American Association of Retired Persons (AARP) has an excellent section on personal finance at its website (www.aarp.org/).

Housing

- The American Association of Retired Persons (AARP) has an excellent section on this topic as well on its website (www.aarp.org/).

- Fannie Mae has an informative website (www.fanniemae.com/).

- The National Center for Home Equity Conversion website (www.reverse.org) also has useful information.

- Visit the National Reverse Mortgage Lenders Association website (www.reversemortgage.org) for more details on reverse mortgages.

- Information regarding not-for-profit retirement communities is available from the American Association of Homes and Services for the Aging and its affiliated organization, the Continuing Care Accreditation Commission, at the CCAC website (www.ccaconline.org; click on "List of Accredited Communities").

- The Federal Housing Administration (FHA) can be contacted at 888-466-3478; also check out its website (www.hud.gov/offices/hsg).

YOU MUST REMEMBER THIS

- Issues of housing, retirement planning, and long-term care can dramatically affect your estate plan.

- Be sure to consider these issues and bring information and questions about these arrangements to your meetings with your lawyer.

CHAPTER 19

Controlling Costs in Your Final Years

Paying for Long-Term Care

Securing a steady retirement income and a place to live, as we discussed in the last chapter, are critical parts of estate planning for your final years. But nothing concerns most older Americans more than paying for the medical needs that often accompany getting older. This chapter discusses some of the major options available. Because the eligibility rules of government programs such as Medicare can be confusing, you might want to include these issues in your estate-planning discussion.

MEDICARE

All Americans become eligible for Medicare at age sixty-five, and you are eligible for Medicare even if you continue to work beyond sixty-five. **Medicare Part A** helps pay for medically necessary hospital care, skilled nursing care, home health care, and hospice care. Knowing that Medicare will meet these expenses makes estate planning and financial planning much easier for most of us.

However, Medicare does *not* pay for most long-term or nursing-home care. Most nursing-home residents do not require the level of nursing services considered "skilled" by Medicare. **Skilled nursing care,** under Medicare, means nursing or rehabilitation services that you need for a limited period of time as an inpatient following a hospitalization of at least three days; it is emphatically not long-term care. Not every nursing home participates in Medicare or is a skilled nursing facility.

Medicare does cover part-time or intermittent skilled nursing; services such as physical, occupational, and speech therapy; med-

MEDICARE AND MEDICAID

It's easy to get them mixed up, but the key difference is that Medicare is open to all individuals sixty-five and older, while Medicaid is open to those whose income is under a certain amount. Medicare won't pay for most long-term care. Medicaid will, but you have to use up most of your assets before you qualify for Medicaid reimbursement. We discuss both briefly in this chapter.

Find out more at www.medicare.gov/ and www.hcfa.gov/medicaid/medicaid.htm; or call 1-800-Medicare or, for Medicaid, your state or local area agency on aging.

ical social services; part-time care provided by a home health aide; and medical equipment for use in the home. It does not cover medications for patients living at home, nor does it cover general household services or services that are primarily custodial.

Hospice care is an important Medicare benefit. A **hospice** provides pain relief, symptom management, and supportive services to people with terminal illnesses. Hospice services may include physician or visiting-nurse services, psychological support, inpatient care when needed, home health-aide services, drugs (including outpatient drugs for pain relief), and respite care. Respite care is short-term inpatient care (less than five consecutive days) in a facility that provides some relief to family caregivers. Respite care is available only on a nonroutine basis.

MEDICAID

Medicaid should not be confused with Medicare. **Medicaid** is a medical assistance program for older or disabled low-income people. The program also covers certain younger people receiving welfare payments.

Unlike Medicare, which offers the same benefits to all enrollees regardless of income, Medicaid is managed by individual states, and the benefits and eligibility rules vary from state to state. Medicaid also benefits many middle-income individuals faced with the devastating costs of nursing-home care.

However, the rules for eligibility and coverage are complex, and the operation of the program is often bureaucratic and frustrating. All states require that adults without dependent children be at least sixty-five, or blind, or disabled, *and* that they meet income and asset tests. Medicaid also imposes a resource test. This means that you will only be eligible for Medicaid if your assets are below a certain amount. In most states, the resource eligibility limits are $2,000 for an individual and $3,000 for married couples, although these amounts may vary. However, not all resources are counted under the resource test. For example, your home is not covered, nor are most household goods and personal effects, your wedding ring, and your car (at least up to a certain value).

MEDICAID ESTATE PLANNING

If you're unable to pay for long-term care, Medicaid planning can help you meet the Medicaid financial eligibility requirements and slow the depletion of your estate or preserve some of it for your spouse or dependents. Medicaid planning uses legally permitted options under Medicaid to preserve assets and try to ensure your survivor some financial security. Some of them include:

• *Transfers of assets.* Transfers of property for less than full consideration (i.e., giving property away in whole or in part), except for transfers between spouses, can result in a period of ineligibility for Medicaid benefits. When you apply for Medicaid, you must disclose any transfer made within the last thirty-six months (sixty months for certain transfers involving trusts). Such transfers trigger a period of ineligibility that varies from location to location. And if you knowingly dispose of assets to qualify for Medicaid, *and* doing so results in a period of ineligibility for Medicaid, you could face criminal penalties.

One rule of thumb when transferring property for less than full consideration, for purposes of Medicaid planning, is to retain enough assets to be able to pay for nursing-home care for the duration of the penalty period. However, this is only a generalization. Every situation is different.

• *Use of trusts.* Irrevocable trusts are another planning tool to help manage the cost of long-term care. Trusts that can be revoked by the creator of the trust are considered countable assets by Medicaid and do have an impact on Medicaid eligibility. However, irrevocable trusts, if created at least sixty months prior to applying for Medicaid (the "look-back" period for trusts) may help establish Medicaid eligibility while slowing down the depletion of your estate, if the discretion of the trustee to distribute income and principal is sharply limited.

Federal law also recognizes certain trusts created for the benefit of persons with disabilities under age sixty-five. Generally, parents who are planning for the long-term care of an adult, disabled child may want to consider this type of trust.

An irrevocable **Miller trust** might help if you live in a state that has an income cap on eligibility and your income exceeds that amount but isn't enough to pay privately for a nursing-home bed. (Some states impose an income cap as well as a resource test to determine eligibility.) Federal law requires those states to exempt (for purposes of Medicaid eligibility) trusts created for a person's benefit if the trust is composed only of pension, Social Security, or other income, and if at the person's death the state is reimbursed by the trust for all Medicaid assistance paid on his or her behalf. Miller trusts work by paying out a monthly income just under the Medicaid cap and retaining the rest of the income. The result is that most of your income, supplemented by Medicaid, goes toward payment of the nursing home, while the rest remains in the trust until your death, when what's left goes to Medicaid.

▶ **GET HELP WITH MEDICAID
   AND NURSING HOMES**

Special income and asset rules apply to persons who need help in paying nursing-home bills. These rules are so complicated that you should talk with someone with expertise in Medicaid—such as a legal-aid lawyer, a benefits counselor at a senior center or health insurance counseling office, a paralegal, a social worker, or a private attorney experienced in handling Medicaid issues.

Other limited trust arrangements may be helpful in some cases, but they all require careful assessment and advice and a good dose of caution—and remember that Congress periodically changes the rules, so your strategy may have to change. Be sure to check with your lawyer. Unfortunately, most of the self-help advice regarding Medicaid planning oversimplifies a very complicated problem. Even with competent advice tailored to your needs, Medicaid planning is not easy.

MEDIGAP INSURANCE

Medicare provides basic health-care coverage but leaves many gaps. Most older persons need to purchase a supplemental (or Medigap) insurance policy to cover some of the costs not covered by Medicare.

If Medicaid already covers you, you do not need a Medigap policy. Medicaid covers the gaps in Medicare and more. If you are not eligible for Medicaid, but your income is low, you may be eligible for help in paying Medicare costs under the **Qualified Medicare Beneficiary** (**QMB**) program. For example, under QMB the government will pay your **Medicare Part B** premiums (insurance for doctor and outpatient services) and provide supplemental coverage equivalent to a Medigap policy if your income and assets fall below a qualification amount (one that is more generous than Medicaid's).

EMPLOYER-PROVIDED RETIREMENT BENEFITS

Your employee benefit package may include a promise to provide health benefits to you after you retire. These benefits are particularly important to you if you retire before age sixty-five because you are not eligible for Medicare until then. Even if you are over sixty-five, an employer-provided benefit might save you a lot on Medigap policies. Unfortunately, many employers have reduced or even eliminated health benefits after employees have retired. (Health benefits do not vest as pension benefits do, and unless the employer made an unqualified contract with employees, you may lose your benefits.)

PRIVATE LONG-TERM CARE INSURANCE

Given the spiraling cost of health care in the last few months or years of life, more and more people are considering whether to buy long-term care insurance. Most employer-provided medical insurance policies, as well as Medicare, fail to cover such long-term care services. Medicaid does, but it requires you to use up most of your savings and other assets to become eligible.

Such plans can cover services for people with disabilities or chronic illnesses, including

- help with daily personal care, such as dressing and bathing;
- assisted-living services, such as providing meals, monitoring your health, and providing some medical care; and even
- full-scale nursing home care.

Long-term care insurance can help you avoid the huge expenses of a nursing home or attendant care if you want to stay in your own home as long as possible. Depending on the policy,

(i) DO I NEED LONG-TERM CARE INSURANCE?

The AARP recommends that you consider a number of factors before deciding whether to obtain long-term care insurance.

- The cost of premiums for someone in your particular circumstances; for example, the older you are, the more expensive the premiums generally will be, and this can affect your standard of living. Costs can range into the thousands of dollars per year for people over age seventy.

- What if your circumstances change?

- Can you qualify for Medicaid (thus eliminating the need for an expensive long-term care policy)?

- What does the policy cover, and what options are available for you? For example, does it cover care in your home, or only in a nursing home, or a wide range of care (including care in assisted-living centers or other congregate housing)?

- What's the benefit period?

- Is it guaranteed renewable?

- Does it require hospitalization prior to receiving benefits? (This is a bad idea because you may need long-term care without ever being admitted to a hospital.)

- Does it cover preexisting conditions?

- What happens if you can't afford the premiums?

long-term care coverage can protect your assets, reduce your dependence on your loved ones, and ensure that you receive whatever long-term care you need.

But such policies can be expensive, ranging from nearly $1,000 per year if you buy before you're fifty to more than $6,000 per year at age seventy-five. Such plans therefore have

> **TIPS FROM THE AARP**

The AARP has a number of suggestions that will help you be an informed buyer of long-term care insurance.

- Read the entire policy—not just an outline—before meeting with a salesperson.

- If you're under age seventy-five, buy 5 percent compounded inflation protection to prevent cost-of-living and expenses increases from eroding your coverage.

- Never buy from a telephone solicitor or a door-to-door salesperson, and never pay cash.

- Know the difference between tax-qualified policies and those that are not and what works best for you.

- Check the stability of the company from which you're considering buying the policy. Rating agencies such as Standard & Poor's, Moody's, and others can provide ratings for the companies. You might also be able to get consumer information about companies through the Better Business Bureau (www.bbb.org).

an impact on your estate plan, because the more you spend on such policies, the less you will make available for your heirs—but if you wind up needing long-term care, you may well save your estate money by reducing the often very high expenses of nursing homes.

THE WORLD AT YOUR FINGERTIPS

There are a number of resources for information on long-term health care and related issues.

- The Centers for Medicare and Medicaid Services can be contacted by telephone at 800-MEDICARE or 410-786-3000; also visit the website (www.cms.gov).

- Medicare maintains a "consumer" website at www.medicare. gov that provides a wealth of information about Medicare, Medigap, Medicaid, and nursing homes.

- Information is also available on educated health-care choices at the AARP website (www.aarp.org/hcchoices/).

- A "Guide to Long-Term Care Insurance" is available on the Health Insurance Association of America website at www.hiaa.org/consumer.

- The National Citizens Coalition for Nursing Home Reform offers publications, fact sheets, advocacy tips, and information on federal laws and regulations focused on nursing homes at its website (www.nccnhr.org/).

- The American Association of Homes and Services for the Aging (AAHSA) also has a website (www.aahsa.org/) that can provide useful information.

YOU MUST REMEMBER THIS

- Even though much of the information in this chapter isn't directly related to estate planning, you need to know what options are available to you in order to make some important estate-planning decisions.

PART SIX

Death and Taxes

Strategies for Holding On to
as Much as You Can

CHAPTER 20

Death and Taxes

Trying to Make Sense Out of Rules That Keep Changing

Ever since Caesar Augustus imposed an estate levy to pay for imperial Roman exploits, death and taxes have walked hand in bony hand. No one really likes paying taxes, but let's not forget that they pay for most of the things we value in modern society: defending the nation; providing health care, jobs, and housing; paving the roads; and so on.

Estate taxes also provide a way of redistributing wealth. Franklin Roosevelt used the estate and gift tax system to do so during the Great Depression. Taxes enabled the transfer of money from those with wealth to those who were unfortunate during those hard times.

This chapter discusses some of the issues everyone, no matter how wealthy, ought to know about death and taxes.

Tax planning is the core of much estate law. It is most important to people with substantial assets, or with assets that will become substantial over time. "Substantial" currently means about $1.2 to $1.5 million. Many people are surprised when they discover that they are in fact "rich" in the eyes of the tax law though they are not "rich" in everyday life.

Even if you aren't rich and don't expect to become so, this chapter provides a very brief discussion of the basic tax-reduction methods for estates. Then, if your estate grows or the law changes, you'll know what to discuss with your lawyer.

Passing an estate at death may also have income tax consequences, and this chapter discusses these briefly. The 2001 tax law presents some new income tax issues at death that we briefly discuss in this chapter and the two that follow. Most estate plans currently do not address these new income tax issues.

THE FEDERAL ESTATE TAX

Your estate isn't liable for federal estate taxation unless it exceeds the **available exemption amount.** This magic number is the value of assets that each person may pass on to beneficiaries without paying federal estate tax. The **Economic Growth and Tax Relief Reconciliation Act of 2001 (EGTRRA)** provides for a gradual increase in the exemption. It is now $1 million; it will go up to $1.5 million in the year 2004, and then to $2 million in 2006.

In addition, you can pass your entire estate, without any estate taxes, to your spouse. (This is called the **unlimited marital deduction.**) If you simply leave your estate to your spouse and don't create an appropriate trust to take advantage of your exemption, your spouse's estate will pay taxes on any amount over the exemption amount when he or she dies. We explain how these trusts work in Chapter 21.

To the extent your estate exceeds the available exemption, the federal estate tax rates start at 41 percent. The assets subject to tax at death may include

- **cash,**
- **stocks and bonds,**
- **the family home,**
- **the family farm,**
- **life insurance,**
- **tangible personal property (such things as clothing, jewelry, furniture, art, china, power tools, computers, etc.),**
- **benefits under employee benefit plans, and**
- **retirement assets such as IRAs, as well as other items that do not produce lifetime income.**

In short, everything that you own is added up to determine your estate. This is why you may be richer than you think for tax purposes.

WHAT ARE YOU WORTH?

How does the government decide what your estate is worth? That depends on the kind of property involved.

• *Real, tangible, and intangible property.* In determining the value of your estate for tax purposes, the IRS currently looks at the fair market value of property you own at your death. In most cases, values at the time of death are used. The tax law also enables the person handling your estate to look at the value of assets six months from the date of death. If this value is lower, the estate can elect to use the alternate valuation date and thus potentially save estate taxes. Volatility in the stock markets makes it wise to look at the alternate valuation date, because taxes could be saved as a result.

• *Insurance policies.* For tax valuation purposes, the government uses the face value of insurance policies in your name, including most group policies from work or professional organizations, but only the cash value of a policy you own on someone else's life if you die before it has matured.

• *Jointly owned property.* The IRS generally divides all joint tenancy property held by spouses equally between them, no matter who paid for it. For example, your estate will be credited with half the value of the family home, even if your wife paid for the whole thing. (In the community property states, married couples hold most property jointly by law.)

Many lawyers counsel against holding property in joint tenancy with your spouse if your assets approach the federal tax limit. For example, Archie and Edith own their house in joint tenancy, and Archie dies. Since for federal estate tax purposes only one-half of the jointly owned property would be included in Archie's estate, only one-half of the property would receive a **stepped-up cost basis** (the cost basis at the time of the owner's death). If the value of the house had greatly appreciated, it would be advantageous to have all of its cost basis be its value at the time of Archie's death, rather than its lower cost many years before. Having half of it with the lower cost basis could give rise to potential capital gains taxes if Edith later decides to sell the house. (Against that detriment, however, you'll have to weigh the benefit of the greater protection against creditors that many states give spousal joint property.)

If you own property in joint tenancy with right of survivorship with someone who is not your spouse, the total value of the property can be included in your estate for estate tax purposes. For example, if you co-own a $90,000 house with your sister, all $90,000 may be considered part of your estate when you die, unless your executor can demonstrate that your sister paid a portion of the purchase price and any improvements. The full value of the property also would be included in her estate for estate tax purposes. For these reasons and many other nontax reasons, lawyers urge clients to avoid owning too much property in joint tenancy—or, if they do own property jointly, to keep detailed records of whose money went toward the purchase and improvement of the property.

If you, or your revocable living trust, co-own property as a **tenant in common,** in contrast, your estate is only liable for tax on the percentage of ownership you had in the property. If you owned 25 percent of a $100,000 house, for example, the government would add $25,000 to the value of your estate.

PAYING THE FEDERAL ESTATE TAX

Any estate whose gross assets exceed the available exemption amount must file an estate tax return, even if deductions and other tax-avoidance methods mean the estate ultimately owes no tax. Federal estate taxes are due nine months from the date of death and must be paid in cash.

If the estate does owe a tax, and nothing in the will or trust specifies which assets will be used to pay it, state law will usually charge the taxes to the beneficiaries on a proportional basis. In other words, the more a beneficiary inherits from an estate, the more tax the beneficiary will have to pay out of the assets he or she inherits. Or state law may mandate taking taxes from the residuary estate first.

▶ **HAVE READY MONEY TO
PAY THE TAXES**

The federal and state governments, as recipients of the tax payments, are given priority over beneficiaries of an estate. It is important for you to consider the liquidity of your estate when designing an estate plan. If you intend to leave certain property, such as a vacation home, to loved ones, your intent would not be met if the property had to be sold to cover tax liabilities.

Some people, however, specify in their wills and trusts that certain funds be used specifically to pay taxes. Often taxes and debts are paid first, and then the estate or trust is divided among the beneficiaries in accordance with the instructions of the will or trust.

THE FEDERAL INCOME TAX

No asset received from a deceased individual is subject to income taxes on receipt. Once received, however, all income generated by that asset is subject to income tax on the tax return of the beneficiary. So your daughter who inherited your MTV stock wouldn't pay tax on the gift itself, but she would pay tax on any income

⚠ **INSURANCE NOT TAX FREE**

Many people believe that life insurance is tax free. Not exactly. The recipient does not pay *income* tax on receipt of the death benefits. However, the value of the insurance is included in the estate of the deceased individual and will incur a tax liability if the estate is larger than the exemption amount. Good planning can lessen the blow.

earned by the stock, such as dividends. The beneficiaries may also owe income taxes on income received by the estate that was eventually paid to them (this is called **distributive net income**).

KEEPING CURRENT

Tax laws frequently change. In fact, in 2001, Congress made the biggest change in estate tax law in decades, especially benefiting the wealthiest taxpayers. Under the new federal tax law (the Economic Growth and Tax Relief Reconciliation Act of 2001), the estate tax only applies to taxable estates of $1 million or more, and the maximum rate of taxation dropped to 50 percent in 2002. The estate tax floor will rise in increments (to $1.5 million in 2004 and $2 million in 2006), and the maximum estate tax rate will drop in increments to 45 percent before the tax is repealed for a year in 2010.

Almost all observers expect Congress to amend this law before 2011. Unless Congress acts, however, the tax law will revert in 2011 to the pre-2001 version. The **Taxpayer Relief Act of 1997** mandated gradual increases in the original exemption from $600,000 in 1997 to $1 million in 2006. Thus, the exemption amount will revert to $1 million in 2011 unless the law changes. Also, the maximum estate tax rate will go back to 55 percent, along with all of the other provisions of the "old" law.

The new law contains some other important changes. While the gift tax exemption is increased to $1 million, it will not increase beyond this. After 2003, there will no longer be a **unified estate and gift tax exemption.** The concept of **step-up in basis** will dramatically change under the new law in 2010. These currently little-known provisions will have dramatic income tax consequences for the unwary.

All of these provisions are complicated, and you'll have to discuss any tax implications for your particular estate with your lawyer. Unfortunately, most people do not review their estate plans regularly. Regular reviews are now imperative in light of the 2001 act. You must check your estate-planning documents to ensure that they still effectively reduce or eliminate your poten-

---

⚠️ SOMEBODY'S GOT TO PAY

It is important to remember that your beneficiaries can be subject to paying taxes on their bequests if the estate is unable to do so. The taxing authorities have priority over your beneficiaries. The taxing authorities will be looking for someone, or something, to pay estate and/or inheritance taxes, depending on the circumstances.

---

tial estate tax liability. If your will or living trust specifies a dollar amount for the available exemption, it will have to be revised. You must also review other specific aspects of your plan to ensure that it is still effective and reflects your needs and wishes.

STATE TAXES ON ESTATES AND INHERITANCES

The federal estate tax rules apply to everyone in the United States. Most states have only a **pick-up tax,** which is equal to the maximum credit the Internal Revenue Code allows to the taxpayer for state inheritance taxes. The state gets a percentage of the federal estate tax, but it comes out of money that the taxpayer owed anyway, and it does not increase the taxpayer's tax burden. To put it another way, it does not change the amount owed, just to whom it is paid.

However, some states charge an additional estate tax similar to the national one, and some impose an inheritance tax. (**Inheritance taxes** are taxes on the receipt of assets and are charged to beneficiaries. **Estate taxes** are taxes on the transfer of wealth at death and are charged to a person's estate.)

Some states also impose a separate gift tax, on top of the federal gift tax. (**Gift taxes** are imposed upon the transfer of wealth during life above a certain amount.)

Taxes and the rate of taxation on intangible personal property depend on the state of **domicile** (residence). Taxes and the

⚠ CAPITAL GAINS TAXES

Death itself produces a large amount of extraordinary expenditures for taxes, expenses of administering the estate, and frequently the forced early payment of outstanding debts. To obtain the cash for such payments, sales of assets are frequently made, and if the sale is for more than the date-of-death value, it may trigger a capital gains tax at the time of sale. The asset selected for sale is critical, as the tax may be deferred or accelerated depending on present or future anticipated tax brackets.

rate of taxation on real estate and tangible personal property are governed by the state in which the property is located.

Unless your state has an inheritance tax, your beneficiaries won't pay such taxes when they receive money from your estate. (They might not pay even if your state does have an inheritance tax if your will or trust provides for payment of the tax.) But they will have to pay income tax on any income that the bequest earns.

Estate planning must increasingly take these state taxes into account. Don't ignore them just because your state doesn't currently impose any death-related taxes. Federal law earmarks a portion of the federal estate taxes for states (the pick-up tax). Under the new federal estate tax law, states will lose from $5 billion to $9 billion in tax revenues each year as the federal tax is eliminated. With the federal tax bite lessened, states stand to get less—and they may make up the difference by taxing the estates of their residents directly. Many states have already enacted legislation designed to address this new revenue shortfall.

TAXES ON EMPLOYEE BENEFITS

Payments under company-deferred compensation and pension plans produce a bewildering array of possible choices (lump sum, installments, etc.) with differing income and estate tax results. Social Security payments to your dependents are not subject to federal estate tax.

Proceeds from pensions and benefit plans generally pass directly to whomever is named as a beneficiary in those plans. Regardless of whether pension and benefit plans pass directly to a beneficiary named in the plan, or are instead payable to the deceased's estate, they are all part of the gross estate for estate tax purposes. You need to ask your lawyer or accountant about the possible tax consequences of your particular plan.

TAXES ON INSURANCE BENEFITS

The proceeds of an insurance policy paid to a named beneficiary are exempt from all federal income taxes, and almost all state income taxes except to the extent that they include interest.

The death benefits of a life insurance policy are included in the estate of the decedent at his or her death if the decedent owned the policy at the time of death. There are ways that life insurance can be made free from federal estate and state death taxes while enabling the owner effectively to control the disposition of the insurance at his or her death. (See chapter 22.)

FEDERAL ESTATE TAX EXEMPTIONS ARE GROWING (FOR A WHILE, AT LEAST)

YEAR	EXEMPTION
2002/3	$1 million
2004/5	$1.5 million
2006/7/8	$2 million
2009	$3.5 million
2010	Unlimited
2011	$1 million

Note: These figures reflect the terms of the law as passed in 2001; Congress could change these numbers. The gift tax exemption was increased to $1 million in 2002 and does not increase beyond this amount.

( ) TALKING TO A LAWYER

Q. *Can you explain briefly the options for selecting the beneficiary of my IRA? Naturally, I want to save as much in taxes as I can.*

A. If you are interested in saving taxes, you want to stretch out the required payments from your IRA over as long a period as possible. Since the earnings in the IRA are not taxed until distributed, your tax savings will grow if you can minimize the distributions. If you are married, the easiest way to do this is to name your spouse as beneficiary. If he or she is alive at your death, your spouse can roll over your IRA into a new IRA in his or her name and name your children as the beneficiaries. This will start a new payout period based on your spouse's age, with a third payout period beginning after your children "inherit" the IRA on your spouse's death. Depending upon the ages of the parties involved, this type of planning can stretch out the payment period for as much as thirty or forty years after your death.

If you are single, it is to your advantage to name a beneficiary who is younger than yourself. This will allow the beneficiary to further stretch out the payments when he or she "inherits" the IRA on your death.

—Answer by Harold Pskowski,
BNA Tax Management, Washington, D.C.

Q. *I'm confused about the tax consequences of my 401(k) plan. How is it taxed when income is withdrawn? Is it taxed at death? Do my beneficiaries pay income tax on it?*

A. You are on the right track in assuming that your 401(k) plan will be taxed under each of these circumstances—these plans are subject to both income tax and estate tax. Any money that you take out of the plan will be subject to tax on your income tax return. Then, at your death, the value of the investments remaining in the plan will be subject to estate tax if your estate exceeds the current $1 million exemption ($1.5 million in 2004). After your death, your beneficiaries will be subject to income tax on any distributions they take from the plan. Fortunately, they will get a partial offsetting deduction for any estate tax that was paid on the plan investments.

—Answer by Harold Pskowski,
BNA Tax Management, Washington, D.C.

Q. *I'm the owner of a business. I understand that my estate would have to pay taxes on the value of the business if I don't do anything—but what can I do to lighten the tax load?*

A. Congress is sympathetic to the plight of business owners and has created several breaks in the tax code for you. One of these allows your estate to pay the estate tax on the business over a period as long as fifteen years, while paying only a 2 percent interest rate on the deferred tax. Another allows your executor to reduce the value of the business by as much as $300,000 for estate tax purposes. Both of these tax breaks have complex requirements, and you should not assume that you will automatically qualify.

But you are not limited to these targeted tax-reduction methods. There are a number of other tested estate-planning techniques—such as annual gifting and placing your business in a family partnership—that can have the effect of reducing the value of the business in your estate. The successful implementation of these techniques will require the services of an experienced estate-planning attorney.

—Answer by Harold Pskowski,
BNA Tax Management, Washington, D.C.

THE WORLD AT YOUR FINGERTIPS

- The IRS is a good source of information about estate tax; access www.irs.gov or get publications from a local office.

- Many estate-planning law firms maintain useful sites with information about taxes and avoidance strategies. One such firm is Lena Barnett and Associates; contact them at www.lenabarnett.com/articles/list.nhtml.

- There are many books for laypeople on the subject of estate taxes. See, in particular, *Protect Your Estate: Definitive Strategies for Estate and Wealth Planning from the Leading Experts,* by Robert Esperti and Renno L. Peterson (McGraw-Hill, 1999), and *J.K. Lasser's New Rules for Estate Planning and Tax,* by Harold Apolinsky and Stuart Welch III (John Wiley & Sons, 2001)

YOU MUST REMEMBER THIS

- The federal estate tax is scheduled to be reduced in the next few years and then eliminated in 2010, but unless Congress acts it will be back in 2011.

- The new tax act presents new income tax issues at death. All plans, especially those of married individuals, must address these new issues.

- State death taxes exist in some states, and other states may impose such taxes in the future. Check with your lawyer about the situation in your state.

CHAPTER 21

Tax Planning 101

Trusts

Now that you know the variety of taxes to which your estate may be subject after you die, you can see why tax planning can be so important. If your estate is likely to exceed the federal exemption threshold, good estate planning can sharply reduce the amount of money that goes to the government instead of to your beneficiaries. The next chapter looks at gifting and ways of sheltering life insurance proceeds from taxation. This one deals with trusts. Read on to find out more.

Of course, no book, not even this one, can show you how to prepare an estate plan that adequately accounts for all the individual needs and peculiarities of your situation—only an estate lawyer can do that. But if your estate approaches the exemption amount set by federal law ($1 million in 2003, $1.5 million in 2004 and 2005) you can help your lawyer work with you to prepare a plan that works for your needs.

MAKING MAXIMUM USE OF THE SPOUSAL EXEMPTION

The best provision of federal estate tax law from the taxpayer's perspective is the **unified credit,** which gives each person a $1 million total exemption from estate taxation ($1.5 million in 2004 and 2005). But what do you do if your wealth exceeds that amount?

One of the most basic tax-planning devices is the **unlimited marital deduction.** This allows one spouse to pass his or her entire estate, regardless of size, to the other, and not pay federal estate taxes. No matter how large the estate, no taxes are due when it is passed to the spouse.

ⓘ DO YOU NEED TO PLAN FOR ESTATE TAXES?

The floor for federal estate taxes is $1 million in 2003, and $1.5 million in 2004 and 2005. If you perform an asset inventory as suggested in Appendix A, you'll have a better idea of the value of your estate and whether you need to see your lawyer for tax planning.

If you only cared about leaving your property to your spouse, that would end your tax worries. Most people, however, want to leave property to their families at the death of the second spouse—and this is where tax planning pays off.

To take full advantage of the unified credit and the unlimited marital deduction, taxpayers with assets above the exemption amount would probably be best advised to use a trust. This is especially important for married taxpayers. Trusts are one of the main ways to minimize taxes upon death.

Using the marital deduction properly, usually in conjunction with a tax-saving bypass trust (as explained below), you should be able to transfer at least double the exemption amount free of estate taxes to your children or other beneficiaries no matter which spouse dies first or who accumulated the wealth.

BYPASS TRUSTS

One of the most common of these is the **credit shelter trust,** also called the **exemption trust** or **bypass trust.** It's called a bypass trust because the entire unified credit (exemption amount) bypasses the surviving spouse's taxable estate, and goes directly to a trust that ultimately benefits the children, the grandchildren, or other beneficiaries when the second spouse dies. The surviving spouse can be an income beneficiary of this trust, too, so it can provide support during his or her life.

Here's how it works. Assume that in 2005, Johnny dies and is survived by his wife, Louise, and several children. The adjusted gross estate (his estate after deducting funeral expenses, expenses of administration, and claims) totals $3 million. Johnny's will (or trust) either creates a marital trust (see the next section) or provides for a direct distribution of $1.5 million for his wife; the remaining $1.5 million goes into a bypass trust. If the will creates a marital trust, the income from the trusts can be payable to her for as long as she lives. On her death, her estate and the trusts will pass to the children free of federal estate taxes as long as her estate has not grown beyond this exemption amount.

When Johnny dies, his estate will not owe estate taxes. The $1.5 million marital trust or direct distribution to Louise is not taxed because of the unlimited marital deduction. The distribution to the bypass trust uses his $1.5 million exemption, so there is no federal estate tax at Johnny's death.

During her lifetime, Louise will be able to maintain her lifestyle, since she can benefit from all of the assets in Johnny's estate. Proper planning can enable people to reduce their tax liability without adversely affecting their lifestyles or those of their loved ones.

At Louise's death, the property in the bypass trust will pass to the children. Again, this trust is free of estate tax. The key question is the size of Louise's estate upon death. The distribution from Johnny's estate was added to Louise's taxable estate. If, at her death, her estate is now larger than the available exemption, she may owe taxes, but far less than if she had inherited all

---

(i) WHAT IF A BYPASS TRUST WON'T BE ENOUGH?

For estates beyond the double exemption amount, there are other tools that estate planners use to limit taxes, such as removing the value of life insurance from the estates and gifting. Both of these are discussed in the next chapter.

of Johnny's estate outright. If her estate is not larger than the available exemption amount, no federal estate taxes will be due as the result of her death.

MARITAL TRUSTS

We mentioned marital trusts in the previous section. They are used to enable the decedent spouse to take full advantage of the unlimited marital deduction while controlling the disposition of the property during the life and after the death of the surviving spouse. The advantage of using such a trust, as opposed to a direct gift in the will, is that the trustee can make distributions from the trust over a period of time (for example, he or she can make annual distributions to the surviving spouse); all the money does not have to pass at one time, with no guidance as to how the money is used.

There are two commonly used marital trusts.

Power of appointment trust

A **power of appointment trust** is structured so that one spouse gives a trustee property to be held for the benefit of the other spouse, providing the other spouse with the use of the principal and all the income. At the death of the first spouse to die, the surviving spouse receives a general power of appointment that permits him or her to determine where the property should go after his or her death—to the children, a charity, or other beneficiaries. Like all trusts, it avoids probate. It will generally qualify

⚠ CITIZENSHIP RESTRICTIONS

Special rules apply to qualify for the marital trust if the spouse is not a U.S. citizen. Check with your lawyer.

for the marital deduction and thus escape taxation at the first spouse's death. The only potential problem (for some people) with a power of appointment trust is that it gives the surviving spouse total discretion over what happens to your money after the death of the first spouse to die.

Qualified terminable interest property trusts (QTIP trusts)

People who are afraid of giving up so much control to their spouses often turn to the second principal marital trust. A **qualified terminable interest property (QTIP) trust** is a marital

---

ⓘ REFUSING BEQUESTS

Don't laugh—to reduce taxes or for other reasons, sometimes your beneficiaries may not want their bequests. For example, if your son already has plenty of money to live on, he might disclaim his inheritance from you so it will go directly to his children (or to a trust that benefits them). This avoids taxing the money twice (once when he inherits it, once when his children do), and could save a huge amount of money. Or perhaps he might disclaim property that you left him that's subject to liens and mortgages greater than its market value.

Most states permit someone to **disclaim** (i.e., renounce or refuse) an inheritance or benefit. The Internal Revenue Code describes how a beneficiary may disclaim an interest in an estate for estate tax purposes. State law also defines how to disclaim for purposes of state death taxes; usually the two standards are the same.

Once you disclaim a gift, the law generally acts as if you died before the testator insofar as the gift is concerned. Should the will or trust provide that if you die before the decedent your share will go to your children, the children will take it if you disclaim the gift. You should see a lawyer if you intend to disclaim any gift.

---

trust that doesn't grant the spouse a general power of appointment. It's especially favored by people who want to make sure their children aren't slighted if their surviving spouse remarries or has her own children or other beneficiaries whom she prefers.

OTHER TRUSTS

There are many other tax-saving trusts, among them **generation-skipping trusts** (sometimes known as **wealth trusts** or **dynasty trusts**). Trusts generally benefit your children, but you can keep saving taxes and provide for your descendants for several generations after your death by using a generation-skipping trust. Such a trust is quite versatile, allowing your family to use the money for college costs, medical expenses, large purchases such as homes, and general support. And it avoids or limits estate taxes on the estates of your children. You'll probably want to include your children as discretionary beneficiaries, as well as more remote generations.

In a generation-skipping trust, instead of distributing all the money in the trust to beneficiaries upon your death, you can use your federal exemption to leave the available amount to future generations. (In 2003, for this purpose, the exemption amount is indexed for inflation and totals $1.1 million.) This way, you can keep at least some of your assets out of the control of children who might squander it or lose it in a divorce. If you put more

HANDY IN SEVERAL WAYS

Not only can irrevocable trusts be used to reduce taxes on an estate, they can also help pay taxes that are incurred. For example, the cash assets in the irrevocable trust can be used to buy assets from the estate, providing the estate with cash to pay taxes.

than the tax-exempt amount in a generation-skipping trust, it may be subject to taxation, either immediately (if no person in your child's generation is a beneficiary) or at a later time, but it can grow tax-free beyond the exemption amount through investments and interest.

As with all tax-saving trusts, be sure to consult a lawyer, because there is a generation-skipping tax that may apply.

Life insurance trusts are also commonly used as a way of assuring that taxes don't have to be paid on the benefits of the policy. (For more details, see chapter 22.)

INCOME TAX PLANNING

Although the federal estate tax is the main concern of estate tax planning, you can't afford to ignore the possible consequences of the federal income tax as well. It is likely that income tax planning during the estate-planning process will become as important, if not more important, as estate tax planning for most people under the new tax law and under new laws that are likely in the future.

An estate and a trust each constitute a separate taxpayer for income tax purposes (there are exceptions for living trusts—see chapter 11), and this offers a broad range of tax-planning options. For example, the timing of estate expense payments and distributions have critical tax implications. Moreover, there are income tax options for Series E and H savings bonds, the filing of a joint return with the surviving spouse, and the deduction of medical expenses, and highly sophisticated techniques for timing distributions to beneficiaries.

GOOD ADVICE CAN MAKE
A BIG DIFFERENCE

The expenses of estate administration may be used as either an income tax deduction on taxes owed by the estate or an estate tax

(i) **SUBJECT TO TAX**

Although the standard bequests in a will pass to the beneficiaries free of income tax, some income is still subject to income tax when received by the estate or its beneficiaries, including:

- Wages, bonuses, and fringe benefits
- Deferred compensation
- Stock options
- Qualified retirement plans
- Some IRAs (other than Roth IRAs)
- Medical savings accounts
- Insurance renewal commissions
- Professional fees
- Interest earned before death
- Dividends declared before death
- Crop shares
- Royalties
- Proceeds of a sale entered into before death
- Alimony arrearages
- Income received through distributions from an estate (distributive net income)

deduction (but not both). In the last year of the estate, such expenses can even be handled so as to be deductible directly or indirectly from the tax returns of the individual beneficiaries.

This means that your survivors may have to make some tough calls about how and when to take certain deductions or make certain tax payments after you die. It's a good idea to plan ahead and obtain competent financial and legal advice.

( ) TALKING TO A LAWYER

GENERATION-SKIPPING BASICS

Q. *The whole generation-skipping thing confuses me. Can you give me a quick picture of what it is and why it might be advantageous from a tax standpoint?*

A. The advantage of a generation-skipping trust is that it can benefit several generations of your descendants while being subject to the gift or estate tax only once. If you create the trust in your will, it will be subject to the estate tax, while a trust created during your life would be subject to the gift tax. But the trust will never be subject to either the estate or gift tax again, only income tax on the earnings of the trust.

Compare this to an outright gift or bequest to your children. This gift will be subject to the same initial gift or estate tax as the trust, and it also will be subject to the gift or estate tax a second time when your children eventually hand the property down to their children. A tax will be imposed on each generation, and within a few generations the property will be taxed to nothing.

There are two things you should note before considering a generation-skipping trust. There is currently an effective cap of $1.1 million ($2.2 million for married couples) on these trusts, since any funding in excess of that amount means that distributions from the trust to grandchildren and younger generations will be subject to a special generation-skipping tax. (Those amounts will go up in 2004, 2006, and 2009.) Also, these trusts are appropriate only for wealthier families whose children already have enough investments to live on. Your children will have only limited access to the trust investments and should be willing to give up control of the property in exchange for the future tax savings.

—Answer by Harold Pskowski,
BNA Tax Management, Washington, D.C.

Tax savings are possible, but no adviser can help if the family member in charge (whether an executor, a surviving spouse, a trustee, etc.) lacks the powers and discretion to make the proper tax choices. Most states give the necessary authority by statute, unless the person making the will provides otherwise.

If you don't specify otherwise in your will, many states have a law that apportions the tax to each person who receives anything from your estate.

◖◗ TALKING TO A LAWYER

Q. I'm told that I should look at my tax-saving trusts in light of the new federal law. How hard are trusts to change? What if they are irrevocable?

A. While you are alive, trusts can be changed by amendment (for smaller changes) and by restatement (for larger changes). Given the new volatility of the tax laws, it is important that all plans be drafted with flexibility in mind. If your will contains tax-saving trusts that come to life at death, these trusts can be changed by codicil or by executing a new will that replaces the current one.

It is important that you review your plan on a regular basis. Many people are now reviewing their plans each year. They are not only looking at the tax laws, but also at changes in personal circumstances such as deaths, births, marriages, and changes in assets.

Trusts established in your will or living trust can easily be changed during your lifetime. It is even possible to change irrevocable trusts. Sometimes it does take a court order; other times, depending on the terms of the trust, it may be possible to modify the trust. For example, some irrevocable trusts give the trustee powers to change the technical portions of the trust in response to changes in the tax law.

—Answer by Lena Barnett,
Attorney-at-Law, Silver Spring, Maryland

THE WORLD AT YOUR FINGERTIPS

- Trust company and bank websites often have good information about charitable trusts, generation-skipping trusts, and other trusts. See, for example, www.nmtrust. com/index.html, the site of Northwestern Mutual Trust Company, and www.lasallebank.com/index.html, the site of LaSalle Bank.

- The site of Cornell University Law School's Legal Information Institute, www.law.cornell.edu/topics/estate_gift_tax.html, has good information and many links on gift and estate tax laws.

- The website of the National Association of Financial and Estate Planning has much useful information; access www.nafep.com/.

YOU MUST REMEMBER THIS

- If you are married and your estate is valued at over the $2 million mark ($3 million in 2004, $4 million in 2006), trusts are the way to save as many taxes as possible.

- By using the marital exemption and the unified credit, you can help shelter much of your money from taxation, but the laws and accounting in this realm are so complicated that you should certainly rely on the advice of a good tax lawyer.

CHAPTER 22

Tax Planning 102

The Benefits of Living Gifts
and Life Insurance

Malcolm and Genevieve were pretty well off, but not so well off that they could easily afford to send their children to the expensive private colleges they wanted to attend. Their son had tentative plans to attend law school. His twin sister's high grades in science and illegible handwriting clearly marked her for medical school. But the parents had planned ahead and made down payments on their children's education. They used prepaid tuition for their daughter's college education at an Ivy League school and other tax-free education savings plans to finance the other college and graduate school tuition.

They also made gifts each year to help Genevieve's sister, who had muscular dystrophy, pay some of her medical bills. And they made substantial gifts to organizations trying to find a cure for the condition. Years later, when they died, with their son (the trial lawyer) and their daughter (the radiologist) at their sides, all their relatives were able to benefit from life insurance that passed to them free of estate taxes, and very little of their wealth went to the taxman.

Some of the most effective tax planning involves making gifts while you're still alive. Not only will the gifts themselves escape taxation if they comply with legal limitations, but any appreciation in value after the gift is given will also escape taxation. All this obviously saves money for your beneficiaries that would otherwise go to taxes. Giving while you're still alive also gives your beneficiaries the chance to express their appreciation for your generosity—and you get the opportunity to see it at work.

If made properly, many gifts may escape taxation under current law. As we saw in the previous chapter, trusts can help a married couple take advantage of both of their unified credits (exemptions). If their combined estates are still large enough to face taxation, even considering the trusts, then a structured gift-giving program may help them reduce their estate to the tax-exempt level.

The law allows you to give up to $11,000 worth of assets per recipient to as many people as you wish each year (married donors giving a gift as a couple are allowed a $22,000 gift tax exclusion per recipient per year). This is called an **annual exclusion** in IRS-speak. There are also ways to structure gifts to transfer value in partnerships or businesses above the $11,000 amount (**discounted gifts**). You can even make gifts that will multiply the actual gift (**leveraged gifts**).

There is no gift tax on any gifts made between spouses in any amount (assuming that the recipient spouse is a U.S. citizen), nor on gifts to charitable organizations. You can also make certain tax-free, direct payments of tuition and medical expenses. These payments must be made directly to the institution involved and cannot be given to the individual for him or her to make the payments. These payments can be made in addition to gifts made directly to the recipient, which are tax free if $11,000 or less per year. We briefly discuss each of these options below.

GIFTS TO SPOUSES

Similar to the estate tax marital deduction, the **gift tax marital deduction** lets spouses (as long as they are both U.S. citizens) transfer an unlimited amount of money to each other any time without gift tax concerns of any kind. (The unlimited marital deduction is not available for gifts to a spouse who is not a U.S. citizen, even if he or she is a U.S. resident.) Your lawyer can use these tax-free gifts to shift ownership of property between you and your spouse so that each spouse may make full use of his or her unified credit.

For example, suppose that Mr. Gotrocks is an old-fashioned fellow who has all the family assets in his name. As the previous chapter shows, he can set up trusts to escape taxes up to the exemption amounts of himself and his wife, if he dies first. But what if his wife dies before he does? She has no assets, so her exemption amount is lost. But if they each have assets of at least the exemption amount, and set up appropriate trusts, then they can use both exemption amounts no matter who dies first. If he gives her the exemption amount (remember, there is no tax on gifts between spouses) and then creates appropriate trusts, they're covered.

GIFTS TO CHARITY

Gifts to approved charities made during one's lifetime, or made at death, are exempt from federal (and almost all state) gift taxes. There are many ways to help a good cause and help yourself at the same time. You can give a charity stock that has appreciated in value, for example. This way you won't have to pay the taxes on the increased value of the stock.

The value of any bequests to charity is subtracted from the value of your estate before the federal estate tax is computed after your death. This means you can reduce estate taxes by giving gifts to charity, though your beneficiaries may not get any more, since the estate is reduced by the amount of the gifts to charity. In essence, you may be substituting the charity for the IRS.

Gifts to charity take all sorts of forms, including stocks, real estate, cash, cars, and life insurance. Some people will buy a life insurance policy that lists a charity as the beneficiary. They pay the premiums and get an income tax deduction for doing so, as long as the beneficiary designation is irrevocable or the charity owns the policy. At their death, the proceeds are paid to the charity, which will create a deduction against estate taxes and can reduce the tax liability for the estate.

Sometimes people make split gifts to charity. A split gift typically occurs when the grantor has retained some interest either for himself or for his beneficiaries and given the other interest to a charity. Be aware that such gifts may be taxed to your estate

▶ GIFT GIVING WITH TRUSTS

The drawback to lifetime gifts is that you may lose control of the money—the beneficiary (usually a child) may not be responsible enough to handle that kind of money wisely. As chapters 9–12 point out, trusts are a good way to avoid this total loss of control.

because you have retained an interest. However, such gifts can provide income tax benefits now as well as estate tax benefits later. Examples of these types of gifts are **charitable remainder trusts, charitable lead trusts,** and **charitable gift annuities.** Consult your lawyer for more information about these powerful planning tools.

GIFTS FOR EDUCATION

Federal tax law permits you to pay a student's tuition directly to the institution and not have the payment be taxed as a gift. New features in federal law give you a number of other attractive alternatives to reduce your gift, estate, and/or income tax liabilities while advancing someone's education.

Prepaid tuition plans, offered by many states, permit you to make payments now toward the tuition of someone not yet enrolled in college. By paying for these tuition credits or certificates at today's tuition rate, you protect yourself against tuition increases in the future. (Tuition has been increasing far more than the inflation rate for many years.) **College savings plans,** offered by almost every state, enable you to save for tuition and other expenses and use them at a wide range of colleges, either in-state or out-of-state.

A federal income tax deduction is not available for your contributions to either of those plans (though you might get a state deduction). However, Section 529 of the Federal Tax Code now gives you a lot of attractive, tax-saving options. **Section 529 plans** allow earnings on your contributions to accumulate tax free until they are withdrawn. This is a significant benefit for taxpayers, especially for high-income taxpayers. Earnings withdrawn to pay tuition and other expenses are now free from federal tax for state-sponsored programs.

Tax benefits are now extended to contributions you make to a qualified plan established by an education institution, along the same lines that they are available to state plans, except that earnings withdrawals will not be tax free until January 1, 2004.

The Section 529 plans allow you to maintain control over the accounts you set up. You even can change beneficiaries (for example, to first cousins of the original beneficiary). Even accounts established under the Uniform Transfer to Minors Act (UTMA) and the Uniform Gift to Minors Act (UGMA) can be reconverted to a restricted form of a 529 plan. However, assets in 529 Plans, unlike the UTMA and UGMA accounts, face a tax penalty if they are withdrawn and not used for educational purposes. State law will govern what can and cannot happen to a UGMA or UTMA account. It is important to check with

---

(i) FRONT-LOADED GIFTS

You can contribute up to $11,000 annually to each education plan you set up and pay no taxes on the gift. Or you can make gifts of up to $55,000 to each plan in one year, excludable from taxation, but this uses your annual exclusion allowance for the next five years. This enables you to shelter more growth from taxation. This is called a **front-loaded gift.** You must live five years for the full $55,000 to be excluded from your estate for estate tax purposes. Thus, if you die at the end of year four, $44,000 will be excluded from the estate, but $11,000 will be included for federal estate tax purposes.

⚠ SAVE SOME FOR YOURSELF

Remember that taxes aren't the only factor in estate planning. Be careful not to give away too much money or too many assets that you might need for emergencies, living expenses after you retire, or even some late-in-life fun.

your lawyer before converting a UGMA or UTMA account to a Section 529 plan.

Coverdell Education Savings Accounts, which used to be known as **Education IRAs,** now can be used to cover expenses in elementary and secondary school, not just higher education. You can give as much as $2,000 in a single year for each beneficiary of one of these accounts. Money withdrawn for qualified expenses is exempt from federal taxes.

You can make contributions to a Section 529 plan and a Coverdell account in the same year for the same beneficiary. (Previously, you could only make contributions to one plan or the other.) However, you could have gift tax consequences if you contribute a total of more than $11,000 to a 529 plan and a Coverdell account in the same year. For example, if you contributed $11,000 to a 529 plan and $2,000 to a Coverdell account in the same year, only $11,000 would be sheltered from gift tax, and there would be a taxable $2,000 gift.

Hope Scholarship Credits and **Lifetime Learning Credits** allow you to claim credits of $1,500 a year in the first two years of your dependent's college years, and up to $1,000 in subsequent years. You can claim one of these credits in the same year that you take a tax-free distribution from a Coverdell account, as long as you meet certain conditions. Unlike the Coverdell accounts, these credits contain income caps so that some high-income individuals cannot claim them.

THE GIFT OF LIFE INSURANCE

Most people don't like to think much about life insurance because it involves two unpleasantries: dealing with insurance companies and thinking about their own deaths. Life insurance can make a great tax-saving gift because it is valued for tax purposes not at what the proceeds will be when you die, but at the cash value—a far smaller amount. And the beneficiary doesn't pay income tax on the proceeds, either. You can also use life insurance to help your charitable giving.

Many people think life insurance proceeds aren't taxable. Wrong! The recipient of life insurance proceeds will not pay income taxes on the receipt of the proceeds, but he or she will pay taxes on any income earned on the proceeds after receipt. Also, the cash value of a life insurance policy counts as an asset of your estate, and so might be subject to the federal estate tax if your estate is large enough.

If you own life insurance, the death benefit is included in your estate for estate tax purposes. If your spouse is the beneficiary, the value of the proceeds will be included in the spouse's estate for estate tax purposes at the death of the spouse. (We will discuss how you can address this problem in the next section.)

INSURANCE CAN BENEFIT YOUR TAX SITUATION

Life insurance proceeds paid to a bona fide charity will create a charitable deduction that will reduce the federal estate tax liability for the estate. Unlike the income tax side, there is no limit to the charitable deduction that can be applied to reduce, or eliminate, the estate tax.

The best way to reduce an estate tax liability that may be created by life insurance is to change the ownership of the policies. Remember, if you own the policies, the death benefit is included in *your* estate for estate tax purposes. There are two common ways to change ownership of insurance policies.

Third-party owners

In the first method, you take out a policy on your life that benefits your children or other beneficiaries.

Next—this is the critical move—you place ownership of the policy not in your name, but in your beneficiaries' names (usually your children). You can then give them the money each year to pay the premiums, making sure to keep your total gift to each person below $11,000 per year to avoid the gift tax. In general, as long as you live more than three years after transferring ownership, the policy is out of your estate.

You will lose control over the policies should you choose this option. For example, if third parties own the policy they have certain rights, including the right to change beneficiaries.

Life insurance trusts

Life insurance trusts are a popular way of accomplishing the same goals while maintaining effective control over the policies and their disposition. Remember, you do not need to own something to control it.

Here's how life insurance trusts work: A married couple has a combined taxable estate that is greater than their combined exemption amounts after using other tax-avoidance devices. They set up a life insurance trust in which the trustee of the trust owns the policy on their lives; they are not the owners. They can do this with an existing policy (by transferring ownership to the trustee) or a new one.

 DO IT RIGHT

Certain factors must be considered when transferring an existing policy. Your lawyer can address these factors while working with a qualified insurance professional.

TALKING TO
A LAWYER

Q. Can you explain how discounted gifts work? What is their advantage?

A. Discounting is a method of reducing the value of an asset that is used to make a gift. As a result, you pay less tax on the gift. There are many kinds of discounts, with the most common being **minority** and **marketability** discounts. A good example of a discounted gift is a fractional interest in real estate. Let's say that you and your spouse want to make a gift of your vacation home, valued at $90,000, to your three children. If you give each child a one-third tenant-in-common interest, you might think that you had made a $30,000 gift to each child. The value of the gift for tax purposes, however, would be considerably less (some courts have said as much as 40 percent less) because there is a marketability discount applied to a transfer of a fractional interest in real estate. Because tax values are determined on a "willing seller, willing buyer" standard, a one-third interest in your vacation home will be valued on the basis of what you would get for it in the marketplace, not on its intrinsic value to you and your family. When you think of it, who would pay $30,000 for only a one-third interest in a vacation home in which a stranger owns the other two-thirds? That is how discounts are created, and they can be used to your advantage to reduce gift and estate taxes.

Discounts, although a valuable tax-planning tool, are not subject to hard-and-fast rules and are often the subject of dispute with the IRS. Be sure to consult a qualified tax attorney before you claim any discount on a gift. He or she will probably recommend that you obtain a written appraisal supporting the discount before you make the gift.

—Answer by Harold Pskowski,
BNA Tax Management, Washington, D.C.

Q. *Can you provide a brief rundown of trusts that we can use to benefit our children and save on taxes?*

A. Some people find it appropriate to establish lifetime minors' trusts for their children and other loved ones. One form of trust is the **2503(c) trust.** This trust is designed to qualify for the annual gift tax exclusion under the rules of Internal Revenue Code Section 2503(c). With such trusts, parents gradually can transfer part of their estate to their children during their lifetimes in a fashion that will reduce potential estate taxes at little or no gift tax cost. These trusts allow parents to keep assets out of a child's control until age twenty-one, and even longer if the child so agrees.

Section **2503(b) trusts** allow parents to control assets until the child has attained adulthood and then some. This trust is required to pay out its income every year. Such income may be paid to a custodial account or directly to the child.

Crummey trusts are another commonly used method of gifting assets to children and other minors. These trusts allow multiple beneficiaries and permit control of assets well beyond age twenty-one under the terms of the trust. There are certain procedures that must be followed with these trusts, but they are not burdensome.

Section 529 plans are a new option that parents and other loved ones can use to make gifts to children. These plans are designed to fund education and have many tax benefits. UTMA and UGMA accounts can be converted to restricted 529 plan accounts.

—Answer by Lena Barnett,
Attorney-at-Law, Silver Spring, Maryland

Each year, for example, the husband buys $11,000 worth of premiums in the policy. When he dies, the policy pays off $400,000—none of it taxable as a part of his gross estate—to the trust. (The premium payments and death benefits are determined by a number of factors and will vary with each case.) The wife lives off the income from the trust. When she dies, the children take the principal remaining—again, tax free—because the wife didn't own the proceeds, and only had a life interest in them. Or the trust may provide for a continuing trust or trusts to benefit the children.

You must follow strict requirements to keep the value of the proceeds from being included in your estate.

- **The life insurance trust must be irrevocable (see chapter 9).**

- **You cannot retain any kind of ownership (the technical term is incidents of ownership), such as making decisions about the policy, or name yourself the trustee.**

- **You must transfer the ownership at least three years before you die; otherwise, the proceeds will be taxed as part of your estate. The three-year rule doesn't apply if you were never the owner of the policy; for example, you could originally take out the policy in the name of the trustee or of your spouse.**

- **It is imperative that your attorney, insurance adviser, and trustee work together to ensure that all of the rules that govern the establishment and management of these trusts are carefully followed. While these trusts are commonly used, many of their advantages will be lost if the rules are broken.**

TAX PLANNING IF YOU KNOW YOU'RE DYING

This may sound morbid, but if you know you're going to die soon, you may be able to give more to your survivors by manipulating your income today. For example, you might choose to take capital losses while you're still alive. Because of tax law treatment at death, this can save your survivors money at tax time.

You can also make your annual, tax-deductible IRA contribution sooner than usual and give charities the gifts you'd planned to leave in your will. This step removes those assets from your estate and also gives you an income tax deduction—though that won't matter to you after you're gone. Nevertheless, you can take heart now in knowing that you left more money in the estate for your beneficiaries. (You can make such gifts even if you're incapacitated, as long as you had the foresight to include such giving powers under a power of attorney.)

You could also make charitable gifts in your will or living trust. These, too, would reduce the value of your estate, and so reduce taxes.

Of course, if you're able, you'll also want to consider quickly implementing some of the other tax-saving devices mentioned in this chapter, like interspousal transfers and annual tax-free gifts. But consider doing all this planning now, instead of on your deathbed, when you'll have other, more eternal concerns to occupy you.

▶ **BULL OR BEAR?**

Sometimes the best of intentions must give way to changing circumstances. Many people grew wealthier than they ever expected during the flush times of the 1990s and wanted to leave some of that windfall to good causes after their deaths. Now that tighter economic times have followed, they are concerned that their children or other beneficiaries will need more from their estates than they'd earlier believed. The kids' businesses might have collapsed, or the value of the stock portfolio you left them might have plummeted. You can avoid having to rewrite your will or living trust every time the economic winds shift by stipulating that your property will pass to a charity contingent upon whether the estate exceeds a certain amount, with anything over that amount going to your favored cause. Even these provisions should be reviewed from time to time as your wishes and preferences change.

THE WORLD AT YOUR FINGERTIPS

- Many websites have information on tax-saving plans for putting money aside for college and other educational expenses. See, for example, www.collegeboard.com/, www.finaid.org/savings, www.collegesavings.org, and www.savingforcollege.com.

- Personal finance sites often have considerable information on life insurance trusts, gift taxes, and other techniques. See, for example, www.invest1to1.com, www.wachovia.com, www.themotleyfool.com, and www.quicken.com.

YOU MUST REMEMBER THIS

- Sometimes the most effective—and rewarding—estate planning involves giving away your money before you die, especially to good causes such as education or charity.

- Be sure to consider these options and possible recipients of your generosity when you consult your attorney about estate planning.

- The tax code gives you a number of attractive options to pay for the education of children and grandchildren.

- Life insurance is an excellent tool for reducing taxes—but be sure you comply with all of the complex rules to get its full benefit.

PART SEVEN

When You Can't Make the Decision

Confronting Your Biggest Fear Now Can

Make a Big Difference Later

CHAPTER 23

Delegating Decisions

Advance-Directives

A sudden stroke has left you unable to move and unable to speak—but in constant pain. You can see and hear, though, and you understand that your condition is probably irreversible, and there's a good chance that you'll die soon. What you see now is your partner and children gathered around your hospital bed, asking each other and your doctor, "What would she want us to do?" You're unable to tell them.

Most of us think of estate planning as something that really doesn't bear fruit until we're dead. But technology has changed all that. Modern medicine can now keep alive indefinitely many people who would have died a few years ago. Alive, but not necessarily able to take care of themselves. Nowadays, a good estate plan must take into account the possibility that you may someday be unable to care for yourself, make decisions, or even regain consciousness—but remain alive.

You may remember the Nancy Cruzan case, in which a Missouri woman suffered a head injury in an auto accident that rendered her unlikely ever to escape from an unresponsive, coma-like state. She had left no written instructions about what doctors were to do if she ever became so disabled. Her family wanted to discontinue intravenous feeding, but the hospital—and the state—refused to allow it. Finally, the U.S. Supreme Court ruled that although individuals do have the right to refuse medical treatment, they must express their wishes clearly enough to meet the standards set by the state in which they live.

The controversy surrounding Jack Kevorkian, the Michigan doctor who assists people to commit suicide, indicates just how touchy and ambivalent our society remains about euthanasia (mercy killing) and the right to die.

Let's hope that you never have to face the choices that the Cruzan family and Kevorkian's patients faced. But there are more-common and less-spectacular situations in which you may have to let someone else make important decisions for you because you aren't able to do so.

Twenty years ago, half of Americans died in institutions such as hospitals or nursing homes; today, it's almost four out of five. The medical personnel in those institutions will look to you for instructions on whether to resuscitate you or let you die in life-threatening situations. If such procedures would only mean great pain for you and prolonged anguish for your family, or would leave you in a vegetative state, you might not want them performed. But you may not be in a condition to refuse them. Or you may be in a situation where you want to live but can't manage your affairs.

THE LEGAL SITUATION

The courts have ruled that all mentally competent adults have the right to refuse medical care. If you're suffering from a condition that leaves you unable to communicate, and there is clear evidence of your wishes regarding treatment (such as a living will or other **advance directive**), those intentions must be obeyed. As a practical matter, your instructions must be written down, preferably in a formal document, if there is to be a good chance that they will be obeyed. And they have to conform to your state's laws. Even then, there's no guarantee.

There are some planning tools that can help. For financial matters, you can use trusts and durable powers of attorney to help you manage. For health-care decisions, you can name a health-care power of attorney (HCPA; sometimes called a **health-care proxy**) to act for you when you cannot act for yourself.

This chapter outlines some of the strategies you can map out right now so that your affairs are managed the way you want when you might not be able to make decisions regarding your

⚠ **DON'T WAIT TOO LONG**

In considering lifetime-planning or advance-directive documents, re-member that they're only valid if made while you are competent—not when you've entered an advanced state of, say, Alzheimer's disease. Also, state laws about how these documents must be created and wit-nessed vary greatly.

While you aren't formally required to use a lawyer to prepare yours, a lawyer experienced in doing advance-directives is very helpful. A lawyer can draft a personalized document that reflects your particular wishes and ensures that all legal formalities are followed. A lawyer is especially helpful if potential family conflicts or special legal or medical concerns are present.

property, your medical treatment, and even your life. The follow-ing section covers situations in which you turn financial decision making over to others; the section after that explains the advance-directives you can create now to guide doctors and others in how to follow your wishes when you may not be able to tell them yourself.

MANAGING YOUR PROPERTY

Even if you become disabled, life will go on. Bills (rent, mort-gage, utilities) will have to be paid. Form 1040 will have to be filed. If you own a business, you may want it to carry on without you. Your property will have to be managed.

You may expect your spouse to do all this for you, but what if he or she is killed or disabled in the same event that renders you unable to manage your affairs? What if he or she dies before you do? What if he or she is simply not capable of handling your affairs? Your estate plan must anticipate such a situation.

⚠ JOINT TENANCIES MIGHT NOT DO IT

One way to give someone else authority to manage your property is to put it into joint tenancy. This will give your co-owner the power to handle your property should you become disabled. But, of course, if your joint tenant is your spouse, he or she might also become disabled and not be up to managing the property; or he or she might die before you, terminating the joint tenancy. In many cases, joint tenancies are a bad idea, or at least insufficient to take care of all possibilities; chapter 5 explains why.

Living trusts

A good method of preserving or protecting assets is through a revocable living trust. (See chapters 11–12.) You name yourself and someone you trust as cotrustees (or name the other person as your alternative trustee). You transfer the assets that need managing (especially things like investments, rental property, and bank accounts) to the trust. You can give the cotrustee or alternative trustee as much or as little power over the assets as you want (you can, for example, require that until you are incapacitated, he or she must obtain your approval before taking any action). If you become incapacitated, your cotrustee or alternative trustee will manage the assets for you. If you die, the assets can pass into your estate, continue in the trust, or be paid to a beneficiary.

However, a living trust may not be appropriate for your situation. It can be cumbersome in that it entails transferring assets into the trust while you're alive.

Durable powers of attorney

A durable power of attorney (DPA) protects against the consequences of becoming disabled. A DPA is a document in which one person (the **principal**) gives legal authority to another person (the **agent**) to act on the principal's behalf. State laws vary, but a DPA generally has to be signed and notarized and state that it shall be "durable"; that is, that it will continue in effect after you become incapacitated. It terminates at your death or at a time you specify. You can also cancel it at any time while you are competent.

Your agent does not have to be a lawyer. In most states, the agent can be any adult or an institution. However, it should be someone who knows you well and whom you trust completely to manage your affairs.

The DPA lets you appoint an agent to manage all or part of your business or personal affairs. The law does impose the responsibility on the agent to act as your fiduciary, but it might be difficult for you or your family to take him or her to court. Since this person can in effect do anything with your money, you should be sure to appoint someone you trust and in whose judgment and ability you have confidence.

A DPA's flexibility is one of its main advantages. You can limit the authority of the agent in the document, giving him or her as many or as few powers over your property as you wish.

While it's not required that you hire a lawyer to draft your durable power of attorney for property, one should be consulted to make sure that your document meets your state's requirements and that the powers you wish to give your agent are actually spelled out in language that will be legally effective.

Some powers may not be presumed to be within the scope of the power of attorney unless they are specifically spelled out— for example, the power to make gifts or loans, or file tax returns. Some states require a specific format or specific wording in the document. Certain states provide a do-it-yourself "short-form durable power of attorney" that allows you to select the powers you wish to grant to the agent, with state law providing an interpretation of what each power means. Even with these simplified forms, legal consultation is advisable.

Another alternative is the springing power of attorney, which becomes operative ("springs to life") if certain conditions are met. (See chapter 14 for more details.)

MAKING TREATMENT DECISIONS

You now have several ways to prepare for the possibility that you may someday be unable to decide for yourself what medical treatment to accept or refuse. This chapter concludes with a discussion of health-care advance directives; the next chapter covers living wills and organ donation.

Remember, federal law now gives you the right to consent to or refuse any medical treatment, and to receive information about

- **the risks and possible consequences of the procedure,**

- **advance-directives (such as living wills), and**

- **life-sustaining medical care and your right to choose whether to receive it.**

ⓘ COMPREHENSIVE HEALTH-CARE ADVANCE DIRECTIVES

The third appendix to this book provides a sample health-care advance directive prepared by the AARP, the ABA, and the American Medical Association (AMA). It not only permits you to name a health-care agent and specify his or her powers (a health-care power of attorney), but it also provides instructions about end-of-life treatment (a living will). It also enables you to state in advance whether you want to donate organs at death, and permits you to nominate a guardian of your person should one be required.

Using this comprehensive single document obviously is more convenient and less prone to confusion than having several documents covering portions of your health-care wishes. It meets the legal requirements of most states. Even if it does not meet the requirements of your state, it may provide an effective statement of your wishes if you cannot speak for yourself.

⚠️ **BUT I'M HIS WIFE . . .**

To many couples, it seems natural that one spouse should be able to speak for the other if he or she is disabled. The law doesn't always see it that way. Many states have **family consent** (or **health surrogate**) laws permitting other family members, in order of kinship, to make some or all health-care decisions on your behalf. Even without such laws, doctors routinely rely on family consent, as long as decisions are not controversial and are made by close family members. But without an advance-directive, decisions may not be made the way you would want, or by the person you would want to make them. Making an advance-directive also benefits your family members, because it spares them the agony of having to guess what you would really want.

No one else, not even a family member, has the right to make these kinds of decisions, unless you've been adjudged incompetent or are unable to make such decisions because, for example, you're in a coma or it's an emergency situation. No one can force an unwilling adult to accept medical treatment, even if it means saving his or her life.

Society has gradually come to a rough consensus on these principles, and almost all medical providers follow them. However, difficulties can still arise when your wishes or intentions aren't clear. That's where the next planning tool comes in.

Health-care advance directives

In an emergency, the law presumes consent. In all other instances, someone else must make decisions for you. The best way to ensure that decisions are made the way you would want, and by the person you want, is to prepare a **health-care advance directive** before you become incapacitated.

An advance-directive is generally a written statement, which you complete in advance of serious illness, about how you want medical decisions made. The two most common forms of advance-directive are a living will and a health-care power of attorney, although in many states you may combine these into a single advance-directive document.

An advance-directive allows you to state your choices for health care or to name someone to make those choices for you should you become unable to make decisions about your medical treatment. In short, an advance-directive enables you to have some control over your future medical care.

A health-care power of attorney (sometimes called a health-care proxy) is a document that appoints someone of your choice to be your authorized agent (or "attorney in fact" or "proxy") for purposes of health-care decisions. You can give your agent as much or as little authority as you wish to make some or all health-care decisions for you.

The health-care power of attorney is a more comprehensive and flexible document than a living will. It can cover any health-care decision and is not limited to terminal illness or permanent coma. More important, it authorizes someone of your choice to weigh all the facts at the time a decision needs to be made and to speak legally for you according to any guidelines you provide.

No one can tell you exactly what to say in your advance-directive. Consider addressing these points:

1. *Alternate proxies.* Whenever possible, name one or more alternate or successor agents in case your primary agent is unavailable.

2. *Life-sustaining treatments.* Are there any specific types of treatment you want or don't want under any circumstances? Your personal or family medical history may make certain conditions or treatments more likely.

3. *Artificial nutrition and hydration.* Some states will presume that you want nutrition and hydration under all circumstances unless you instruct otherwise.

4. *Organ donation.* In many states, you can include instructions about donating organs in your advance-directive or, better yet, on the back of your drivers' license. The idea is to have the

▶ **TALK IT OUT**

The most important point to remember about forms is that they are supposed to aid discussion and dialogue, not take their place. Therefore, a form ought to be a starting point, not an end point, for making your wishes known. There is no ideal form. Any form you use should be personalized to reflect your values and preferences. Before doing an advance-directive, talk with your doctor, family members, and advisers. Opening yourself up to different perspectives will help you to understand the medical possibilities you may face and clarify your values and choices.

information known while there is still time to harvest the organs and put them to use.

AFTER YOU'VE COMPLETED YOUR DIRECTIVE

In most states, lawyers recommend that you tell your doctor and lawyer about your decisions regarding health care in the event that you later become unable to speak for yourself, and give each of them a copy of any document you have prepared to keep in your file or permanent medical record. It's also a good idea to give a copy to the executor of your regular will and, of course, to the person you've chosen to act for you if you cannot act for yourself.

You may also want to make a small card for your purse or wallet that states that you have an advance-directive and provides the name, phone number, and address of your agent or another person who can provide a copy of it.

You can revise or revoke the HCPA at any time, including during a terminal illness, as long as you are competent. To revoke it, notify the people to whom you gave the copies, preferably in writing. To change it, execute a new document. The same formalities of signing and witnessing are required for changes.

It's a good idea to prepare the DPA, the HCPA, and living will all at once, and make sure they're compatible with each other and the rest of your estate plan. These days, all should be regarded as essential components of any estate plan.

Some attorneys advise using different people to serve as agents under your HCPA and DPA. The former is usually a spouse, a child, or another close relative who can make health-care decisions; the latter, a lawyer or other moneywise friend, relative, or professional competent to make business and financial decisions.

One final issue. Do you need more than one advance-directive if you spend considerable time in more than one state? In many states, the law expressly honors out-of-state directives. But in some states, the law is unclear. Realistically, providers will normally try to follow your stated wishes, regardless of the form you use or where you executed it. However, if you spend a great deal of time in more than one state (for example, summers in Wisconsin, winters in Arizona), you may want to consider executing an advance-directive for each state. Or you may want to find out whether one document meets the formal requirements of each state. As a practical matter, you may want different health-care agents for each state if one agent is not readily available in each location.

GUARDIANSHIPS AND CIVIL COMMITMENT

The goal of many of the devices described in this section is to enable you to avoid court-appointed guardianships. The law authorizes courts to designate **guardians** (or **conservators**) for adults judged to be incompetent. Guardians are usually appointed to protect people who are mentally ill or mentally challenged, who are senile, or who are addicted to drugs or alcohol. Depending on

▶ SOME QUESTIONS TO ASK YOURSELF

Advance-directives are tools to make sure that your wishes are carried out. Here are some of the issues you need to explore (perhaps with your family, friends, spiritual adviser, or doctor) before preparing an advance-directive.

1. What are my values?
   - How important is independence and self-sufficiency in your life?
   - What role should doctors and other health professionals play in medical decisions that affect you?
   - What kind of living environment is important to you?
   - What role do religious beliefs play in such decisions?
   - How should your family and friends be involved, if at all, in these decisions?

2. Who should be my agent?
   This is the person who will have great power over your health if you become incapacitated. Who can you trust to know what you would want if unexpected situations arise? Who will be able to handle the stress of making such decisions? (Remember, state laws sometimes prevent doctors and others from acting as agents in these circumstances.)

3. What guidelines should I impose?
   You don't have to spell out every contingency. In fact, you need to leave your agent some flexibility should unexpected circumstances arise. But if you have specific intentions (not being kept alive by feeding tubes if you are brain-dead, for example) you can help your agent by writing those out.

4. How can I deal with reluctant doctors?
   The medical establishment has been slow to recognize a patient's right to make these kinds of decisions in advance. If you have a regular physician or hospital, you might want to discuss these issues with your health-care providers now to make sure your wishes, and those of your agent, will be carried out.

the law, there can be two kinds of guardians: **guardians of the estate,** who are authorized to manage property, and **guardians of the person,** who make medical and personal decisions for the incompetent person, who is known as a **ward.** (The latter is similar to the guardianships set up for children, which are discussed in chapter 13.)

You establish a guardianship by petitioning a court to hold a competency hearing, at which testimony (usually medical) is introduced to prove that the person can't handle his or her own affairs. If the court agrees, it appoints a guardian (usually the petitioner). The guardianship continues until the ward regains the capacity to handle his or her own affairs, which seldom happens. The ward loses most of his or her civil rights, often including the right to make a binding contract, to vote, and to make medical decisions.

A guardian's power varies with the state and the court's decree. It may be broad or limited. The duties and responsibilities will be enumerated in the appointment document. Usually the guardian will be required to post a bond, and an inventory of the ward's property will be required. Annual reports will have to

---

ⓘ WHO MAY BE A GUARDIAN?

Laws vary from one state to another. In most states, the courts may appoint almost anyone as guardian if the person meets legal requirements. The court often appoints the person filing the petition. Most courts like to appoint a relative who knows the person and is most likely to act in his or her best interests. However, the courts may appoint a friend or an attorney, especially if no family members are available. The courts also may appoint co-guardians, who either share the duties or split the responsibilities between them. If there are no friends or family members willing or able to serve as guardian, many states permit public or private agencies to act as the guardian and to charge fees for that service if the estate of the incapacitated person is able to pay.

---

be filed with the court. The guardian may receive a fee, which is often waived by family members.

Guardianships are relatively clumsy and inefficient ways of taking over decision-making power. For example, the guardian usually must get the court's permission before spending money or selling assets. Notice, public hearings, or other red tape may be required. You should explore (with a lawyer's advice) the other possibilities listed in this chapter before undertaking one.

If you are afraid someone is seeking a guardianship over you against your wishes, you should see a lawyer. If you agree with the need for guardianship, you can ask the court to appoint a guardian of your choice. The best protection against involuntary guardianship, though, is to have a health-care power of attorney and a durable power of attorney in place before someone tries to impose one on you.

The same goes for commitment to a mental hospital. State laws govern the circumstances in which someone may be invol-

A LEGAL TEST OF CAPACITY

There is no universal legal test of mental capacity or incapacity. Laws vary from state to state, but some general principles apply everywhere.

Incapacity is always evaluated in connection with specific tasks. The question is always "Incapacity to do what?" Different legal standards of capacity may apply to different tasks, such as the capacity to do a will, to drive, to enter contracts, to manage money, or to make medical decisions. In a typical guardianship proceeding, most but not all states use a two-part test to determine incapacity (sometimes called incompetency). First, some type of disability must be verified—for example, mental illness, mental retardation, and/or Alzheimer's disease. Second, there must be a finding that the disability prevents the person from performing activities essential to take care of his or her personal needs or property. Most courts will also insist that all feasible alternatives to guardianship must have been explored before appointing a guardian.

untarily committed to institutional care. A court hearing is required; the standard is whether a person is dangerous to him- or herself or others, or can't care for him- or herself. A lawyer is usually appointed to represent the person whose commitment is sought. If you are committed to an institution, you retain certain rights. If you feel someone is wrongly seeking to have you committed to an institution, see a lawyer immediately.

THE WORLD AT YOUR FINGERTIPS

- Information about health-care advance directives is available from most area agencies on aging and from many state bar associations and medical societies.
- State-specific information and forms are also available from Partnership in Caring, an organization concerned with excellent end-of-life care, at www.partnershipforcaring.org.
- The ABA's Commission on Law and Aging has a consumer tool kit for health-care advance planning available at www.abanet.org/aging.
- Americans for Better Care of the Dying (www.abcd-caring.org) publishes *Handbook for Mortals,* an excellent guide for dealing with serious and eventually fatal illness.
- Last Acts provides a wealth of similar information on its website (www.lastacts.org).

YOU MUST REMEMBER THIS

- Advance planning for financial and health-care decision making is the most effective means of ensuring that your wishes will be followed if you become incapacitated.
- Methods for dealing with financial incapacity or difficulties in managing finances include a durable power of attorney, a living trust, and joint ownership.
- You can use health-care advance directives, such as a living will and a health-care durable power of attorney, to provide instructions about your medical care in the event you are incapacitated.
- In the absence of advance planning, a petition for guardianship may be necessary in cases of serious incapacity.

CHAPTER 24

Planning for End-of-Life Decisions

Living Wills and Organ Donation

Most elder-law specialists recommend that you execute documents that authorize someone to act for you in the event you are unable to act for yourself. That's the point of the previous chapter, where we discuss health-care advance directives, trusts, durable powers of attorney, and other ways of having a person stand in for you. But maybe there is no one you trust to act for you. In this chapter, we look at documents that state your wishes but don't name someone to stand in your stead.

A living will is a written declaration that lets you state in advance your wishes about the use of life-prolonging medical care if you become seriously ill and are unable to communicate. It lets your wishes be carried out even if you cannot state them. If you don't want to burden your family with the costs (medical expenses in the last month of life average over $20,000) and the prolonged grief that are involved in keeping you alive when there's no reasonable hope of revival, a living will typically authorizes withholding or turning off life-sustaining treatment if your condition is irreversible.

Living wills typically come into play when you are incapable of making and communicating medical decisions. Usually you'll be in a medical state such that if you don't receive life-sustaining treatment (intravenous feeding; breathing with a respirator), you'll die. If your living will is properly prepared and clearly states your wishes, the hospital or doctor will normally abide by it, and will in turn be immune from criminal or civil liability for withholding treatment. If the doctor or institution cannot go along with your wishes as a matter of conscience, they must make an effort to transfer you to another provider.

Some people worry that by making out a living will, they are authorizing their own abandonment by the medical system. They need to understand that a living will can also be used to state their desire to receive life-sustaining treatments. Thus, even if you prefer to receive all possible treatment whatever your condition, it's a good idea to express those wishes in a living will.

All states recognize living wills, or **medical directives** as they are sometimes called, but such documents are far from uniform. There are two kinds of living wills: **statutory** (those that comply with the state's statute) and **nonstatutory** (those that don't). The principal difference is that statutory living wills are thought to give medical providers more-certain immunity from liability if they comply with your wishes. Moreover, statutory living wills generally address only terminal illness and permanent unconsciousness. Depending upon the state you live in, they may not address advanced illnesses, such as late-stage Alzheimer's disease, in which death is not yet imminent.

A statutory living will complies with all the formalities required under the living-will statute of your state. Typically, the requirements involve detailed witnessing or notarization requirements and sometimes the use of specific warnings or other language. Most of the statutes include a form that may be mandatory or merely optional. But even if the form is mandatory, you have the opportunity to add to or expand on its instructions, and it is usually advisable to do so. Standard living-will language is usually too broad and general to be of much guidance when a real decision about continuing treatment has to be made. It is important to individualize your living will by stating your preferences and adapting the general language to the specifics of your medical condition, if that is possible.

The form required for a valid living will differs in each state. Be sure to get advice from a lawyer. You can also obtain a copy of a living-will form and instructions (as well as other advance-directive forms) valid for your state by contacting Partnership for Caring at 800-989-9455 or www.partnershipforcaring.org.

Usually, the decision to write a living will should be made after consulting with your doctor and a lawyer. Your particular

▶ **IF I HAVE A LIVING WILL, DO I STILL NEED A HEALTH-CARE POWER OF ATTORNEY?**

Absolutely. An HCPA (see chapter 23) appoints an agent to act for you; a living will doesn't. Moreover, an HCPA applies to all medical decisions (unless you specify otherwise); most living wills typically apply only to a few decisions near the end of your life, and are often limited to use if you have a "terminal illness," which has become a slippery term. An HCPA can also include specific instructions to your agent about the issues you care most about, or what you want done in particular circumstances.

medical history may make some treatments more likely in your future. If you are writing a living will yourself, consider explaining the kinds of circumstances in which you believe continuing to live would be worse than death. That will help you to explain when you would or would not want any form of life-sustaining treatment. Also describe what you would want at the end of life (e.g., good pain management; expressions of forgiveness or thanks) and not just what you don't want. You do not have to list particular treatments you want or don't want unless you wish to do so, although it is advisable, and in some states necessary, to make clear your wishes about artificial nutrition and hydration. If you have a medical condition that makes certain unwanted treatments more likely, you may want to address those treatments. (For example, someone with chronic obstructive pulmonary disease may want to be very specific about when a respirator is to be used or not used.)

SOME PROBLEMS WITH LIVING WILLS

Living wills are typically either vague ("I don't want to be kept alive if I'm a burden to anyone." What does that mean?) or so specific as to be inflexible. In the twilight world at the end of life, all lines are blurred, all colors are gray. It's simply impossible to predict every possible contingency.

Since living wills are so limited, it is definitely better to use a health-care power of attorney unless you have no one whom you can trust to make life-and-death decisions for you. Some lawyers recommend that you have both a living will and an HCPA, with the HCPA handling other kinds of disability, or gray-area cases in which it's not certain that you're terminally ill or your doctor or state law fail to give your wishes due weight. A living will by itself wouldn't have helped Nancy Cruzan (see chapter 23) in 1990, for instance, because she wasn't considered terminally ill by her doctors, and with artificial nutrition and hydration she could have lived as long as thirty more years in a persistent vegetative state. Today, most states cover persistent vegetative states in their living-will laws. In any case, a health-care power of attorney would have permitted a designated person to make the decision for Nancy Cruzan.

If you use a living will, be sure to update it every few years. Your values and wishes may change, and the law itself may change. A very old living will may not be given as much weight as a more current one.

Finally, despite recent changes in laws, old habits die hard, and many doctors and nurses are still reluctant to turn off life

---

⚠ WHAT HAPPENS IF I DON'T HAVE A LIVING WILL OR AN HCPA?

If you don't have a living will or an HCPA, someone who is not of your own choosing will be making the most important decisions of your life—or death. As a result, those decisions will not necessarily be made the way you would have made them. The consequence can be continued suffering with unwanted treatment or, conversely, the refusal of treatment you may have wanted. Yet most Americans still don't have advance-directives such as living wills or HCPAs.

( ) TALKING TO A LAWYER

Q. In protecting assets in case of disability, is a living trust preferable to a durable power of attorney?

A. I think so. Your living trust will provide a trustee or trustees to protect your property. The trustees will follow the instructions you have set out in the trust. Your trustees will be held to the highest standard of care under the law. Also, your trust will be coordinated with your health-care documents to ensure that your interests are protected.

A trust can provide extensive instructions for disability planning, and the trustees are held to a much higher standard of care than an agent under a power of attorney. A trust is appropriate for smaller estates because it will better protect the client in the event of disability and save the costs inherent in probate. Also, most powers of attorney contain a list of powers with little or no instruction. They are like giving someone a blank check to one's assets.

I use special durable powers of attorney in conjunction with my trusts to address issues in which it may be inconvenient, imprudent, or inappropriate to get the trust involved. Resigning from fiduciary positions is an example of a matter addressed by my special powers of attorney.

Q. I'm concerned about the disadvantages of joint bank accounts. Is there another way that I can give someone access to my bank account without giving that person ownership of my money?

A. You can put your account into your revocable trust. Your trustees will then have access to your account. As trustees, they will be held to the highest standards under the law, and they will follow the instructions you established in your trust.

Q. I believe very strongly that healthy organs should be donated to help others—but how can I ensure that my wishes in this regard are followed for my organs?

A. There is a great need for **anatomical gifts** (transplantable organs and tissues). Besides filling out the donation information on your driver's license (if that's permitted by your state), you can see that your living will and health-care power of attorney also express your wishes regarding organ donation. It is also important to point out to your family that your directions have been expressed in your documents.

Q. I absolutely don't want rescue personnel to try to save me. Besides executing a health-care power of attorney and a living will, what can I do?

A. Many states have passed laws that protect individuals from unwanted intervention by rescue personnel. These states enable doctors to issue emergency medical system "do not resuscitate" (EMS DNR) orders for patients who want to die at home. Some states only enable doctors to issue DNR orders for those patients who are terminally ill or chronically ill.

Without such orders, emergency medical personnel are legally bound to resuscitate any patient who has a chance of being revived. Even with a living will, unless a doctor writes a DNR order, medical personnel are still required to do everything to resuscitate the patient.

If the patient has a DNR order, medics will not perform cardiopulmonary resuscitation (CPR) if the patient's heart or breathing has stopped, but they will treat other symptoms.

EMS DNR orders can be revoked by patients or by the person acting as the patient's attorney in fact under a durable power of attorney for health care.

—Answers by Lena Barnett,
Attorney-at-Law, Silver Spring, Maryland

support—even if that's what a patient wants. Surveys show that medical institutions still routinely overtreat patients with no realistic hope of recovery, in the process ignoring living wills and often angering and tormenting the dying person's loved ones. That's why you need an advocate appointed by your HCPA to press your intentions.

ORGAN DONATION

The Uniform Anatomical Gift Act, along with similar provisions in most state laws, sets forth your wishes about whether, after your death, you want your organs donated to help other people who may need them to survive. Donating your body or organs to science or medicine has been called the greatest gift, as the thousands of people now on waiting lists to replace their failing organs would attest. You can direct hospitals to donate your organs by filling out a donor card, witnessed by two people. The card is often attached to the back of your driver's license. A card can be obtained at your state's motor vehicle department or by contacting the Living Bank in Houston, Texas, at 800-528-2971, or at www.livingbank.org. Doctors may also ask your family whether they will consent to organ donation on behalf of a terminally ill patient.

THE WORLD AT YOUR FINGERTIPS

- Partnership for Caring (www.partnershipforcaring.org) is a national nonprofit organization that partners individuals and organizations to improve how people die in our society. Among other services, Partnership for Caring operates a national crisis and information hot line dealing with end-of-life issues and provides state-specific living wills and health-care advance directives.

- Aging with Dignity (www.agingwithdignity.org) is a nonprofit organization that provides practical information, advice, and legal tools you need to ensure your wishes and those of your loved ones will be respected.

- U.S. Living Will Registry (http://www.uslivingwillregistry.com) stores living wills and other advance-directives that are made available to health professionals. The idea is to make advance-directives more readily available when needed. The registry electronically stores advance-directives, along with organ donor and emergency contact information, and makes them available twenty-four hours a day to health-care providers across the country through an automated computer-facsimile system.

- The ABA's Commission on Law and Aging (COLA) (www.abanet.org/aging) examines law and policy issues affecting older persons. It seeks to improve legal services for the aging, particularly through involvement of the private bar.

YOU MUST REMEMBER THIS

- Living wills enable you to specify the treatment you want or do not want.

- They should be carefully worded and specific to your medical history if it is relevant.

- They should be reviewed periodically to see that they still reflect your wishes and are in accord with the law of your state.

PART EIGHT

Putting the Plan into Action After Your Death

Steps You Can Take Now

to Help Your Survivors

CHAPTER 25

Easing the Burden on Your Family

There's a Lot You Can Do to Help—Now

When the renowned baseball player Ted Williams died in 2002, the acclaim over his career was somewhat shadowed by the ugly legal battle over what would happen to his remains. One of his children insisted that Williams wanted to be cremated, while another contended that the old slugger had decided to have his body cryogenically preserved.

Although few such conflicts become so bizarre, or so public, far too many children and other survivors often face the agonizing question of deciding what kind of funeral arrangements Mom or Dad would have wanted. This chapter gives you some tips on how to make things easier for your family in the days and weeks after your death.

Where will Mom be buried? How much should we spend on the funeral? Where are the important records—bank accounts, safe-deposit boxes, and the like—needed to make sense of her affairs after she's gone? What insurance policies are affected? Which friends and relatives need to be informed, and how can they be reached?

Putting together the threads of anyone else's life after they're gone is hard enough—but having to do so when you're suffering from the grief over a loved one's departure, and while maintaining your own family and work responsibilities, can be overwhelming.

So once the hard part of your estate planning—writing a will, setting up a trust, tax planning, and so on—is done, it's vital to take a little more time to ease the burden on your family by providing them with clear final instructions about how to handle the myriad loose ends during the trying months after your departure.

YOUR FINAL INSTRUCTIONS

You can make your survivors' task easier by leaving a letter containing burial instructions and your other last wishes in a place where your family can find it.

The most important decision is what to spend on a funeral. The average funeral costs more than $5,000, and other burial costs can push the bill up to $7,500 and well beyond, depending on how elaborate you and your family want to get. Although cremation or very simple burial can run less than $3,000, death is usually one of the largest single expenses a family incurs. Unfortunately, a grieving family may spend more than it can really afford to show how much they loved the departed.

To protect your estate and survivors from this sort of tension, set a limit on funeral expenses, and arrange the service while you're alive (through a funeral home) with the help of someone you trust, such as your spouse, executor, or religious leader. Funeral homes are legally required to send you a written price list; use it to comparison shop. The options range from basic cremation to elaborate memorial ceremonies. If you get a prepaid or "preneed" plan, make sure you sign a fixed-price contract. If you don't, your family could be surprised by charges above the amount you've already paid.

A warning: If your body will have to be transported out of the state in which you die, a permit may be required. The funeral home or health department can advise your survivors. Most states have laws concerning embalming, cremation, and other aspects of burial. Occasionally, an unscrupulous funeral director will tell survivors falsely that the law requires certain procedures (such as the purchase of a casket before cremation). So it's a good idea for you or your lawyer to research these requirements before you die and make sure your survivors know them.

Remember, oral or written instructions about burial *aren't legally binding* on your family or executor. The spouse or next of kin is entitled to handle burial arrangements; if no one comes forward to do so, state law takes over.

Where should you keep these instructions? Not with your will; sometimes wills aren't read until after the funeral. And not in a safe-deposit box, because that might be sealed pending the reading of the will. You should keep a copy with your will *and* give another to your lawyer, the executor of your will, your spouse, and any other close family members or beneficiaries. The main thing is that it be accessible and that everyone who needs it will know in advance where to find it.

THE LITTLE THINGS

Families can fight over things as trivial as a favorite lamp or a wedding dress, as well as valuable antiques or jewelry. That's why, as much trouble as it seems now, you'll be doing everyone a favor if you make a list (sometimes called a **precatory list** because it's not necessarily legally binding and can be altered easily) of personal property items that are too inexpensive (and change too often) to put in the will. Off to the side, write down the name of the person who you want to inherit each item—in short, who gets what. (See also the discussion of tangible personal property memoranda in chapter 7.)

You might also need to think about what will happen to personal or business items that will outlive you. The widow of Sir Richard Francis Burton, the great explorer and translator of *Arabian Nights*, burned all his unpublished manuscripts—to the anguish of scholars and adventure lovers ever since. Franz Kafka's dying injunction to his friend to burn his manuscripts was fortunately ignored; that's the only reason his legacy has come down through history. One of the sons of Johann Sebastian Bach sold many of his father's irreplaceable manuscripts to support his drinking. A descendant of Thomas Jefferson used some of the former president's private papers for kindling.

Few of us will reach the exalted status of these men. But you might want to consider whether a local university, library, museum, or other institution would be interested in your stamp collection, private correspondence with a celebrity, or other items of potential historical import. Your heirs and executors may not appreciate their value to posterity. So be sure to spell out what you want to happen to such items.

CUSHIONING THE BLOW

Many people are as concerned with sparing their survivors grief and financial stress as they are about dying themselves. Especially in families where one spouse is the primary wage earner, the loss of income from that spouse's death can be as devastating financially as it is emotionally. For that reason, your estate planning should include some provision for an emergency fund for your survivors, to tide them over the period immediately following your death. Life insurance is one method for doing this (see chapter 4), but there are others. A joint bank account, a Totten trust, or a marital trust will provide your spouse with income on your death. And some states have pay-on-death accounts that can accomplish the purpose.

Finally, you might locate the name of a counselor or a psychiatrist to help your family cope with grief. Your loved ones

---

 NOTE TO HUSBANDS

Widows sometimes find it hard to obtain credit after a husband dies, especially if they've been homemakers all their lives. Therefore, add your wife's name to any credit cards currently held in your name only. After you die, your widow should notify credit card companies of your death, and change all cards held in both of your names to her name alone. After your death, she probably should pay any debts that are owed jointly by you and herself (e.g., mortgage, utility bills), to shore up her credit rating. (An exception to this rule of thumb would be if she's advised not to do so for tax purposes—it may be preferable to have such bills paid by the estate.)

---

don't have to call, but at least they'll know that help is there. You might also put the names of local or national support groups for the newly bereaved in your list of final instructions. If you can't find one in the phone book or from friends, contact the American Association of Retired Persons (AARP).

Insurance policies demand special attention. If you were covered through a health plan provided by your employer, your spouse and dependent children may be entitled to continue that coverage for up to three years. Check with your employer and leave written instructions. Your loved ones may need to buy more insurance, or to reduce the amount of life insurance needed now that you're gone. They will need to change the beneficiaries of their policies if you were one of them.

A final checklist

Here are some suggestions about what you should tell or provide your survivors in your final instructions.

- What you want done with your body—for example, whether you want it buried, cremated, or donated to science
- Information about any funeral arrangements you've made, including the details of any funeral plan you've bought or account you've set up to pay burial expenses; information about burial vaults, caskets, or other specifics if included in the plan; the location of the cemetery and the burial plot; the location of the services; the names of any members of the clergy or others you wish to speak; and your preferences as to music, flowers, and aspects of the service
- The name of any charity or cause to which you wish contributions sent in your name
- The location of your will and the identity and phone number of the executor and lawyer
- The location of your safe-deposit box, the key to it, and any important records not located in it, such as your birth certificate; marriage, divorce, and prenuptial documents;

important business, insurance, and financial records; and pension and benefit agreements

- An inventory of assets (like the one in Appendix A), including documents showing debts owed and loans outstanding; credit card and car information; information about your post office box and the key to it; information on any investments; the deed to your home; IRA, pension, and bank account information; a list of expected death benefits; and so on

- Important information, such as names, addresses, dates and places of birth for you and your spouse and family members (including ex-spouses, if any), Social Security numbers for you and your spouse and dependent children (and the location of your Social Security card), policy numbers and phone numbers and addresses of insurance companies and agencies that control your death benefits (employer, union, Veterans Affairs office), and so on

- The name and address of your lawyer, executor, and employers

- Information you want included in your obituary

(i) PICK THE FUNERAL SERVICE YOU WANT

Here are some of the options funeral homes offer. Find out how much each funeral home charges for each service, pick the ones that fit your needs and budget, and purchase a plan that provides them. It will save your loved ones needless turmoil and expense. You can join a memorial society now that will help you plan your own funeral. Some offer preneed plans (oh, the euphemisms for the D-word) that allow you to prepay the funeral costs.

- Burial, cremation, or gift of body for science
- Transporting the body to the funeral home
- Embalming and other preparation of the body
- Selecting flowers
- Selecting headstone, plaque, or tomb
- Providing a hearse for the body and limousines for the family
- Renting facilities for viewing the body
- Memorial cards and guest book
- Transporting the body to the cemetery
- Tents and chairs for the funeral
- Copies of the death certificate
- Assistance in notifying insurance companies, newspapers, and organizations to which the deceased belonged

Other choices you'll have to make:

- Open or closed casket?
- Indoor memorial service or graveside service (or both)?
- Elaborate or simple service?
- Who conducts the service: family member, religious leader, or funeral home?
- Who speaks at the service?
- Should music be played? If so, what music?
- Should there be a reception after the funeral? If so, where?

THE WORLD AT YOUR FINGERTIPS

- The Funeral Consumers Alliance is a group "dedicated to protecting a consumer's right to choose a meaningful, dignified, affordable funeral." Its website (www.funerals.org/) has much information and many links.

- Beyond Indigo (www.death-dying.com/) has much information on funerals, last instructions, and coping with grief.

YOU MUST REMEMBER THIS

- Psychologists say that most of us live in denial of our own deaths, and it's not something anyone really wants to think much about. But planning the details of your final arrangements now will greatly ease the burden on your family at a time when they're under the most stress.

- You won't be there to provide it in person, but the planning you do now will help your loved ones immensely when they need it most.

CHAPTER 26

Choosing the Executor

Some Tips on Getting the Right Person

Okay. Let's assume you've followed this book's advice and, working with your lawyer, have crafted a well-thought-out estate plan, one that protects your assets from unintended taxes; provides for your loved ones, business interests, and favored causes; and leaves clear final instructions for your funeral and other final arrangements. Secure in the knowledge that you've tied up all the loose ends and done everything you could to ease the burden on your family, you close your eyes for the last time.

Now what?
What, if anything, happens to you after death is a matter for metaphysics, spirituality, and other subjects beyond the scope of this book. Right now, though, you need to pick the person (or persons or institution) to be in charge of your assets after you're gone: the executor of your will and the trustee of any trusts you set up (see chapter 27).

WHAT EXECUTORS DO

The law requires that an executor be appointed because someone must be responsible for

- collecting the assets of the estate,
- protecting the estate property,
- preparing an inventory of the property,
- paying valid claims against the estate (including taxes),
- representing the estate in claims against others, and, finally,
- distributing the estate property to the beneficiaries.

▶ ## THE WORKHORSE EXECUTOR

The will can impose additional duties on the executor that are not required by law. These include planning postdeath tax strategies, choosing which specific property goes to which beneficiaries, and even investing funds.

These last two functions may require liquidating assets; that is, selling items like stocks, bonds, or even furniture or a car to have enough cash to pay taxes, creditors, or beneficiaries.

Sounds like a lot of work, doesn't it? It can be, and some of it can be complicated. However, the executor doesn't necessarily have to shoulder the entire burden. He or she can pay a professional out of the estate assets to take care of most of these functions, especially those requiring legal or financial expertise, but that will reduce the amount that goes to the beneficiaries. Therefore, handling an estate is often a matter of balancing expertise, convenience, cost, and other factors.

There's no consensus, even among lawyers, about who makes the best executor; it all depends upon your individual circumstances.

THE CASE FOR A PAID EXECUTOR

One approach is to appoint someone with no potential conflict of interest—that is, someone who doesn't stand to gain from the will. For this reason, many testators avoid naming family members or business partners. This helps the estate to avoid will contests from disgruntled relatives who might accuse the executor of cheating. If you have several beneficiaries who don't get along, you may want an outside executor who's independent of all factions. The larger the estate, the more the potential for conflicts, and the more you should consider naming an outside executor. You should also consider the possibilities of conflicts of interest if you have several beneficiaries.

There are other reasons for choosing a paid executor—usually a lawyer—instead of a family member. If the family member is your spouse he or she may be incapacitated by grief, illness, or disability. Nonetheless, he or she as executor will be personally liable for unpaid estate taxes and fines for late filings, even if he or she has delegated such tasks to a lawyer.

Furthermore, since the executor must gather all the estate assets, your spouse may be faced with the odious duty of retrieving money or property you lent to other family members or friends.

If you think your spouse may not be up to the job (considering that he or she may also be saddled with sole responsibility for any minor children), you might choose a lawyer or other professionals, even though it means paying a fee. Remember, this is a job that can take more than three years of involvement, primarily because of tax procedures, though most estates take far less. In any event, the first few months are by far the hardest, and your spouse might not be up to the task.

For larger estates, it's often advisable to use a lawyer or a bank. A complicated estate that involves temporarily running a business often demands an institutional fiduciary, such as a bank, that can call on the advice of lawyers, tax experts, accountants, investment counselors, and even business administrators. An institution is impartial and immortal.

You might also consider hiring your lawyer as executor if you anticipate a will contest or know that the estate is going to require a lot of legal work. However, not every lawyer would welcome the responsibility, since possible exposure to liability for performance on the job is a concern.

THE CASE FOR AN UNPAID EXECUTOR

Most of the time, where there is little possibility of a contest, the fees that lawyers and other paid executors charge may make it too expensive to hire such outsiders. Many people choose a friend or family member who will waive (refuse) the executor's fee to which he or she would be entitled—and which comes out of your estate.

For people whose assets amount to less than a million dollars or so, your spouse or a mature child may be your choice. This person naturally will be interested in making sure the probate process goes as quickly and smoothly as possible. Some lawyers caution that choosing one child to be the executor can cause animosity among siblings.

If you do decide to appoint an interested person as the sole executor and give that person discretionary powers to determine who gets which items of personal property, it may be wise to include a method for making these discretionary decisions. Drawing lots or arbitration by a third party can help avoid any abuse of discretion and eliminate undue pressure on the executor.

One compromise popular with small-business owners is to appoint coexecutors, such as one personal friend who's close to your family and one person with business expertise, and specify

▶ BUT I DON'T WANT TO BE AN EXECUTOR!

If you learn after a relative has died that you've been named executor, and you don't want to serve, you should file a document called a **declination** with the court. If the will named a contingent executor (and if the deceased followed our instructions in the sample will in Appendix B he or she did), that person will take over. If none was named, the court will appoint one.

If you are a family member who has been named executor—a surviving spouse, for example—you might find out whether in your case it's advisable to start probate quickly. It may be possible to delay beginning the executor's duties until grief subsides. A competent lawyer can relieve many of the burdens of the executor.

which executor will be responsible for which duties. Or, to prevent family dissension, your will may provide that all of your children serve as coexecutors.

Coexecutors can be a good idea if the main beneficiary lives in another state and it would be inconvenient for him or her to make frequent trips to handle clerical details. You could appoint another relative or friend who lives in the same city as the one in which the probate court is located to handle local details. If you choose this course, be sure to pick people or entities that can work together. You must also choose a successor in case your first choice dies or is unable to serve.

WHAT TO LOOK FOR IN AN EXECUTOR

It's important to be sure the executor is capable of doing the job. Think of the appointment as employment—not a way to reward (or punish) a friend or a relative.

The quality most desirable in an executor is perseverance in dealing with bills (especially the hospital, Medicare, ambulance, and doctor charges incurred in an illness). Paying bills and then filing for reimbursement from insurance companies often requires a lot of paperwork. Pick someone who has the time and inclination to deal with bureaucrats and forms. Also, the executor may have to cope with relatives who may be wondering why it's taking so long to receive their inheritance, or why their bequests are smaller than they expected. This can happen if, for example, the decedent's money was aggressively invested in the stock market, and those stocks nose-dived after he or she wrote the will.

The executor will probably hire a certified public accountant (CPA) or lawyer to handle

- the income tax return for income the deceased person accrued before death,
- the estate tax return, and
- the *estate* income tax return for income taxes incurred after the person's death.

⚠ THEY CAN'T SERVE

The executor cannot be a minor, a convicted felon, or a non–U.S. citizen. Some states require a nonresident executor to be a primary beneficiary or close relative. Others require a surety bond or require that the out-of-state executor engage a resident to act as his or her representative.

If the estate includes stocks or other investments, the executor may have to hire an investment adviser, particularly if the value of the estate has changed substantially because of fluctuations in the market.

In most estates, no significant legal expertise is required to serve as executor; the issues are all financial. The executor will generally work with a lawyer to probate the will. Your will can direct that your executor use a lawyer's services for court appearances, filings, and other technical matters requiring legal expertise. The lawyer handles all the court appearances and filings while the executor provides information and input. Estate fees paid to the lawyer may be set by law (some states specify an hourly rate, some a fee based on a percentage of the estate).

If you run a business, or are self-employed, consider making someone knowledgeable in your field your executor or coexecutor. Sometimes the specialized knowledge of accounting or tax laws applicable to your area of business is easier for a colleague than for your spouse or another family member to master.

Take the example of a self-employed writer. Even in a profession notorious for its practitioners' lack of business acumen, certain specialized knowledge is often required. Some tasks must still continue after the writer is dead: recording copyrights, negotiating contracts for reissues of previously published material, deciding which publisher should (and equally important, should not) get rights to reprint articles, determining which works should be completed by others, figuring out television and

▶ **HIRING A LAWYER**

What lawyer should the executor hire to help with probate? It's critical to find a lawyer who's competent in estate law, preferably in the probate court that's handling your will. Your executor may be tempted to use your regular lawyer, or a friend or relative who is a lawyer. But if that lawyer primarily handles business transactions, say, or practices in another state, he or she may not be familiar enough with estate law in your area to handle the job efficiently.

movie rights, deciding what happens to manuscripts, letters, and other unpublished material (perhaps a university or library or historical society would be interested in them).

In short, there are many specialized decisions to be made if you own your own business. Would your executor know how to handle them? If not, appoint a coexecutor who does or authorize your executor to employ the necessary experts.

Whoever you choose, be sure to provide in your will for a replacement executor in case the original executor dies or is unwilling to act. Otherwise, the court will have to choose someone.

What if you also have a living trust? It's generally preferable to name the same person as the executor and the trustee or successor trustee (see chapter 27). If you don't want to do this, discuss your reasons with your lawyer. After hearing about the difficulties splitting these jobs among different people might cause, you may change your mind.

GIVING THE EXECUTOR MORE POWERS

The law defines, and sometimes restricts, the powers of an executor. For this reason, it's often a good idea to specify in your will that your executor will have certain powers beyond those normally granted by state law. What powers should you give the executor? It depends on how much you trust your executor, how much expertise he or she has in legal and financial matters, your state's law, and what your estate consists of. Many lawyers put some or all of the following powers into the boilerplate language of the wills they write for their clients:

• *Power to hire professional help.* You can state, in your will or final-instructions letter, that you expect your executor to appoint a competent attorney and other appropriate counselors to speed the process of settling your estate. Besides taking the burden off your executor (especially important if it's your spouse) and bringing expertise to your estate administration, it will also forestall any second-guessing or complaints by relatives or beneficiaries about the money spent on hiring a lawyer or accountant.

• *Power to retain certain kinds of property in the estate.* This is necessary because the state law may mandate that certain kinds of property be sold (e.g., "unproductive assets," which might be interpreted to include, say, the family forest preserve).

• *Power to continue running your business.* The executor can keep your business operating until a new chief executive is chosen, unless you want it liquidated.

• *Power to mortgage, lease, buy, and sell real estate.* This ability is often limited by law, if not otherwise specified in the will.

• *Power to borrow money.* The executor can arrange for loans to the estate, usually to pay its debts.

• *Power to take advantage of tax savings.* The executor can accomplish this by exercising the various options permissible in tax law, such as filing a joint tax return with your surviving spouse.

EXECUTOR'S COMMISSIONS

In most states, an executor who is also a lawyer cannot receive both an attorney's fee and an executor's commission. In such cases, it's often to your advantage to use an attorney as executor;

( ) TALKING TO A LAWYER

Q. Do executors have to be bonded? Is this expensive? Can it be avoided?

A. Bonding requirements vary from state to state, but all states require some type of bond unless your will directs the probate court to waive it. The purpose of the bond is to protect the estate and the heirs if your executor decides to run off with the assets of the estate. If this should happen, the bonding company would reimburse the estate and then pursue the executor for restitution. A bond, however, can be expensive, running into the thousands of dollars for a large estate.

If you trust your executor, or if your executor is a beneficiary of a significant portion of the estate (and has no interest in stealing from it), you should consider stating in your will that you are waiving the bond requirement. Even if you neglect to waive the bond in your will, your heirs can still join together and request the court to waive the bond if they trust your executor. The court may still require a bond, but it will be an inexpensive "nominal bond" that only guarantees that the state will receive its probate fees and inheritance taxes.

—Answer by Harold Pskowski,
BNA Tax Management, Washington, D.C.

otherwise, if your nonlawyer executor must hire an attorney, your estate may pay both the executor's commission and the attorney's fee. Many attorneys will waive their executor's commission and take only the attorney's fee.

You can agree with your executor (either in a contract or by will) to fix an executor's fee that's different from (and usually lower than) the one imposed by the state.

RESPONSIBILITIES OF THE EXECUTOR

- Guiding the will through probate to legal acceptance of its validity, including defending it against will contests

- Collecting the assets of the dead person

- Transferring legacies and gifts to the beneficiaries

- Evaluating and paying claims against the estate, especially bills and taxes

- Raising money to pay these claims, often by selling estate assets

- Preparing and filing a budget and accounting for the court

THE WORLD AT YOUR FINGERTIPS

- An online brochure and useful links can be found at the site of the Federal Citizen Information Center, www.pueblo.gsa. gov/cic_text/money/executor/executor.htm.

- Personal finance sites often have good information, too. Try out www.moneycentral.msn.com/articles/retire/estate/1232.asp on the MSN site.

YOU MUST REMEMBER THIS

- Choosing the executor of your will is one of the single most important decisions you can make in your estate plan.

- There's no simple formula for picking an executor—it all depends on the nature of your estate, your family situation, and other factors mentioned in this chapter.

- The main thing to remember is to have some idea of potential executors and the pros and cons of each when you meet with your lawyer to plan your estate.

CHAPTER 27

Trustees

You Can Choose a Person or a Company to Get the Job Done

If you have a living trust, you'll probably name yourself trustee. But what about other kinds of trusts? The Rockefellers and other millionaires probably have big institutions as trustees. The little guy in the top hat in the Monopoly game probably has them, too. But what about you? If you have a trust, who should your trustee be?

If you have a will, and it leaves assets to a trust upon your death, the executor will transfer those assets to the trustee for distribution to the beneficiaries or for continued management. While an executor's duties can be onerous, at least they're over within at most a few years. A trustee's duties can continue for generations.

⚠ WHAT IF THE TRUSTEE BLUNDERS?

A trust is a binding legal contract, so the trustee—whether a bank or a relative—has a legal obligation to follow your instructions and to manage the trust funds in a reasonable and prudent manner. If the trustee mismanages the funds, any beneficiary can demand an accounting of how the money in the trust has been spent. If any beneficiary doesn't think the trustee acted reasonably, he or she can sue for reimbursement of any ill-gotten proceeds or improper losses, and have the trustee removed from that position. However, the beneficiary will have to show more than, say, that stocks the trustee bought lost money. The dissatisfied beneficiary has to show that investing in those stocks was unreasonable at the time.

And they require expertise in collecting estate assets, paying taxes, protecting assets, investing money, paying bills, filing accountings (quarterly or annual), and managing money for beneficiaries.

There's also a human side to the relationship. The trustee consults with your beneficiaries about the size of the checks that are issued periodically, what expenses will be paid, and what withdrawals against principal will be permitted.

A trustee's powers can vary greatly, depending on how your trust is worded. In general, it's a good idea to give wide latitude to the trustee, because the economy changes so quickly. And because the law may limit what kinds of investments a trustee can make, you may have to spell out these powers in the trust agreement.

WHO SHOULD BE YOUR TRUSTEE

The biggest decision to make in designating a trustee is whether to use a family member or a professional. Most, though not all, of the following discussion applies primarily to trusts other than living trusts; those are discussed separately at the end of this chapter.

Many people setting up a trust prefer to make decisions about trustees themselves, if for no other reason than to preserve their privacy. An alternative that makes a lot of sense, though, is to allow everyone in the family to see the fee schedule and other records of any professional trustee you're considering hiring so that together you can make an informed decision about who will make the best trustee. If the beneficiaries are old enough, they could be involved as well. After all, when the creator of the trust is enjoying eternal rest, they're the ones who'll have to live with this decision.

Family members as trustees: pros and cons

Many people choose family members to serve as trustees. They usually don't charge a fee, and they generally have a personal stake in the trust's success. If a family member is competent to handle the financial matters involved, has the time and interest to do so, and you're not afraid of family conflicts if one relative is named trustee, using that person can be a good move for a small to medium-sized trust. If you do make a relative a trustee, be sure to consider who the successor will be in the event of death, incapacity, divorce, or other family strife.

Here's the downside to choosing family members.

• *Lack of expertise.* Relatives often lack the financial acumen of professional trust officers, and so they must often hire professional help.

• *Mortality.* Trusts can last for many years. Human trustees die; banks don't. And if your bank merges with another, the new company automatically will succeed to the former one's trust operations.

• *Family conflicts.* Depending on their relationship with the beneficiary, family trustees may have problems with what the beneficiary wants and what's best for him or her. Sibling rivalries may also complicate arrangements in which one brother or sister serves as trustee for others. A professional manager doesn't face such pressures.

Institutional trustees: pros and cons

A good rule of thumb: If the trust assets amount to more than a few hundred thousand dollars or involve any complicated problems, you at least should explore the option of using a professional trustee—a bank, a trust company, or a lawyer.

Banks and trust companies are permanent institutions that can manage your trust for decades. They also have professional knowledge of and experience with investment options. They're objective and regulated by law. If you question the honesty or reliability of friends or family members, a bank is the better option. It can also handle the investments, tax preparation, management, and accounting. Because institutions are immortal (in a legal sense), one is usually designated the ultimate successor trustee after the first (human) trustee dies.

The disadvantages?

- *Cost.* If you do use a bank or trust company to manage the assets, expect to pay a fee for those services. These institutions sometimes have a minimum fee that makes them costly for a small trust. Ask your trust company for its schedule of fees or discuss its fee structure with a trust officer. Find out what services are included and those for which additional fees are charged, including a termination fee. Fees are deductible for income tax purposes, to the extent the income is taxable to the trust or beneficiaries.

- *Conservatism.* Bank investments are generally conservative, with all the advantages and disadvantages that implies. While you, the trust creator, can program the kind of investment strategy you want the professional trustee to follow, that can cause problems because of changed circumstances after your death. For example, investing in tech stocks and dot-coms was a great idea in the 1990s—but a prescription for disaster a few years later.

- *Impersonality.* While a bank probably won't die, that doesn't mean your beneficiaries will always be dealing with the same person there; personnel move around, or move on. As depositors in many banks have learned, the bank itself can change hands. And your beneficiaries will want someone who's willing and able to listen to and discuss their needs and questions; impersonal institutions are sometimes weak in these interpersonal areas. On the other hand, when squabbling relatives are involved, impersonality can be a boon.

 THE BEST OF BOTH WORLDS?

An increasingly popular middle course between naming an institutional trustee and naming a family member is choosing a relative as trustee and hiring a bank or investment company as an independent adviser, rather than naming it as cotrustee. The fees for investment advice may be smaller than the fees it charges to serve as trustee.

If you do choose an institutional trustee, make sure you and your beneficiaries are comfortable with the people with whom they'll be dealing.

YOUR LAWYER CAN HELP YOU CHOOSE

When the time comes to choose an institutional trustee, cotrustee, or investment adviser, your lawyer may be able to give you some names of such companies, and may be willing to accompany you as you make the rounds, asking the trust officer the hard questions: What are all the possible fees you might charge? What is your record of rate of return on trust investments? What is the mechanism for changing the successor trustee? What happens if the person assigned to your trust account leaves the bank or trust company? What if the beneficiary needs emergency cash from the trust? You may be able to judge how responsive the company will be to your beneficiaries by their responses to such questions.

Banks and large financial institutions intimidate a lot of people, but since you're putting a lot of money in their care, you have a right to demand good service. Your lawyer should help you obtain it. Remember, doing the hard work now will save your children or other beneficiaries much grief later.

USING A LAWYER AS TRUSTEE

If you pick a lawyer to serve as trustee, he or she may charge a trustee's fee at the usual hourly rate for legal services, which may prove either less or more expensive than a bank's fee.

Another alternative is to have the lawyer serve as one of the cotrustees, perhaps with the role of preparing tax returns and providing advice on how to minimize taxes. Or perhaps the attorney for the trustees can handle the tax problems without being a cotrustee. Be aware that fiduciary tax returns can be complicated, and the IRS likes to scrutinize them.

SPLITTING THE DIFFERENCE: COTRUSTEES

It's possible to split the job among several persons, professional and nonprofessional. You might pick someone who's good with investments, another who knows taxes, and a third who can talk to the beneficiaries.

You (the trust creator) can decide how the multiple trustees will make decisions. Be sure to establish some mechanism for resolving disputes. Obviously, too many cooks can spoil the broth, and you shouldn't make someone a trustee just to keep him or her from feeling left out. Make sure he or she can be useful.

Any cotrustees should be familiar with the nuances of this particular trust. Also, they should be sensitive to present or potential conflicts between family members.

If you designate a family member as cotrustee, be sure to designate another family member as successor cotrustee to take over after the original family member cotrustee dies or becomes incapacitated.

A warning: The IRS prohibits using family members (especially spouses) as cotrustees in some tax-saving trusts, and using your spouse as trustee could destroy the tax benefits. That's why you should be sure to have a lawyer's advice in naming a trustee. Even if the IRS does not prohibit family members from serving as trustees or cotrustees, it may still be advisable not to have family members serve in those roles.

REMOVING A TRUSTEE

Some grantors write in a procedure for removing a trustee if the beneficiaries should become dissatisfied, but that could let irresponsible beneficiaries circumvent your wish to have the funds invested and maintained in a responsible manner. Such decisions depend on your confidence in the trustee and the beneficiaries.

(i) SHOULD THE TRUST CREATOR OR A BENEFICIARY BE A TRUSTEE?

The creator of a revocable trust may serve as trustee, but the grantor of an irrevocable trust should rarely be a trustee as well. (An exception: the trustee of a **grantor retained annuity trust [GRAT]** may be and usually is the grantor.) Not only will you almost always risk losing the tax benefits, you're also inviting IRS scrutiny. If you want that personal touch, use your spouse, a partner, or a close friend.

Should the trustee be a beneficiary? It depends. A beneficiary who is also a trustee may be liable for estate taxes, unless the trust is set up to avoid this. A key issue is whether to give beneficiaries who are also trustees the authority to make discretionary payments to themselves out of the trust principal or income. (Some states automatically disallow this power.) Such arrangements may limit the freedom to invest or pay out the trust principal. Generally, beneficiaries who are also trustees can only pay themselves principal under an ascertainable standard of support for health, maintenance, and education.

This may be a good situation for cotrustees: one could be a beneficiary, whose powers are limited to what the tax law allows; the other could be a disinterested trustee, maybe an institution, that can make decisions about investments and disbursements without jeopardizing tax advantages.

Some states don't allow the sole beneficiary of a trust to be its sole trustee. Check with a lawyer before making a beneficiary a trustee.

Also, if you make it too easy for yourself (the grantor) or the beneficiaries to fire the trustee of an irrevocable trust, you might endanger the trust's tax advantages, depending on how the replacement process is handled and what type of trust is involved. The key is whether the new trustee seems subordinate to the grantor and the beneficiaries. The IRS might think that the grantor or the beneficiaries never really intended to give up control of the funds, but wanted instead to fire and hire trustees until one did it the way the real power behind the trust wanted. Solution? Limit the appointment of substitute trustees to people who are independent, or give the power of substitution to another person. And remember that removing a trustee can spark a legal fight, or at least a potentially expensive accounting, and can also trigger termination fees and charges.

TRUSTEES AND LIVING TRUSTS

Choosing a trustee for a living trust

Living trusts are frequently created for disability planning, for probate avoidance, and for property management. The creator is usually named the trustee. If it's a joint marital living trust, both spouses are frequently cotrustees; when one spouse dies or becomes unable to act, the other becomes sole trustee. If the married couple has a separate trust for each spouse, the spouses may be cotrustees with each other; in that case, the nondisabled or surviving spouse becomes sole trustee of both trusts upon the death or incapacitation of the other.

If you depart from this pattern, you need to check with your lawyer. For example, naming a third party as trustee could complicate things by requiring the keeping of separate trust and tax records and controlling the trustee's discretion. At the same time, don't feel as though you must be the trustee; you can designate a relative or a friend with more time or knowledge than you, and you can always change your mind later.

Revocable living trusts are not used for tax avoidance, and the tax-reporting requirements are greatly simplified if the trust grantor also is the trustee. However, if having tax-saving features is a goal, the living trust should be *irrevocable* and, of course, contain appropriate tax-planning language. If you are using the living trust primarily to avoid taxes, you generally should not make yourself the trustee. Instead, you may want to make the beneficiary the trustee or designate an independent trustee.

(i) AUTHORITY TO ACT

If the successor is required merely to transfer property to the beneficiaries, a copy of the original trust agreement and the death certificate of the original trustee should be sufficient for banks, stockbrokers, government agencies, and other entities that control the assets to enable them to be transferred to the successor or beneficiaries entitled to receive them. Sometimes, especially when real estate is involved, the successor trustee will have to sign over deeds transferring property from the living trust to the beneficiaries.

Choosing successor trustees

When you create the living trust, you should designate a successor trustee in addition to naming yourself trustee. Depending on the trust, the successor trustee distributes the trust assets to your beneficiaries after you die or continues to administer the trust for one or more generations. He or she could also take over management of the trust if you become incapacitated.

Whom should you choose? The successor trustee may be the primary beneficiary of the trust, someone who has the incentive to handle the transfers promptly and efficiently. However, it can be anyone you trust: a close friend, an adult child, your spouse, your lawyer, an accountant, or a corporate trustee.

You have to specify the successor's powers, which normally will be broadly phrased: the ability to transfer assets to people or institutions, to pay debts and taxes, and to spend trust principal for maintenance, education, support, and health. Be sure to get a lawyer's advice if you feel the need to control the powers of the successor trustee or the beneficiaries. Your lawyer can help write into the agreement special rules that will carry out your wishes.

▶ **CLOSE TO HOME?**

A successor doesn't have to live in the same state that you do, but it's usually more convenient if he or she does. You should take into account the amount of time and effort the successor will have to expend and his or her ability to perform the duties of the trustee and to deal with the beneficiaries.

In any event, don't forget to name an alternate successor trustee in case your first choice predeceases you or otherwise is unwilling or unable to serve.

SPECIAL CIRCUMSTANCES

In some cases, you will want the successor trustee to have special expertise, or at least the ability to hire professional help. For example, if any of your beneficiaries are minors or disabled, or if the trust is to continue, the successor will have to manage the trust property until the beneficiaries reach the ages at which you specified the property would be distributed to them or to their **remaindermen** (i.e., people who have a future interest in the trust). This may involve the successor in preparing tax returns, investing funds, and so on.

How about naming co–successor trustees? The discussion in the previous paragraph can give some guidance here. When children are beneficiaries of the living trust, parents often choose to make them all equal co-beneficiaries, and therefore it makes sense to name them co–successor trustees as well. However, if you fear the children may fail to agree, this can be a bad idea. You may have to choose one child as trustee, or put in a mechanism (such as arbitration) for resolving conflicts between

▶ **YOUR CHILDREN AS COTRUSTEES OF THEIR TRUSTS**

If you establish continuing trusts for your children, you may want to consider giving them the right to serve as cotrustees of their trusts if certain conditions have been met. This will enable them to become accustomed to the responsibilities of managing assets.

co-successors. In any case, be sure to have a lawyer advise you if you fear such conflicts.

Conflicts or the size or complexity of the trust frequently make an independent trustee, such as a lawyer or a trust company, necessary. Since no individual can be certain to serve for the duration of the trust, a trust company always should be designated as the ultimate successor trustee. Otherwise, an expensive court proceeding may be necessary to appoint a successor.

DUTIES OF THE SUCCESSOR TRUSTEE

Usually, the successor trustee will be taking over from the creator of the trust, who may be the original trustee. Therefore, some of the duties are similar to those of an executor. Those duties will vary depending on the nature of the trust property and also, of course, on whether the original trustee has died or become disabled. A successor trustee will need to do the following:

- **Know the contents of the trust agreement, which should spell out specific duties and instructions.**

- **Obtain a medical opinion confirming the original trustee's incapacity (if he or she has become disabled), or obtain a certified copy of the death certificate if the original trustee has died. The latter can be obtained from the funeral home.**

- Notify the lawyer who prepared the trust of the original trustee's death or incapacity, and explain that he or she is now the trustee.

- Inform any banks holding trust assets that he or she is now the trustee.

- Notify all entities that control pensions, insurance, or government benefits that the original trustee has died.

- Tell the family that he or she is the successor trustee.

- Send copies of the trust agreement to the beneficiaries.

- Inventory the trust property. (The successor trustee will need a list of the property, keys to any safe-deposit boxes, dwellings, businesses, or storage areas, and the like.)

- Take care of business transactions as needed if the original trustee has become incapacitated.

- Collect and pay all bills and taxes.

- Keep accounts of money paid out and income received.

- Hire a lawyer or an accountant to prepare any tax returns, if necessary.

- Distribute the property to beneficiaries in the order indicated in the trust agreement and get receipts.

- Make a final accounting record and send copies to the beneficiaries.

TALKING TO A LAWYER

Q. I'm confused about what trustees do. Is there anything like a job description?

A. With a living trust, think of three potential circumstances. First, you are alive and well. Second, you are no longer able to take care of your financial affairs. This is known as disability planning. Third, you have passed away. If you establish a living trust, you can be your own trustee. You could then appoint **disability trustees** in the event of disability and **death trustees** who will serve upon your death. Your trustees will handle your financial matters in accordance with the instructions set out in your trust.

Think of everything that you do to manage your financial affairs. Your trustees are your financial managers and will be responsible for doing all that you do to protect your financial interests.

—Answer by Lena Barnett,
Attorney-at-Law, Silver Spring, Maryland

Q. In general, what should be the balance between family member trustees and professional trustees?

A. Some of my clients choose a combination of family members and professional trustees. This way the family members know the personal side of the beneficiaries while the professional trustees are aware of the legal, financial, and technical sides of serving as trustee. These days, a professional trustee can be an institutional trustee or a CPA or an attorney.

Other clients work this combination in a different fashion. They may have family members selected as trustees with instructions that such family members must seek professional assistance.

Sometimes the trust specifies that a beneficiary, such as a particular family member, serve as one of the trustees, but that his or her role be limited to certain tasks, such as investment decisions and selecting the professional trustee from a somewhat-restricted group noted in the trust.

In all cases, it is important to have a line of backup trustees in case a trustee dies, resigns, or goes out of business.

Also, if a trustee, professional or otherwise, is not performing, the beneficiaries can remove him or her but must replace the bad trustee with someone or some institution that is listed in the trust or that meets certain requirements that have been spelled out in the trust.

—Answer by Lena Barnett,
Attorney-at-Law, Silver Spring, Maryland

Q. *I'm the trustee for my brother's living trust. Can I distribute assets immediately to the beneficiaries, or do I have to wait?*

A. That depends upon the terms of the trust. A well-drafted trust should provide you with specific guidelines for making distributions to the beneficiaries. If you became the trustee as the result of your brother's death, the trust may provide that you are to distribute the assets within a reasonable period after his death. But before you do so, you should be certain that all debts and taxes have been paid. The trust may provide that it is responsible for your brother's death taxes; if so, you should not make any distribution until his estate has received closing letters from the IRS and state tax authorities verifying that all taxes have been accounted for. If you distribute the trust to the beneficiaries before all the taxes have been paid, you could end up being responsible for those taxes out of your own pocket.

—Answer by Harold Pskowski,
BNA Tax Management, Washington, D.C.

THE WORLD AT YOUR FINGERTIPS

- *How to Settle an Estate: A Manual for Executors and Trustees,* 3rd edition, by Charles K. Plotnick and Stephan R. Leimberg (Plume, 2002), is a practical guide to the duties of a trustee.

- *The Truth About Trusts: A Trustee's Survival Guide,* by Jack W. Everett (FTPC Publishing, 1999), *How to Settle Your Living Trust,* by Henry W. Abts (McGraw-Hill, 1999), *Executor and Trustee Survival Guide,* by Douglas D. Wilson (Fiduciary Publishing, 2001), and *Your Trustee Duties,* Tax Guide 305 (Series 300, Retirees and Estates), by Holmes F. Crouch (Allyear Tax Guides, 1998), are also recommended.

YOU MUST REMEMBER THIS

- The decision about whom to name as trustee (and successor trustee) is one of the most important estate-planning choices you can make.

- More than most such decisions, the choice of trustee depends on individual circumstances, such as the nature and size of your estate, your family circumstances, and so on.

- Be sure to involve your family and your lawyer, and be sure you—and they—are comfortable with whomever you choose.

CHAPTER 28

Probate

A Quick Primer on How It's Done

We all know about traffic court and criminal court and small-claims court. But no one does TV shows about probate court. What is this institution that most of us can live without but not die without?

Probate is the court-supervised legal procedure that determines the validity of your will.

As a verb, "probate" is also used to mean the process of settling an estate (e.g., "probating the estate"). In this sense, probate is the process by which assets are gathered, applied to pay debts, taxes, and expenses of administration, and distributed to those designated as beneficiaries in the will. The purpose of probate, put bluntly, is to take the ownership of your assets out of your dead hands and put them into those of a living person or institution.

Even more than most law, probate law varies by state—but which state's law applies? If you have a second home, or a winter home, your will will be probated in the state of your primary residence. But any real estate you own in another state must go through probate in that state, unless it's jointly owned or held in a trust. If it is jointly owned, the property passes immediately to the co-owner, avoiding probate entirely. Since real property must go through probate in the state in which it's located (even if the owner didn't live in that state), you should make sure your will meets the requirements of that state. If it doesn't, the real estate may pass as though you'd died without a will.

PROBATE: TO AVOID OR NOT TO AVOID

The first probate-related question you have to decide is whether to try to avoid probate. For years, a nonfiction book entitled *How*

KINDS OF PROBATE

• *Supervised.* This is the most formal and expensive method. The court plays an active role in approving each transaction. In states where it's optional, supervised administration is used for contested estates, when an interested party requests it, or when the executor's ability is questioned.

• *Unsupervised or independent.* This is a simpler, cheaper method in which the number of duties and procedures is reduced and the court's role is diminished or eliminated. It's used for estates that exceed the asset limit for small-estate administration but don't require heavy court supervision. It often requires consent of all beneficiaries, unless the will specifically requests unsupervised administration.

• *Small-estate.* This is the simplest and fastest form of probate, but it's not available in every state. Small estates range in value from $1,000 to $100,000, depending on state law. In this type of administration, property is often transferred by affidavit. Small-estate administration often lasts only a few weeks.

to Avoid Probate was a big seller. But the need to avoid probate has been lessened in recent years as simplified procedures (such as independent executor provisions) in some states have reduced or eliminated many of the hassles and charges. Though delays are possible, the average estate completes the probate process in six to nine months, depending on state law. And the reformed probate procedures in many states now make it possible for your spouse, minor children, and disabled children to obtain the money they need to live on almost immediately, without waiting for the entire estate to clear probate.

For some people—such as those who own considerable property in states other than the one in which they reside, or those who need rapid administration of their assets (such as stock speculators or people who own businesses in volatile markets), or those who live abroad, and some others—probate avoidance should be the primary goal of their estate plan. They might be well advised to put their property into a living trust. But for many other families, especially those of moderate means, it actually can be more trouble to avoid probate than to go through it.

Despite its sometimes cumbersome nature, probate does help assure that those—and only those—entitled to receive part of your estate do so, even if it takes them a year to get their shares. It reduces the time for creditors to present claims against the estate. It is a public proceeding, but how many of us are really worried about someone going through our estate records? Probate privacy, though highly touted by living-trust salespeople, is usually the concern of celebrities and the ultrarich, not the rest of us.

If you do intend to save money by avoiding probate, be sure to use one of the methods outlined in this book. That probably means seeing a lawyer. Don't make the mistake so many people eager to avoid probate have made: using a one-size-fits-all-estates form from a book or a computer program that doesn't take into account all your estate-planning needs (such as providing for your family) and the peculiarities of your individual situation.

And please understand that you can't avoid probate by not having a will. Even if you don't write a will (i.e., if you die intes-

---

▶ **BE A WISE CONSUMER**

For most people, the complexity of the probate procedures of the state they live in is probably the single most important factor in deciding whether to use probate-avoidance techniques. Ask your lawyer to advise you about the probate system in your state (and in any other state in which you may own property) and whether probate avoidance should be one of your principal estate-planning goals.

tate), you'll still have one—the one the state writes for you. The court will appoint a personal representative—the administrator. The administrator's job is essentially the same as the executor's; the only difference is that he or she is appointed by the court instead of being selected by you in your will. Probate will take place, but it will cost more and take more time because you didn't leave a will.

▶ HOW TO SAVE MONEY IN PROBATE

For most people, it's seldom necessary to use a lawyer as the executor. Instead, the preferred course is to allow a nonlawyer executor (usually but not always a family member) to do most of the work, which is gathering information and records. The family member files the required forms, calculates and pays the taxes, and distributes the estate assets. If the family member has any questions, he or she can consult a lawyer. He or she may also pay the lawyer to review final documents for legal accuracy or to do a few specific tasks that a lawyer can do best.

For some estates, this will take no more than a few hours of a lawyer's time. It's the best way to save money in probate, but it does mean a trade-off for the executor: his or her time for your estate's money. Only you and your executor can decide whether the trade-off is worth it under the circumstances.

To save time for your executor, prepare your own inventory before you die. After you die, your executor (if he or she is a family member who's waived a fee) can do as much of the work as possible, such as preparing an updated inventory and notifying creditors.

If you live in a state that assesses probate fees based on the value of the estate, it may be to your advantage to get property out of your estate by using a living trust, joint tenancy, gifts, and so on. This, along with getting your own financial affairs in order before you die, will also reduce the billable hours an attorney for the estate will have to charge.

Probate isn't all bad, but if you can minimize the court's involvement, you should, especially if you live in a state that doesn't have alternative or simplified procedures, or if your estate doesn't qualify for them. Probate-avoidance tools include living trusts, joint tenancy, and life insurance. Using these techniques, most of your assets will be distributed outside the probate process. Even though you still need a will, it will likely be so simple and dispose of so little property that the cost and time it takes to see it through probate will be minimal.

One potential probate-related problem worth worrying about is the freezing of assets that automatically occurs in some states when a person dies and his estate goes into probate. Even jointly held bank accounts are sometimes frozen until state tax authorities can assess their value. Some state laws allow the spouse to receive some or all of the funds within a few days of death, but some do not. There is a lesson here: When planning your estate, find out your state's law, and make sure your survivors have some freeze-proof method of getting hold of money during whatever the period of delay is in your state.

THE ESTATE ADMINISTRATION PROCESS—STEP BY STEP

Let's assume that probate is the best choice for your estate, or at least unavoidable. Now that you've designated your executor, here's a general outline of what she'll face after you die.

Step 1: Opening the estate

If you left a will, your executor's first job is to submit the original copy to the probate court having jurisdiction; that would be the court in the county where you lived. In some states, it may be necessary to prove, in a brief hearing, that the will is valid. This is usually routine, but if there is a will contest—that is, someone disputes that your will is valid, or that this is your last will—or if there are complications, a lawyer's help definitely will be needed. In many states, the probate court may require you to have a lawyer for courtroom appearances.

To "open the estate," the executor completes certain forms that notify the court and interested parties of your death. At this stage, depending on state law, the executor may have to choose among several types of probate: supervised, unsupervised, and small-estate. This decision is important, and it may be a good idea to get your lawyer's analyses of the pros and cons of each.

Step 2: Collecting the estate's assets

The next step is to inventory the assets of the estate. If you've already prepared the inventory described in chapter 2, your executor will be quite grateful—and if he or she is being paid, your estate might save a lot of his or her time and your money. A lawyer might be helpful in differentiating the property that passes through probate from the property that is out of the probate process (see chapters 3–5 for information on property that's transferred without a will).

For assets that do pass through probate (assuming they are held in sole ownership), the value of stocks and bonds depends on their value on the date of death. The same is true of bank balances. The value of other forms of property, such as real estate, antiques, collections, and art objects, may have to be set by professional appraisers.

Step 3: Managing the estate's assets

If you owned a business, income-producing real estate, or an active portfolio of stocks and bonds, your executor might well have to take on the responsibility of managing this property. That's why it's a good idea to specify in a will that the executor has the authority to retain certain kinds of property in the estate, continue running the business, buy or sell real estate, borrow money, and take advantage of tax savings. All of these decisions may have significant legal dimensions, and the executor may benefit from legal help.

(i) PROPERTY THAT AVOIDS PROBATE

Not all property needs to go through probate. Here's a partial list of things that don't.

- Property in a trust
- Property that's jointly held (but not community property)
- Death benefits from insurance policies, the government, and employers and other benefits controlled by contract
- Property given away by gift before you die
- Money in a pay-on-death account
- Retirement accounts with a named beneficiary
- Transfer-on-death beneficiary deeds
- Deeds with reserved life estates

Step 4: Handling taxes

Your executor must notify the IRS of his or her appointment by sending in a form and applying for a separate taxpayer ID number for the estate. The executor must file a form to pay the federal estate tax for estates whose value exceeds the threshold (see chapter 20). There may also be state estate taxes to pay, sometimes even on smaller estates. On the federal estate tax return, there is a credit for state death taxes. That credit, which is scheduled to expire in 2005, is paid directly to the state (the so-called pick-up tax).

The executor must also file some income tax returns. A personal return covers income the deceased person earned in the tax period before dying. This final income tax return (Form 1040) is due by April 15 of the year after the year of death, unless the executor obtains an extension. A return for the estate covers income earned by the estate while it is being administered, such as through dividends, royalties, income from the sale of property, and so on. Taxes may have to be paid before money and other assets can be distributed to the beneficiaries. The executor has many decisions to make regarding how and when to pay taxes, a number of which could significantly affect the amount of taxes that are due.

Step 5: Closing the estate

This process could vary from state to state, but generally it involves filing various forms with the court. These forms require the executor to show that all interested parties—including creditors—received timely notice of the death, that the time period in which claims can be filed against the estate (specified by state law) has passed, and that all valid claims (including taxes) were paid. A final accounting—the totaling up of all the estate's assets, minus expenses—will also be required. The final accounting will also indicate the amounts to be distributed to beneficiaries.

Step 6: Distributing the assets

Again, state laws may vary on details, but the general pattern is that all the assets are not paid out to beneficiaries until the court has approved the executor's filings regarding assets, claims, taxes, and so on. In many states, a portion of the assets can be paid out by way of partial distributions before the final stages. This helps minimize financial hardship for the family.

TEN FACTORS THAT REDUCE THE COST OF PROBATE

The more you answer "yes" to these questions, the less probate should cost.

1. Has the estate been planned as recommended in this book?

2. Is the will up-to-date, properly prepared (see the sample will in Appendix B) with bequests made in a clear, simple, and predictable manner, and self-proving?

⚠ **POSSIBLE PITFALLS**

Administering estates can be routine, but thorny legal issues may arise. They can take many forms, besides those specified in this chapter:

- Bonding requirements for the executor (have they been waived in the will?).

- Methods of serving notice of the death and proving that all interested persons received such notice.

- The spouse's right of election. State law generally gives surviving spouses the right to a certain percentage of the estate, despite what the will says (see chapter 14). Therefore, a disinherited spouse may have the right to claim a percentage of assets of the estate. Also, the family homestead is usually shielded from creditors, and that could be an issue in certain estates.

- Out-of-state vacation homes or other real property, which can necessitate ancillary probate.

- Disputes over what certain provisions of the will mean (is it clear which person is to get which property?).

- Discovery of assets (Have they all been located? Has the executor shown proper diligence?).

- Letters of administration for the executor.

- Disputes among beneficiaries.

- Disputes regarding creditors' claims.

When these or other difficulties surface, a lawyer's help can be invaluable.

3. Have you prepared an inventory of all your assets for your executor?

4. Is the fair market value of all the probate assets below $1 million?

5. Is there only one beneficiary of the will?

6. If there is a surviving spouse, are all your children also the children of the surviving spouse?

◖◗ TALKING TO A LAWYER

HOW LONG DOES THE CLOCK RUN?

Q. How long is the period for notifying creditors in most states? How do you notify them? What if one of them files a claim after the period is over?

A. The probate rules of virtually all states require that the executor of an estate publish a notice of her appointment in a local newspaper. The probate court usually assists the executor in doing this. This publication is treated as notice to creditors of the decedent's death and starts the clock ticking on the state's official claim period. Depending upon the state in which the probate occurs, a creditor will have anywhere from three months to a year after the date of publication to file a claim with the estate. Any claim filed after that period of time will be barred.

Some states also require that the executor mail a notice to any creditors of the decedent of which the executor is aware. If you have been appointed executor in such a state, this requires that you go through the decedent's records to find out who may have a claim against the estate, and then mail a claim form to each creditor. This actually offers an extra measure of protection to the estate, because any creditor receiving the mailed notice cannot later claim that he was unaware of the decedent's death and the need to file a claim.

7. If your state has simplified (small-estate or unsupervised) probate procedures, does the fair market value of the estate fall below the ceiling for those procedures?

8. Is the probate estate free of real estate in another state, or a family business?

9. Was the estate plan discussed with the family and other beneficiaries before death?

10. Can the estate debts and taxes be resolved without delay or controversy?

If a creditor files a claim after the end of the claim period, the executor is not required to pay the claim, no matter how meritorious. Some states, however, give the probate court the power to extend the claim period under exceptional circumstances. As a result, the executor should consult the estate's attorney before denying what seems to be a late claim.

Q. *What if one of the beneficiaries thinks that the executor is not diligent or is biased? Can an executor be replaced?*

A. The probate court always has the power to remove the executor, but only under carefully delineated circumstances. If the decedent named the executor in the will, the court will generally respect that decision and, in the words of one court, will remove the executor only under "extreme circumstances." Some of the factors that may be considered by the court are whether the removal would be in the best interest of the estate; whether the executor has misled or disregarded the court; whether the executor is incapable of performing his duties; and whether the executor has mismanaged the estate. As you can see, "bad blood" is not a sufficient reason for replacing the executor; a beneficiary must present objective evidence of malfeasance or neglect before the court will consider removal.

—Answers by Harold Pskowski,
BNA Tax Management, Washington, D.C.

THE WORLD AT YOUR FINGERTIPS

- IRS Publication 559 has tax information for executors and survivors. You can access it online at www.irs.gov/pub/irs-pdf/p559.pdf.

- Insurance company websites often have useful information for executors and family members. For example, www.usaaedfoundation.org/family/coping/cp04/cp04.htm (the USAA site) covers the duties of an executor, the probate process, and suggestions for coping with grief.

- Helpful books that take you through the process include *The Executor's Handbook*, by Theodore E. Hughes and David Klein (Facts on File, 2001), *Probate and Settling an Estate: Step-by-Step*, by James John Jurinski (Barron's, 1997), and *How to Administer an Estate: A Step-by-Step Guide for Families and Friends*, by Stephen G. Christianson, (Career Press, 2001). See chapter 27 for books that will help trustees.

YOU MUST REMEMBER THIS

- For most people, probate isn't nearly the monster that it used to be, so think carefully and consult your lawyer before investing in schemes to avoid it.

- At the same time, you can take steps now to minimize the probate court's involvement in administering your estate so that the process is as quick and painless as possible.

WHERE DO YOU GO FROM HERE?

RESOURCES

Throughout this book, we've given you resources to help you find more information on a variety of topics associated with wills and estates. But we're not done just yet; here are even more resources for you to check out. (Some of these may have been mentioned in previous chapters, but we think they're your best places to start.) Also included are some reminders and tips you can use to go about getting more information. This section is broken up into the following subsections:

Twelve Websites to Get You Started

Elder Law: Aging, Health Care, Guardianship, and Living Wills

A Novel Idea: Read More About It

Don't Forget

Twelve websites to get you started

Some of these websites are housed within larger sites—but they do contain rather lengthy sections on topics associated with wills and estates. You're bound to find what you're looking for at one of these sites, or from one of their links.

The 'Lectric Law Library's Laypeople's Law Lounge: *www.lectlaw.com/lay.html*

Crash Course in Wills and Trusts: *www.mtpalermo.com*

Nolo's Wills and Estate Planning: *www.nolo.com*

FindLaw's Wills, Trusts, Estates, and Probate: *www.findlaw.com/01topics/31probate/index.html*

Cornell's Legal Information Institute's Estate Planning: *www.law.cornell.edu/topics/estate_planning.html*

Cornell's LII's **Estates and Trusts:** *www.law.cornell.edu/ topics/estates_trusts.html*

KinderStart Search Engine (legal and financial information for parents): www.kinderstart.com/ legalandfinancial/willsestatestrusts.html

AARP's Estate Planning: www.aarp.org/estate_planning/

Family Files' Resource Center: www.familyfiles.com/ resource/resource.asp

ABA Real Property, Probate, and Trust Law Section's Information for the Public: www.abanet.org/rppt/public/ home.html

National Association of Financial and Estate Planning: www.nafep.com

OutEstatePlanning.com: www.outestateplanning.com

Elder law: aging, health care, guardianship, and living wills

Some of these sites may also include sections related to the more general aspects of wills and estates, but they are noted here for their particular attention to the subtopic at hand.

National Academy of Elder Law Attorneys: www.naela.com

Elder Web: www.elderweb.com/

Growth House: www.growthhouse.org

Partnership for Caring: www.partnershipforcaring.org

Elder Law Answers: www.elderlawanswers.com

Virtual Law Office: www.virtuallawoffice.com/

Shape Your Health Care Future with Health Care Advance Directives: www.ama-assn.org/public/booklets/ livgwill.htm

Seniors-Site.com: www.seniors-site.com/home/sitemap.html

Deni.net: www.deni.net/care_giving.html

A novel idea: read more about it

While none of the books below is actually a novel, each one makes for informative and valuable reading. Here are a few picks to start with, on a variety of topics having to do with wills and estates. Don't forget to check out what your local library has to offer, in addition to Amazon.com and other online bookstores.

The Complete Idiot's Guide to Wills and Estates, **2nd edition,** *by Stephen M. Maple (Alpha Books, 2002)*

Plan Your Estate, **6th edition,** *by Denis Clifford and Cora Jordan (Nolo Press, 2002)*

Estate Planning for Baby Boomers and Retirees, *by Stewart H. Welch (John Wiley & Sons, 1999)*

J. K. Lasser's New Rules for Estate Planning and Tax, *by Harold Apolinsky and Stewart H. Welch III (John Wiley & Sons, 2001)*

The Elder Law Handbook: A Legal and Financial Survival Guide for Caregivers and Seniors, *by Peter J. Strauss and Nancy M. Lederman (Checkmark Books, 1996)*

Consumer Reports Complete Guide to Health Services for Seniors, *edited by Trudy Lieberman (Three Rivers Press, 2000)*

Don't forget . . .

While websites and books are great places to get information, you might also want to see if any local venues are offering courses, lectures, seminars, or expert panels related to the topic of estate planning. Check with your local library, bar association, colleges, senior citizens' centers, and hospitals (to name just a few) to see if anything is in the works. Your local radio and television stations may provide some salient programming as well.

Don't forget about the countless posting boards, user groups, mailing lists, and chat rooms that exist on the Internet—many of these could help you in your quest for knowledge and/or provide a network of support, depending on the issues you're facing. Communicating with others who have been in your position is a great way of learning about other avenues to explore, and what pitfalls to avoid.

We hope we've provided you with enough information to get you started, and we welcome your comments and suggestions for future editions of this book. Please visit us on the Web at www.abanet.org/publiced/ or drop us a line via e-mail at abapubed@abanet.org.

APPENDIX A

ESTATE-PLANNING CHECKLIST

This initial estate-planning questionnaire is presented in a narrative form. The detailed explanations and the space provided for answers are designed to garner more complete and helpful information than would be afforded by merely filling in blanks.

Your lawyer will use the information you provide in this questionnaire:

1. To help you organize personal and financial information so that you can assess your current estate plans and evaluate whether changes are desired or required.

2. To provide your estate-planning attorney with the information needed to make a similar analysis.

3. To help you evaluate your lawyer's estate-planning recommendations. The estate plan is your plan, not your lawyer's, and you must be satisfied that it is workable.

The information you provide must be as accurate as possible. If you are uncertain about exact information, tell your lawyer that and give your best assessment. If your lawyer believes that exact information is required, he or she will ask you to be more precise. You may provide as much or as little information as you want. We recognize that this questionnaire is a fairly intrusive document. Keep in mind, however, that the more complete the information is, the better equipped you and your lawyer will be throughout the planning process to come up with the best possible estate-planning alternatives. Your information will be kept confidential by your lawyer unless you authorize or request its release to others.

PERSONAL AND FAMILY INFORMATION

State the names requested below exactly as you want them to
appear in your will and other estate-planning documents. Where
the space on the form is insufficient, please use the reverse side.

Your name: _____ Date of birth:_____

Spouse's name: _____ Date of birth:_____

Home Address: _____

Telephone No.: _____ E-mail Address:_____

Are you a United States citizen? _____
   If not, of what country are you a citizen?_____

Is your spouse a citizen of the United States? _____

If not, of what country is he/she a citizen? _____

Your children, their spouses, and their children

Indicate which, if any, of your children is your child but not your
spouse's, or vice versa. Also show the date and place of adoption
of any adopted child. Be sure to include any deceased child and
indicate the date of the child's death and his or her surviving
spouse and children.

1. (a) Child: _____ Date of birth:_____

   (b) Personal data (specify whether the child is from a prior
marriage, adopted, deceased, etc.):

   _____

   _____

   (c) Child's spouse: _____

   (d) Child's children (and their dates of birth):

   _____

   _____

2. (a) Child:_____ Date of birth:_____

(b) Personal data (specify whether the child is from a prior marriage, adopted, deceased, etc.):

_____

_____

(c) Child's spouse:_____

(d) Child's children (and their dates of birth):

_____

_____

3. (a) Child:_____ Date of birth:_____

(b) Personal data (specify whether the child is from a prior marriage, adopted, deceased, etc.):

_____

_____

(c) Child's spouse:_____

(d) Child's children (and their dates of birth):

_____

_____

4. If either you or your spouse has been married previously, state the name of each prior spouse and indicate whether he or she is now living (if living, give his or her address):

_____

_____

If either you or your spouse has been divorced, attach a copy of the divorce decree.

5. Is there other important personal information that might affect your estate plans? For example, does a member of your family have a serious long-term medical or physical problem that will require special care or attention in the future?

PERSONAL AND FAMILY
FINANCIAL ASSETS

The following questions do not require detailed responses. For example, shares in publicly traded companies might be shown simply as common stocks. On the other hand, for property interests that are more or less unique, such as interests in real estate, greater detail will be helpful. With regard to real estate, it is important for your lawyer to know the location (city and state) of the real estate, how the title is held, and the character of the property (e.g., residence, shopping center, apartment house, or similar description).

The following abbreviations may be used to describe certain attributes of particular assets:

JT = Joint tenancy with right of survivorship

TE = Tenancy by the entirety

TC = Tenancy in common

H = Husband's name alone

W = Wife's name alone

LT = Land trust

FMV = Fair market value (or your best estimate)

CV = Cash value of life insurance policy

PV = Proceeds of life insurance policy

1. Personal residence:

   Address: _____

   Description (e.g., single family, condo, or co-op, or similar description): _____

   _____

   How you hold title: _____

   FMV: _____ Mortgage balance, if any: _____
   Mortgage life insurance? _____

2. **Other personal residences or vacation homes:**

   Address: _____

   Description: _____

   _____

   How you hold title: _____

   FMV: _____ Mortgage balance, if any: _____

   Mortgage life insurance? _____

3. **Personal and household effects:** If you think that the general categories do not provide an adequate description, please provide additional detail. Also state your best estimate of the value of each kind of property and who owns it (how you hold title).

   (a) Automobiles:

   _____

   _____

   (b) General personal and household effects such as furniture, furnishings, books, and pictures of no special value:

   _____

   _____

   (c) Valuable jewelry (indicate if insured):

   _____

   _____

   (d) Valuable works of art (indicate if insured):

   _____

   _____

   (e) Valuable antiques (indicate if insured):

   _____

   _____

   (f) Other valuable collections, such as coins, stamps, or gold (indicate if insured):

   _____

   _____

(g) Other tangible personal property that does not seem to be covered by any of the other categories:

_____

_____

4. Cash, cash deposits, and cash equivalents: State the name and address of each bank or institution and who owns each item.

(a) Checking accounts, including money market accounts:

You: _____

Spouse:_____

Jointly with:_____

(b) Ordinary savings accounts:

You: _____

Spouse:_____

Jointly with:_____

(c) Certificates of deposit:

You: _____

Spouse:_____

Jointly with:_____

(d) Short-term U.S. obligations (T-bills):

You: _____

Spouse:_____

Jointly with:_____

5. Pension and profit-sharing plans, 401(k) accounts, IRAs, Roth IRAs, SEP IRAs, SIMPLE IRAs, Keogh plans, ESOPs, or other tax-favored employee benefit plans:

(a) Pension plans:

You:_____ Vested: _____ Current value: _____

Spouse: _____ Vested: _____ Current value: _____

(b) Profit-sharing plans:

You:_____ Vested: _____ Current value: _____

Spouse: _____ Vested: _____ Current value: _____

(c) Individual retirement accounts (IRAs)—specify which type:

You: _____ Current value: _____

Spouse: _____ Current value: _____

You: _____ Current value: _____

Spouse: _____ Current value: _____

You: _____ Current value: _____

Spouse: _____ Current value: _____

_____

(d) 401(k) plans:

You: _____ Current value: _____

Spouse: _____ Current value: _____

(e) **Other tax-qualified employee benefit plan interests. Please provide similar information.**

_____

(f) **Education savings plans, such as prepaid tuition plans, college savings plans, Section 529 plans, and Coverdell Education Savings Accounts. Please provide similar information.**

_____

6. Life insurance on your life:

(a) **Ordinary life insurance: List company name, address, and policy number.**

_____

_____

_____

Face amount of policies (proceeds): _____

If you do not own it, who does? _____

Beneficiaries: _____

Cash value: _____

Loans, if any, against it: _____

Amount of accidental-death benefits, if any: _____

(b) Term/group term insurance: List company name, address, and policy number.

_____

_____

_____

Face amount of policies: _____

Owner other than you: _____

Beneficiaries: _____

Accidental-death benefits, if any:_____

(c) Please supply similar information with respect to other life insurance or other insurance having life insurance features:

_____

_____

_____

7. Life insurance on your spouse's life:

(a) Ordinary life insurance: List company name, address, and policy number.

_____

_____

_____

Face amount of ordinary life insurance:_____

Owner other than spouse: _____

Beneficiaries: _____

Cash value: _____

Loans, if any: _____

Accidental-death benefits, if any:_____

(b) Term/group term insurance: List company name, address, and policy number.

_____

_____

_____

Face amount of term/group term insurance: _____

Owner other than spouse: _____

Beneficiaries: _____

Cash value: _____

Loans, if any: _____

Accidental-death benefits, if any:_____

(c) Other insurance on spouse's life:

_____

_____

_____

_____

8. Closely held business interests: Describe any interest you have in a family or other business with limited shareholders. Include the nature of the business, its form of organization (e.g., corporation, partnership, or the like), whether you are active in its operations, and your estimate of its value. If it is a corporation, please indicate whether an "S election" is in force with respect to the federal taxation of the corporation.

_____

_____

_____

_____

   With respect to any such business, do you believe it would continue to operate successfully in the event of your permanent absence from it or the permanent absence of some other key person?_____

9. Investment assets: With respect to each category, please state the owner (how title is held) and the approximate value.

(a) Publicly traded stocks and corporate bonds:

You: _____

Spouse:_____

Jointly with:_____

(b) Municipal bonds:

You: _____

Spouse:_____

Jointly with:_____

(c) Long-term U.S. Treasury notes and bonds:

You: _____

Spouse:_____

Jointly with:_____

(d) Limited partnership interests:

You: _____

Spouse:_____

Jointly with:_____

(e) Other investments: Please describe the general nature and value of other investment interests.

You: _____

Spouse:_____

Jointly with:_____

Other interests of current or future value

1. Interests in trusts. Describe any trusts created by you, or by any other person, such as a parent or an ancestor, in which you or a member of your immediate family has a right to receive distributions of income or principal, whether or not such distributions are actually being received or anticipated in the future. Be as specific as you can. If possible, submit a copy of the trust agreement. If the trust agreement is not available, show the date the trust was created, whether it can be amended or changed, whether someone has a power of appointment over it, when the trust terminates, and who will receive the trust property upon

termination. Also, state the approximate current value of the trust and the annual income from it.

_____

_____

_____

2. Anticipated inheritances. If you or any other members of your immediate family are likely to receive substantial inheritances in the foreseeable future from persons other than yourself or your spouse, describe your best estimate of the value and the nature of each inheritance.

_____

_____

_____

3. Other assets or interests of value. Describe the general nature, form of ownership, and your estimate of the value of any asset or interest of value that does not seem to fit in any of the categories above.

_____

_____

_____

Liabilities

Describe here substantial financial liabilities not reflected in the asset information you have provided above. If they are secured, indicate the nature of the security. Also show any substantial contingent liabilities, such as personal guarantees you have made on the obligations of a business, a family member, or any other person. Indicate whether you have insured against any of these obligations in the event of your death, or if the obligations do not survive your death.

_____

_____

_____

PERSONAL ESTATE-PLANNING OBJECTIVES

1. How would you dispose of your estate at your death if there were no such thing as estate or inheritance taxes?

_____

_____

_____

2. In the event of your death, would your spouse or children be likely to receive income from sources other than your estate, such as the continuance or resumption by your spouse of his or her vocation or profession?

_____

_____

_____

3. Describe any personal objectives you have for your family and your estate that override possible adverse tax consequences arising from trying to achieve them.

_____

_____

_____

GUARDIANS, EXECUTORS, AND TRUSTEES

1. **Guardians for minor children. If you have minor children, you may designate in your will a guardian or guardians of the person and their estate in the event of your death and/or your spouse's.**

   (a) Guardian of the person.

   Name(s): _____

   Address: _____

(b) Guardian of the estate, if different.

Name(s): _____

Address: _____

(c) Substitute guardian of the person.

Name(s): _____

Address: _____

(d) Substitute guardian of the estate.

Name(s): _____

Address: _____

2. Executor. Your executor has the responsibility to wind up your affairs at your death, see to it that your assets are collected, that claims, expenses, and estate and inheritance taxes are paid, and then distribute your property to trustees or others you have named. It is a task of limited duration, substantial responsibility, and much work.

   (a) Principal executor.

   Name(s): _____

   Address: _____

   (b) Substitute executor.

   Name(s): _____

   Address: _____

3. Trustees. Your trustees are responsible for the long-range management of property that is to be held in trust for the benefit of the beneficiaries of trusts you may create.

   Depending on the terms of the trust, there may be adverse tax consequences if a trustee has an interest or possible interest in the trust, although usually if the trustee's discretion is limited those adverse tax consequences are similarly limited. A trustee can be a corporation (qualified to act) or individual. You may choose to have cotrustees, one of which may or may not be a corporation. Because corporate trustees must charge fees for their services, they may decline to accept small trusts. Their fees to administer a small trust may turn out to be dispro-

portionately large if they are to cover their costs in handling
the trust.

In general, choose a trustee with the following qualities:
integrity, mature judgment, fiscal responsibility, and reasonable
business and investment acumen. If you wish to select
cotrustees, you may want to choose them for how well their
individual strengths complement each other. Frequently, the
same person(s) or corporation selected as executor(s) may be
designated as trustee(s).

(a) Principal trustees.

Names:

_____

_____

_____

Addresses:

_____

_____

_____

(b) Substitute trustees (to act if one or more of the principal
trustees cannot or will not act).

Names:

_____

_____

_____

Addresses:

_____

_____

_____

OTHER MATTERS

1. Other factors. Describe or list here any facts or matters that do not seem to be covered by the other sections of this questionnaire and that you believe may be important for your estate-planning attorney to know.

_____

_____

_____

_____

2. Community property. If you now live in or have lived in one of the states listed below, or if you own real estate in one of these states, please circle the name of the state and indicate whether you and your spouse have entered into any agreement about whether that property is separate property.

States: Alaska, Arizona, California, Idaho, Louisiana, Nevada, New Mexico, Texas, Washington, Wisconsin

3. Powers of attorney. Have you given a power of attorney to your spouse, a child, or any other person authorizing them either to do specific things on your behalf or to act generally on your behalf? If so, please indicate to whom it was given, the nature of the power (specific or general), the date, and the location of the document granting the power.

_____

_____

_____

_____

4. Living will. Have you signed any document indicating your wishes concerning "heroic" or extraordinary measures to save your life in the event of a catastrophic illness or injury? If not, would you like to do so?

_____

5. Health-care power. Have you signed any document specifically authorizing another person such as your spouse to make decisions with respect to your health care in the event that you are unable to do so? If not, would you like to do so?

_____

_____

Date completed: _____

APPENDIX B

SAMPLE BASIC WILL (ANNOTATED)

There is no standard, legally foolproof will. State laws vary, as do the needs of people making wills. This sample is designed to give you an idea of what a will might look like and why certain language is in it.

I, Tess Tatrix, residing at 1 Wilthereza Way, Any Town, Any State, declare this to be my Will, and I revoke any and all wills and codicils I previously made.

[The opening sentence should make it clear that this document is intended to be your will, give your name, place of residence and revoke any previous wills and codicils (amendments to previous wills). This can help your beneficiaries to avoid a court battle if someone should produce an earlier will.]

ARTICLE I: FUNERAL EXPENSES AND PAYMENT OF DEBTS

I direct my executors to pay my enforceable unsecured debts and funeral expenses, the expenses of my last illness, and the expenses of administering my estate.

[By law, debts must be paid before other assets are distributed. This clause gives your executor the authority to pay the funeral home, court costs, and hospital expenses. Using the term "enforceable" prevents creditors from reviving debts that you are no longer obliged to pay, usually those discharged in bankruptcy. And the term "unsecured" prevents a court from interpreting this clause to mean that your estate must pay off your mortgage or other secured debts that you probably don't want to be immediately paid off.

Note: in many states, the executor is required by law to pay enforceable unsecured debts. In these states, this clause is unnecessary and may create problems.]

ARTICLE II: MONEY AND PERSONAL PROPERTY

I give all my tangible personal property and all policies and proceeds of insurance covering such property to my husband, Tex. If he does not survive me, I give that property to those of my children who survive me, in equal shares, to be divided among them by my executors in their absolute discretion after consultation with my children. My executors may pay out of my estate the expenses of delivering tangible personal property to beneficiaries.

[This gives your personal property to your spouse. If there are particular items that you want to go to other people (such as heirlooms, jewelry, professional equipment, and so on) you should enumerate them and the people to whom you want them to go in a separate clause (e.g., "I give my Beatles albums to my friend William Shears"), and note that Article II excludes those items. Some people will use separate clauses for **legacies** (disposition of money) and **bequests** (disposition of tangible personal property).

Note the important clause that accounts for the possibility that your spouse will die first. The clause on insurance means that if some property you owned was destroyed (perhaps in the event that caused your death, like a car wreck), your heirs will receive the insurance proceeds, not the mangled car.]

ARTICLE III: REAL ESTATE

I give all my residences, subject to any mortgages or encumbrances thereon, and all policies and proceeds of insurance covering such property, to my husband, Tex. If he does not survive me, I give that property to _____.

[Most people want their spouse to keep the family home. In some states, particularly community property states, it's sometimes preferable to leave your residence to your spouse in a marital trust.]

ARTICLE IV: RESIDUARY CLAUSE

I give the rest of my estate (called my residuary estate) to my husband, Tex. If he does not survive me, I give my residuary estate to those of my children who survive me, in equal shares, to be divided among them and the descendants of a deceased child of mine, to take their ancestor's share per stirpes.

[Usually, the residuary clause begins "I give all the rest, residue, and remainder of my estate . . ." because lawyers are afraid to change tried-and-true formulas, and for decades, legal documents never used one word when a half-dozen would do. However, this plain-English form will also work. This clause covers any property you own or are entitled to that somehow wasn't covered by the preceding clauses.]

ARTICLE V: TAXES

I direct my executors, without apportionment against any beneficiary or other person, to pay all estate, inheritance, and succession taxes (including any interest and penalties thereon) payable by reason of my death.

[One common mistake made by people who use a living trust as well as a will is to make the beneficiaries of the estate different from the people benefiting from the trust. The same problem exists when there are significant specific gifts and the residuary beneficiaries are different from the recipients of the specific gifts.

In such cases, the people who end up paying the taxes are not those who receive the most property, an arrangement that unfairly can saddle some beneficiaries with the whole tax bill, and at worst can even bankrupt the estate. The goal should be to see that the taxes are paid by those who benefit from gifts. Often, a provision apportioning taxes to taxable transfers is used to make sure that each recipient of a taxable gift pays his or her fair share. Additional language is sometimes used to apportion credits.]

ARTICLE VI: MINORS

If under this will any property shall be payable outright to a person who is a minor, my executors may, without court approval, pay all or part of such property to a parent or guardian of that minor, to a custodian under the Uniform Transfers to Minors act, or may defer payment of such property until the minor reaches the age of majority, as defined by his or her state of residence. No bond shall be required for such payments.

[This clause gives your executors discretion to make sure any gift to a minor will be given in a way that's appropriate to his or her age. The "no bond" language is intended to save the estate money.]

ARTICLE VII: FIDUCIARIES

I appoint my spouse, Tex, as executor of this will. If he is unable or unwilling to act, or resigns, I appoint my daughter, Alice, and my son, John, as successor coexecutors. If either coexecutor also predeceases me or is unable or unwilling to act, the survivor shall serve as executor. My executor shall have all the powers allowable to executors under the laws of this state. I direct that no bond or security of any kind shall be required of any executor.

[If you set up a trust in the will, you could name the trustees in this clause as well. The "no bond or security" clause is designed to save the estate money.]

ARTICLE VIII: SIMULTANEOUS DEATH CLAUSE

If my spouse and I shall die under such circumstances that the order of our deaths cannot be readily ascertained, my spouse shall be deemed to have predeceased me. No person, other than my spouse, shall be deemed to have survived me if such person dies within thirty days after my death. This article modifies all provisions of this will accordingly.

[This clause helps your beneficiaries to avoid the sometimes time-consuming problems that occur if you and your spouse die together in an accident. Your spouse's will should contain an identical clause. Even though it seems contradictory to have two wills each directing that the other spouse died first, since each will is probated by itself, this allows the estate plan set up in each will to go forward as you planned. The second sentence exists to prevent the awkward legal complications that can ensue if someone dies between the time you die and the time the estate is divided up. Instead of passing through two probate processes, your gift to a beneficiary who dies shortly after you do would go to whomever you would have wanted it to go had the intended beneficiary died before you did. Most such gifts go into the residuary estate.]

ARTICLE IX: GUARDIAN

If my husband does not survive me and I leave minor children surviving me, I appoint as guardian of the person and property of my minor children my uncle-Ernest Entwistle. He shall have custody of my minor children, and shall serve without bond. If he does not qualify or for any reason ceases to serve as guardian, I appoint as successor guardian my cousin-Kevin Moon.

I have signed this will this ____ day of _____, 20___.

_____ (legal signature)

SIGNED AND DECLARED by Tess Tatrix on _____ to be her will, in our presence, who at her request, in her presence and in the presence of each other, all being present at the same time, have signed our names as witnesses.

_____ (signature)

Blair Witness

Address _____

_____ (signature)

I. Witness

Address _____

SELF-PROVING AFFIDAVIT

STATE OF _____

COUNTY OF _____

Each of the undersigned, Blair Witness and I. Witness, both on oath, says that:

The attached will was signed by Tess Tatrix, the testator named in the will, on the ____ day of _____, 20___, at the law offices of Lex Juris, 5440 Orfite St., Geo, Washington.

When she signed the will, Tess Tatrix declared the instrument to be her last will.

Each of us then signed his or her name as a witness at the end of this will at the request of Tess Tatrix and in her presence and sight and in the presence and sight of each other.

Tess Tatrix was, at the time of executing this will, over the age of eighteen years and, in our opinions, of sound mind, memory, and understanding and not under any restraint or in any respect incompetent to make a will.

In our opinions, Tess Tatrix could read, write, and speak in English and was suffering from no physical or mental impairment that would affect her capacity to make a valid will. The will was executed as a single original instrument, and was not executed in counterparts.

Each of us was acquainted with Tess Tatrix when the will was executed and makes this affidavit at her request.

_____ (signature)

Blair Witness

Address _____

_____ (signature)

I. Witness

Address _____

Sworn to before me this ____ day of _____, 20___.

_____ (signature and official seal)

Notary Public

APPENDIX C

HEALTH-CARE ADVANCE DIRECTIVE

CAUTION:

This health-care advance directive is a general form provided for your convenience. While it meets the legal requirements of most states, it may or may not fit the requirements of your particular state. Many states have special forms or special procedures for creating health-care advance directives. If your state's law does not recognize this document clearly, the document may still provide an effective statement of your wishes if you cannot speak for yourself. The directions for filling out the form are given first, followed by the form itself on page 357.

SECTION 1. HEALTH-CARE AGENT

Print your full name in this spot as the principal or creator of the health-care advance directive.

Print the full name, address, and telephone number of the person (age eighteen or older) you appoint as your health-care agent. Appoint *only* a person with whom you have talked and whom you trust to understand and carry out your values and wishes.

Many states limit the persons who can serve as your agent. If you want to meet all existing state restrictions, *do not* name any

This appendix is adapted from the booklet *Shape Your Health-Care Future with Health-Care Advance Directives.*

of the following as your agent, since some states will not let them act in that role:

- your health-care providers, including physicians;
- staff of health-care facilities or nursing-care facilities providing your care;
- guardians of your finances (also called conservators);
- employees of government agencies financially responsible for your care;
- any person serving as agent for ten or more persons.

SECTION 2. ALTERNATE AGENTS

It is a good idea to name alternate agents in case your first agent is not available. Of course, only appoint alternates if you fully trust them to act faithfully as your agent and if you have talked to them about serving as your agent. Print the appropriate information in this section. You can name as many alternate agents as you wish, but place them in the order in which you wish them to serve.

SECTION 3. EFFECTIVE DATE AND DURABILITY

This sample document is effective if and when you cannot make health-care decisions. Your agent and your doctor determine if you are in this condition. Some state laws include specific procedures for determining your decision-making ability. If you wish, you can include other effective dates or other criteria for determining that you cannot make health-care decisions (such as requiring two physicians to evaluate your decision-making ability). You also can state that the power will end at some later date or event before death.

In any case, you have the *right to revoke,* or take away, the agent's authority at any time. To revoke, notify your agent or health-care provider orally or in writing. If you revoke, it is best to notify in writing both your agent and physician and anyone else who has a copy of the directive. Also destroy the health-care advance directive document itself.

SECTION 4. AGENT'S POWERS

This grant of power is intended to be as broad as possible. Unless you set limits, your agent will have authority to make any decision you could make to consent to or to stop any type of health care.

Even under this broad grant of authority, your agent still must follow your wishes and directions, communicated by you in any manner now or in the future.

To limit or direct your agent's power specifically, you must complete Part II of the advance-directive, section 6, on page 360.

SECTION 5. MY INSTRUCTIONS ABOUT END-OF-LIFE TREATMENT

The subject of end-of-life treatment is particularly important to many people. In this section, you can give general or specific instructions on the subject. The four main paragraphs are options—*choose only one.* Write your desires or instructions in your own words if you choose paragraph four. If you choose paragraph two, you have three additional options, from which you can choose one, two, or all three. If you are satisfied with your agent's knowledge of your values and wishes and you do not want to include instructions in the form, initial the first option and do not give instructions in the form.

Any instructions you give here will guide your agent. If you do not appoint an agent, they will guide any health-care providers or surrogate decision makers who must make a decision for you if you cannot do so yourself.

Directive in Your Own Words: If you would like to state your wishes about end-of-life treatment in your own words instead of choosing one of the options provided, you can do so in this section. Since people sometimes have different opinions on whether nutrition and hydration should be refused or stopped under certain circumstances, be sure to address this issue clearly in your directive. Nutrition and hydration means food and fluids given through a nasogastric tube or tube into your stomach, intestines, or veins, and *does not include* nonintrusive methods such as spoon feeding or moistening of lips and mouth.

Some states allow the stopping of nutrition and hydration only if you expressly authorize it. If you are creating your own directive and you do not want nutrition and hydration, state so clearly.

SECTION 6. ANY OTHER HEALTH-CARE INSTRUCTIONS OR LIMITATIONS OR MODIFICATIONS OF MY AGENT'S POWERS

In this section, you can provide instructions about other health-care issues that are not end-of-life treatment or nutrition and hydration. For example, you might want to include your wishes about issues such as nonemergency surgery, elective medical treatments, or admission to a nursing home. Again, be careful in these instructions not to place limitations on your agent that you do not intend. For example, while you may not want to be admitted to a nursing home, placing such a restriction may make things impossible for your agent if other options are not available.

You may guide your agent in any way you wish. For example, you can instruct your agent to refuse any specific types of treatment that are against your religious beliefs or unacceptable to you for any other reasons. These might include blood transfusions, electroconvulsive therapy, sterilization, abortion, amputation, psychosurgery, or admission to a mental institution. Some states limit your agent's authority to consent to or to refuse some of these procedures, regardless of your health-care advance directive.

Be very careful about stating limitations because the specific circumstances surrounding future health-care decisions are impossible to predict. If you do not want any limitations, simply write in "*No limitations.*"

SECTION 7. PROTECTION OF THIRD PARTIES WHO RELY ON MY AGENT

In most states, health-care providers cannot be forced to follow the directions of your agent if they object. However, most states also require providers to help transfer you to another provider who is willing to honor your instructions. To encourage compliance with the health-care advance directive, this paragraph states that providers who rely in good faith on the agent's statements and decisions will not be held civilly liable for their actions.

SECTION 8. DONATIONS OF ORGANS AT DEATH

In this section, you can state your intention to donate bodily organs and tissues at death. If you do not wish to be an organ donor, initial the first option. The second option is a donation of any or all organs or parts. The third option allows you to donate only those organs or tissues you specify. Consider mentioning the heart, liver, lungs, kidneys, pancreas, intestines, corneas, bones, skin, heart valves, tendons, ligaments, and saphenous veins. Finally, you may limit the use of your organs by *crossing out* any of the four purposes listed that you do not want (transplant, research, therapy, or education). If you do not cross out any of these options, your organs may be used for any of these purposes.

SECTION 9. NOMINATION OF GUARDIAN

Appointing a health-care agent helps to avoid a court-appointed guardian for health-care decision making. However, if a court becomes involved for any reason, this paragraph expressly names your agent to serve as guardian. A court does not have to follow your nomination, but normally it will honor your wishes unless there is good reason to override your choice.

SECTION 10. ADMINISTRATIVE PROVISIONS

These items address miscellaneous matters that could affect the implementation of your health-care advance directive.

Required state procedures for signing this kind of document vary. Some require only a signature, while others have very detailed witnessing requirements. Some states simply require notarization.

The procedure in this book is likely to be far more complex than your state law requires because it combines the formal requirements from virtually every state. Follow it if you do not know your state's requirements and you want to meet the signature requirements of virtually every state.

1. *Sign and date the document* in the presence of two witnesses and a notary. Your witnesses should know your identity personally and be able to declare that you appear to be of sound mind and under no duress or undue influence.

   In order to meet the different witnessing requirements of most states, do *not* have the following people witness your signature:

- **Anyone you have chosen to make health-care decisions on your behalf (agents or alternate agents).**

- **Your treating physician, health-care provider, health-facility operator, or an employee of any of these.**

- Insurers or employees of your life/health insurance provider.

- Anyone financially responsible for your health-care costs.

- Anyone related to you by blood, marriage, or adoption.

- Anyone entitled to any part of your estate under an existing will or by operation of law or anyone who will benefit financially from your death. Your creditors should not serve as witnesses.

    If you are in a nursing home or other institution, a few states have additional witnessing requirements. This form does not include witnessing language for this situation. Contact a patient advocate or an ombudsman to find out about the state's requirements in these cases.

2. *Have your signature notarized.* Some states permit notarization as an alternative to witnessing. Doing both witnessing and notarization is more than most states require, but doing both will meet the execution requirements of most states. This form includes a typical notary statement, but it is wise to check state law in case it requires a special form of notary acknowledgment.

HEALTH-CARE ADVANCE DIRECTIVE

PART I
APPOINTMENT OF HEALTH-CARE AGENT

1. Health-care agent

I, _____, hereby appoint

PRINCIPAL

_____

AGENT'S NAME

_____

ADDRESS

_____

HOME PHONE #   WORK PHONE #

as my agent to make health- and personal-care decisions for me
as authorized in this document.

2. Alternate agents

If

- I revoke my agent's authority; or

- my agent becomes unwilling or unavailable to act; or

- my agent is my spouse and I become legally separated or
  divorced,

I name the following (each to act alone and successively, in the
order named) as alternates to my agent:

A. First Alternate Agent_____

   Address _____

   Telephone _____

B. Second Alternate Agent _____

   Address _____

   Telephone _____

3. Effective date and durability

By this document I intend to create a health-care advance directive. It is effective upon, and only during, any period in which I cannot make or communicate a choice regarding a particular health-care decision. My agent, attending physician, and any other necessary experts should determine that I am unable to make choices about health care.

4. Agent's powers

I give my agent full authority to make health-care decisions for me. My agent shall follow my wishes as known to my agent either through this document or through other means. In interpreting my wishes, I intend my agent 's authority to be as broad as possible, except for any limitations I state in this form. In making any decision, my agent shall try to discuss the proposed decision with me to determine my desires if I am able to communicate in any way. If my agent cannot determine the choice I would want, then my agent shall make a choice for me based upon what my agent believes to be in my best interests.

Unless specifically limited by Section 6, below, my agent is authorized as follows:

A. To consent to, to refuse, or to withdraw consent to any and all types of health care. "Health care" means any care, treatment, service, or procedure to maintain, diagnose, or otherwise affect an individual's physical or mental condition. It includes, but is not limited to, artificial respiration, nutritional support and hydration, medication, and cardiopulmonary resuscitation;

B. To have access to medical records and information to the same extent that I am entitled, including the right to disclose the contents to others as appropriate for my health care;

C. To authorize my admission to or discharge from (even against medical advice) any hospital, nursing home, residential care, assisted-living facility, or similar facility or service;

D. To contract on my behalf for any health-care-related service or facility on my behalf, without my agent incurring personal financial liability for such contracts;

E. To hire and fire medical, social service, and other support personnel responsible for my care;

F. To authorize or refuse to authorize any medication or procedure intended to relieve pain, even though such use may lead to physical damage or addiction or hasten the moment of (but not intentionally cause) my death;

G. To make anatomical gifts of part or all of my body for medical purposes, authorize an autopsy, and direct the disposition of my remains to the extent permitted by law;

H. To take any other action necessary to do what I authorize here, including (but not limited to) granting any waiver or release from liability required by any hospital, physician, or other health-care provider; signing any documents relating to refusals of treatment or the leaving of a facility against medical advice; and pursuing any legal action in my name at the expense of my estate to force compliance with my wishes as determined by my agent, or to seek actual or punitive damages for the failure to comply.

PART II
INSTRUCTIONS ABOUT HEALTH CARE

5. My instructions about end-of-life treatment
(Initial only ONE of the following FOUR main statements)

1. ____ NO SPECIFIC INSTRUCTIONS. My agent knows my values and wishes, so I do not wish to include any specific instructions here.

2. ____ DIRECTIVE TO WITHHOLD OR WITHDRAW TREATMENT. Although I greatly value life, I also believe that at some point life has such diminished value that medical treatment should be stopped, and I should be allowed to die. Therefore, I do not want to receive treatment, including nutrition and hydration, when the treatment will not give me a meaningful quality of life.

   (If you initialed this paragraph, also initial ANY or ALL of the following three statements with which you agree)

By this I mean that I do not want my life prolonged . . .

_____ . . . if the treatment will leave me in a condition of permanent unconsciousness, such as in an irreversible coma or a persistent vegetative state.

_____ . . . if the treatment will leave me with no more than some consciousness and in an irreversible condition of complete, or nearly complete, loss of ability to think or communicate with others.

_____ . . . if the treatment will leave me with no more than some ability to think or communicate with others, and the likely risks and burdens of treatment outweigh the expected benefits. Risks, burdens, and benefits include consideration of length of life, quality of life, financial costs, and my personal dignity and privacy.

3. _____ DIRECTIVE TO RECEIVE TREATMENT. I want my life to be prolonged as long as possible, no matter what my quality of life.

4. _____ DIRECTIVE ABOUT END-OF-LIFE TREATMENT IN MY OWN WORDS:

_____

_____

_____

_____

_____

6. Any other health-care instructions or limitations or modifications of my agent's powers

_____

_____

_____

_____

_____

7. Protection of third parties who rely on my agent

No person who relies in good faith on any representations by my agent or alternate agent(s) shall be liable to me, my estate, or my heirs or assigns for recognizing the agent's authority.

8. Donations of organs at death

Upon my death: *(Initial one)*

____ I do *not* wish to donate any organs or tissues, OR

____ I give *any* needed organs, tissues, or parts, OR

____ I give *only* the following organs, tissues, or parts:
    (Please specify)

_____

_____

_____

My gift (if any) is for the following purposes:
(Cross out any of the following you do not want)

- **Transplant**
- **Research**
- **Therapy**
- **Education**

9. Nomination of guardian

If a guardian of my person should for any reason need to be appointed, I nominate my agent (or his or her alternate then authorized to act), named above.

10. Administrative provisions

(All apply)

- **I revoke any prior health-care advance directive.**
- **This health-care advance directive is intended to be valid in any jurisdiction in which it is presented.**
- **A copy of this advance-directive is intended to have the same effect as the original.**

Signing the document

BY SIGNING HERE, I INDICATE THAT I UNDERSTAND THE CONTENTS OF THIS
DOCUMENT AND THE EFFECT OF THIS GRANT OF POWERS TO MY AGENT.

*I sign my name to this health-care advance directive on this
_____ day of _____, 20___.*

_____
MY SIGNATURE

_____
MY NAME

_____
MY CURRENT HOME ADDRESS

Witness statement

I declare that the person who signed or acknowledged this document is personally known to me, that he/she signed or acknowledged this health-care advance directive in my presence, and
that he/she appears to be of sound mind and under no duress,
fraud, or undue influence.

I am not:

- **the person appointed as agent by this document;**
- **the patient's health-care provider;**
- **an employee of the patient's health-care provider;**
- **financially responsible for the person's health care;**
- **related to the principal by blood, marriage, or adoption; and,**
- **to the best of my knowledge, a creditor of the principal or
  entitled to any part of his/her estate under a will now existing
  or by operation of law.**

Witness #1:

_____
SIGNATURE   DATE

_____
PRINT NAME

_____
RESIDENT ADDRESS

_____
TELEPHONE

Witness #2:

_____

SIGNATURE   DATE

_____

PRINT NAME

_____

RESIDENT ADDRESS

_____

TELEPHONE

Notarization

STATE OF _____.

COUNTY OF _____

On this _____ day of _____, 20____, the said
_____, known to me (or satisfactorily proven to be
the person named in the foregoing instrument) personally
appeared before me, a Notary Public, within and for the State
and County aforesaid, and acknowledged that he or she freely
and voluntarily executed the same for the purposes stated
therein.

_____ NOTARY PUBLIC

MY COMMISSION EXPIRES: _____.

INDEX